Slings and Slingstones

Slings & Slingstones

The Forgotten Weapons of Oceania and the Americas

Robert York and Gigi York

The Kent State University Press

Kent, Ohio

© 2011 by The Kent State University Press, Kent, Ohio 44242
ALL RIGHTS RESERVED
Library of Congress Catalog Card Number 2011030817
ISBN 978-1-60635-107-9
Manufactured in the United States of America

LIBRARY OF CONGRESS CATALOGING-IN-PUBLICATION DATA

York, Robert, 1944–
  Slings and slingstones : the forgotten weapons of Oceania and the Americas /
Robert York and Gigi York.
    p. cm.
  Includes bibliographical references and index.
  ISBN 978-1-60635-107-9 (hardcover : alk. paper) ∞
1. Slings—History. 2. Slingstones—History. 3. Oceania—History. 4. America—
History. I. York, Gigi, 1944– II. Title.
  GN498.S55Y67 2011
  799.2'028'2—dc23
                          2011030817

British Library Cataloging-in-Publication data are available.

15 14 13 12 11   5 4 3 2 1

For Adrian, JDY, Brandy, Brandi, Toby, Dora, Valdo,

and all of our Marys.

Contents

List of Figures   ix
List of Maps   xiii
Preface   xv
Acknowledgments   xix
Abbreviations   xxiii

Part 1   Setting the Stage
    1   Time Out, or a Brief Try at Locating the World's First Slings and
        Slingstones   5

Part 2   Oceania/The Islands of the Central Pacific
    2   Micronesia   19
    3   Melanesia   31
    4   Polynesia   43
    5   Oceania Summary   63

Part 3   The Americas
    6   South America and Mesoamerica   75
    7   North America   89
    8   The Americas Concluding Remarks: Questions and Issues   145

References   153
Index   183

Figures

1   Linus demonstrating the advantages of the sling

2   Roman lead sling bullets

3   Four probable Paleoarchaic slingstones, Mt. Hebron Archaeological Site, Butte Valley, northern California

4   Bipointed stones, Nightfire Island Site, Klamath Basin, northern California

5   Jean Baptiste Cabri

6   Exhibit of Marianas slingstones (*acho atupat*)

7   Revised Thompson-Marianas Slingstones Classification (T-M)

8   Chamorro sling (*atupat*) replica and T-M Slingstone Types 1, 3, and 4

9   Chuuk (Truk) sling and three slingstones

10 Sling and slingstone, Port Moresby area, Central Province, Papua New Guinea

11 New Ireland warriors

12 Nine New Ireland slingstones

13 Possible jagged-edged or unfinished slingstone, Malaita, Solomon Islands

14 Three probable slingstones, Santa Cruz Islands, Solomons

15 Eleven slingstones and carrying bag, New Caledonia

16 Fiji sling

17 Samoan (Tutuila) slingers battle LaPerouse's men 1787

18 Tahitian slingers engage HMS *Dolphin*, Matavai Bay, 1767

19 Two probable basalt slingstones, the Marquesas

20 Display of slingstones, Rarotonga, the Cook Islands, at the Otago Museum, Dunedin, New Zealand

21 "Masked Man of the Sandwich Islands"

22 Three Hawaiian slingstones

23 Modern-day Andean slinger

24 Three depictions of Inca sling use from Felipe Guamán Poma's chronicle, ca. 1615

25 Inca, wool, solid-pocket sling, Coyungo Site, Peru

26   Inca, wool, split-pocket sling, Coyungo Site, Peru

27   Pre-Columbian (Inca?) slingstones

28   Inca spherical slingstone

29   Inca wool, plaited sling

30   Historic Brazilian sling

31   Plan and side views of lenticular slingstone recovered from "excavations on site of Casa del Gobierno Nacional, Federal District, Buenos Aires, Argentina"

32   "Domed" or cone-shaped slingstone recovered from "excavations on site of Casa del Gobierno Nacional, Federal District, Buenos Aires, Argentina"

33   Caribbean Venezuela Manicuaroid Series bipointed slingstones

34   *Soldato Mexicano* armed with *macana,* shield, and sling

35   Pre-Columbian Zapotec (?) spherical slingstone

36   Two Zuni Pueblo, New Mexico, and Tarahumara, Mexico, leather slings

37   Two typical pre-Columbian stone balls, North America Southwest

38   Two more typical pre-Columbian Southwest stone balls

39   "Belly of Sling" (i.e., sling pocket) representational art designs, Tewa Pueblos, New Mexico

40   "Gaming stones," Clear Lake, Modoc County, California

41   T-M Type 3, biconical/diamond-shaped slingstone of argillaceous coral limestone, LauLau Beach, Saipan

42   Basalt, diamond-shaped "charmstone," Kramer Cave, Falcon Hill, Winnemucca Lake, Nevada

43   Two bipointed stones actually cataloged as "slingstones," Stiles Ranch Site, Lassen County, California

44   Two basalt bipointed stones, Lassen County, California

45   Two bipointed stones of unidentified rock, Sonoma County, California

46   Seven "bipointed charms" of limestone and igneous rocks, Alpaugh vicinity, Tulare County, California

47   "Plummet" of unidentified stone, probably igneous, San Miguel Island, California

48   Lovelock Cave, Nevada

49   Sling recovered from Lovelock Cave, Nevada

50   Two bipointed stones, Lovelock Cave, Nevada

51   "Elliptical and globular clay balls," Lovelock Cave, Nevada

52   Three basalt bipointed stones, Pyramid Lake, Nevada

53   Three more basalt bipointed stones, Pyramid Lake, Nevada

54   Stone (tuff) balls classified as "slingstones," Indian Island Site, Lake County, California

55   Replicated baked clay sling balls used by Eastern Pomo for hunting water-fowl

56   Eastern Pomo tule basket for carrying clay sling balls

57   Eastern Pomo buckskin war or hunting sling

58   Eastern Pomo tule and milkweed fiber waterfowl sling

59   Bipointed stones, Nightfire Island Archaeology Site, Klamath Basin, California

60   "Elliptical baked clay balls," Gunther Island Site (HUM-67), Humboldt Bay, California

61   Two more probable baked clay sling missiles, Gunther Island Site

62   "Slinger Man" petroglyph at Little Petroglyph Canyon, China Lake Naval Air Weapons Station, California

63   Inuit sling, Greenland

64   Inuit sling, Kotzebue, Alaska

65   Arapaho sling, Wind River Reservation, Wyoming

66   Uintah Ute decorated sling, Whiterocks, Utah

67   Two Cheyenne leather slings, Darlington, Okalahoma

68   Seneca Iroquois sling, New York

69   Common forms of Poverty Point Objects recovered from the Poverty Point Site, Louisiana

70   Fired clay objects, Pecos Pueblo, New Mexico

71   Volcanic bomb, unmodified or slightly modified, recovered ca. 1927 from Summer Lake, Lake County, Oregon

72   "Tuff ball," spherical volcanic ejecta, unmodified manuport recovered from the Chance Gulch Archaeological Site (5GN817), Colorado

Maps

1   Korfmann's sling worldwide distribution
2   Oceania
3   Micronesia
4   Melanesia
5   Polynesia
6   Mesoamerica and South America sling distribution
7   South America
8   Mesoamerica
9   North America slingstone survey areas
10   North America Southwest
11   Locations of Native American groups claiming use or knowledge of the sling in part of western North America
12   North America West Coast and Great Basin
13   North America Arctic-Subarctic
14   North America interior
15   North America southeastern and eastern coasts

Preface

Although not every one of the Old and New World peoples knew the sling, its distribution is sufficiently wide so that no serious doubt may be entertained as to its near-universal distribution among man. Those people who did not use this implement may once have possessed it and later given it up.

—*Robert F. Heizer and Irmgard W. Johnson, "A Prehistoric Sling from Lovelock Cave, Nevada" (1952)*

Through the first half of the twentieth century, slings and slingstones garnered some interest among anthropologists and archaeologists. For reasons that we will explore throughout the text, the implications of the above communication passed down by the eminent California archaeologists Robert F. Heizer and Irmgard W. Johnson, was relegated to archaeology limbo.

Our introduction to and pursuit of slingstones began in 1998 on Saipan, while serving as collections curators at the Northern Mariana Islands Museum of History and Culture (CNMI Museum). For us, archaeologists who had spent their careers among projectile points and potsherds in the western United States, the prevalence of worked slingstones (artifacts totally unfamiliar to us), coupled with the absence of projectile points, was a revelation.

Of the many wonders of our new tropical home, the island's native peoples (Chamorros and Carolinians) and their ancestors' slingstones fascinated us most. Saipan's coral sand beaches are alternately lapped and torn by calm aqua waters and savage typhoons. Waves deposit among the shoreline boulders long-stored booty, including Spanish galleons' gold, sea shells, and warriors' missiles—from ancient slingstones to WWII munitions.

Curt Klemstein, sling enthusiast and one of our new Saipan friends, knowing of our interest in slingstones, brought to our attention Manfred Korfmann's 1973 *Scientific American* article on slings and slingstones. Korfmann focused largely on the use of slingstones by classical Old World armies, but what caught our attention was his worldwide sling distribution map displaying a rash of dots indicating that the sling was widely known throughout the Pacific and the Americas (see map 1).

Our first hands-on slinging experience happened on a typical steamy tropical afternoon. We joined Curt and Paul Oberg (CNMI Museum director) at the nearby high school athletic field to test our skills with the sling by hurling coral stones (fashioned by Curt to replicate typical Marianas football-like slingstones) at a cardboard target. Without disclosing the results of our slinging contest, we can say that an impromptu audience of Saipan teens was highly amused.

Back Stateside in 2002, on the windswept high plains near our home in Laramie, Wyoming, we gave the sling another whirl. On this outing, naturally egg-shaped granite stones that we had collected from California beaches and streambeds served as our ammunition. We had painted these stones bright red and yellow to, we trusted, enhance our ability to retrieve them. After a couple cautious attempts, Gigi power-fired a stone whose flight path could never be determined and landing place never found. Fortunately, it had not come to rest in one of our skulls. That day we retired the slings to our hallway coat rack and the stones to the walkway flower bed.

Our pathetic attempts at slinging awakened us to the many hours—years—of practice required of slingers to master this weapon for effective use in the hunt and combat, whose employment spanned across continents and the millennia.

We have had a rewarding and continuing archaeological and ethnohistoric research journey, encompassing more than a decade of gleaning data from hundreds of library volumes and surveying numerous artifact collections housed in museums from Laramie to Auckland. The written history begins with retrieved European accounts penned in sixteenth- and seventeenth-century sea captains' logs and explorers' journals detailing their early contacts with Pacific Islanders and Native Americans—which were often punctuated with a barrage of slingstones.

Certainly most of us have known since childhood the Old World story of David slaying Goliath with his shepherd's sling and stream-polished pebbles. Few, however, know the significant role this weapon also played in the prehistory and history of Oceania and the Americas. Sling missiles, rather than simply being naturally occurring rocks, were often fashioned from stone and clay (and, in the case of the Greeks and Romans, lead) into a number of purposeful shapes.

Our primary objective here is to supply a long-overdue survey of existing knowledge regarding use of the sling and particularly slingstones in the Americas and Oceania. In this respect, we trust this work will serve as a valuable reference for archaeologists, ethnologists, and other interested parties. Beyond that, we will pose many questions, particularly of archaeologists. Unless we totally miss the mark, we trust this work will challenge, if not radically change, archaeological thinking about this humble weapon's importance in understanding the prehistory and history of the Pacific islands and the Americas and accordingly spur renewed interest and research.

Many of our ideas will prove controversial. Good. For we wish this work to provoke discussion and, as said, hoped for concomitant research. Study of slingstone technology, as we will point out, if diligently pursued by archaeologists and allied disciplines, will rewardingly inform arguments relative to such topics as warfare and pre-Columbian Oceania-Americas contacts, which have reemerged as "respectable" for scholarly inquiry after many years in the wilderness.

Potentially of more importance, our admittedly elementary sling research questions an underlying assumption of much archaeology: adoption/rejection of technology by ancient peoples was largely determined by environment and utilitarian needs. Rather, it appears that cultural factors such as politics and traditionalism were at least of equal value in the acceptance of technological innovations, just as in the modern world.

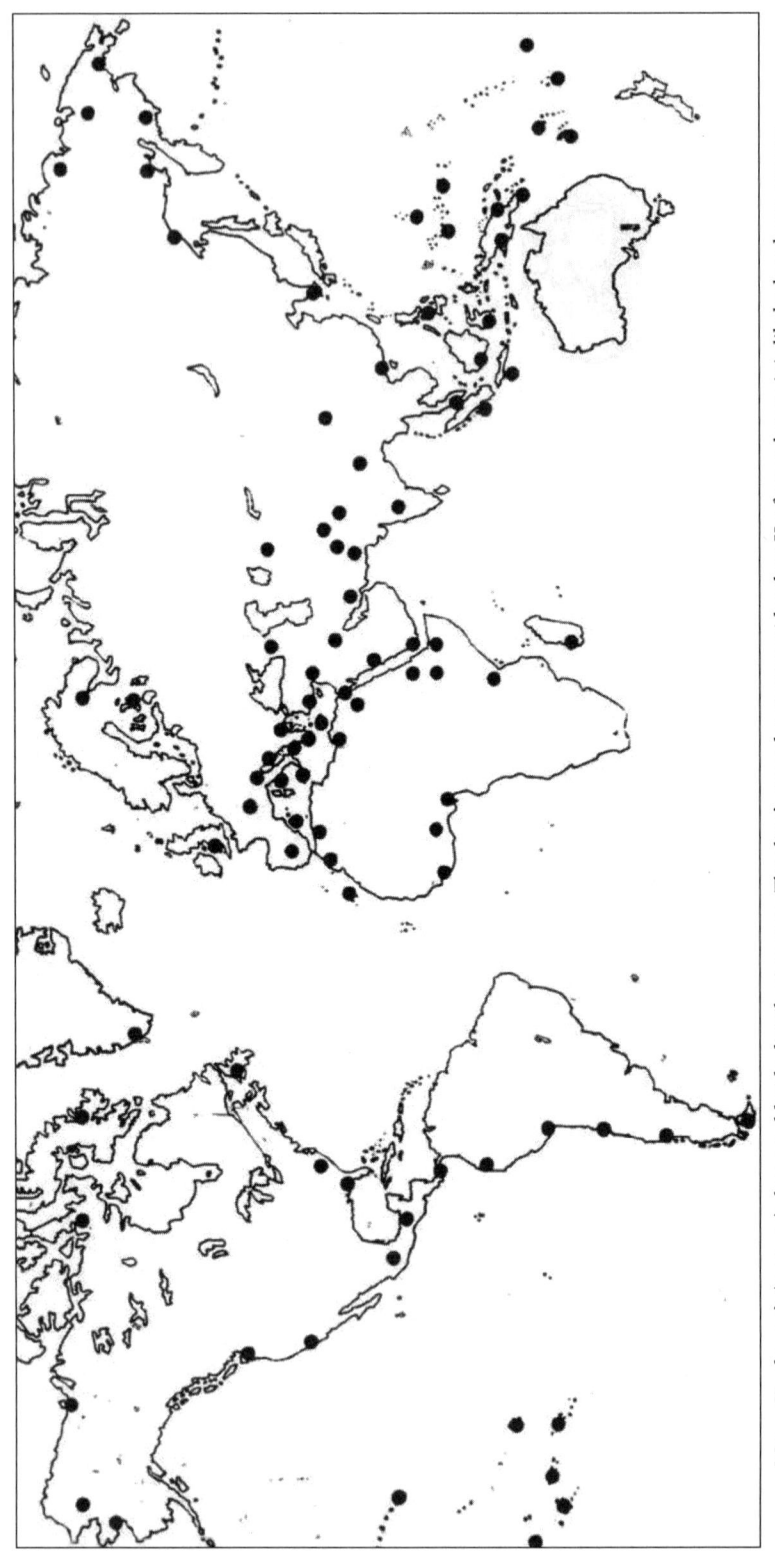

Map 1. Korfmann's (1973; 42) sling worldwide distribution map. The sling's spread was even wider then Korfmann knew; it is likely that there were no areas in the Americas where it was unknown. Reprinted with permission. Copyright © 1973 *Scientific American*, a division of Nature America, Inc. All rights reserved.

Acknowledgments

We owe our enduring gratitude to a formidable list of individuals and personnel of numerous libraries, museums, and universities, from Boston to Brisbane, who facilitated our decade-long research project. In particular, we are indebted to the helpful staffs of the University of Wyoming libraries, where much of our literature search was accomplished. To those individuals or institutions we may have unwittingly overlooked, please accept our most sincere gratitude and apology.

Our deepest appreciation goes to Saipan friends Curt Klemstein and Lisa Hacskaylo, for sharing their Pacific-wide sling research. Their data rekindled questions first spawned and mulled over with anthropologist Kathy Helmer and fellow world traveler Paul Robinson on the eve of our departure for Saipan in 1998. And thus it began.

We wish to thank all former and current staff, volunteers, and board members of the Northern Mariana Islands Museum of History and Culture on Saipan (CNMI Museum), where we served as collections curators from 1998 to 2002 and Gigi as director for a time. We are extremely grateful for their continuing support of our research. Expressly, we wish to thank former board chairman Herman T. Guerrero, former directors Paul Oberg and Genevieve Cabrera, and current director, Robert Hunter, as well as former museum colleague, great friend, and guide in all things Marianas, Linda Torres. Thanks also to our Saipan friends Jim and Grace Belyea, Nancy Gottfried, Ruth Tighe, Nancy and Dick Weil, and Sam McPhetres for their insights, wit, and encouragement.

We extend our gratitude to long-time Guam-based archaeologist Rosalind Hunter-Anderson for sharing her broad knowledge of Pacific archaeology. She patiently reviewed and offered many useful suggestions that aided in our development of the manuscript.

We also thank Gary Heathcote, University of Guam physical anthropologist, for furnishing us with data particularly relevant to sling-related physical anomalies of the peoples of Oceania. We thank Dave DeFant, who shared with us his data from a Guam archaeological site that dramatically testified to the lethality of ancient

Marianas slingers. And we wish to thank Lawrence J. Cunningham, long-time Guam history scholar, and the staffs of the Guam Museum and Guampedia.com for their assistance.

Before moving on from the Marianas, we must express our great appreciation to Will Shapiro, who expanded our research horizon by apprising us of artifacts remarkably similar to Marianas slingstones that existed across the Pacific in California.

We are grateful for all the assistance—from lodging to data sharing—we received from "Down Under" friends and colleagues: Roger Green and Moira Doherty of the University of Auckland; Pandora Fulimato Pereira at the Auckland Museum; Dimitri Anson at the Otago Museum, Dunedin, New Zealand; Roderick Ewins of the University of Tasmania; Jen Davis at the University of Queensland Anthropology Museum, Brisbane; and our good friends Pippa and Andrew Hooper of Cairns, Australia.

We especially want to recognize Barry Craig of the South Australian Museum (SAM), Adelaide, for his many valuable contributions to our Oceania research. Barry graciously and most expeditiously supplied images taken by SAM photographer Tony Vlavogelakis, hard-to-find references, helpful reviews of our various drafts, and, maybe most importantly, continuing insistence that we were engaged in a most worthy endeavor that would lastingly add to archaeological knowledge.

Our special thanks also goes to John Topic of Trent University, Perterborough, Ontario, for supplying a wealth of data on slingstone use related to the west coast and Andes areas of South America. Moreover, we thank John for his enthusiasm for the project, for supporting our work relative to the Americas in much the same way as Barry Craig did relative to our Pacific research.

We also thank our other Canadian contacts who generously supplied us with information regarding use of slingstones along North America's northwest coast, particularly in British Columbia: Ryan Sagarbarria with Antiquus Archaeological Consultants, Maple Ridge, B.C.; Knut Fladmark and Barbara J. Winter of Simon Fraser University, Vancouver; Grant Keddie of the Royal B.C. Museum, Victoria; and Karen Murchison of the Canadian Museum of Civilization, Gatineau, Quebec.

Numerous individuals facilitated our study of collections at the American Museum of Natural History, New York. We especially want to recognize the super assistance of Dave Thomas, Lorann Pendleton, Paul Beelitz, Anibal Rodrigues, and Craig Morris.

Our very special thanks go to Pat Nietfeld and staff at the Smithsonian's National Museum of the American Indian, Washington, D.C. Pat's extensive and resourceful long-distance research on our behalf was rivaled only by her outstanding ingenuity in providing assistance during our on-site research at the NMAI. We also gratefully acknowledge the most helpful assistance afforded us by James Krakker at the Smithsonian's Department of Anthropology Curatorial Facility.

Steven LeBlanc and Susan Haskell at Harvard University's Peabody Museum generously gave of their time, imparting useful information and study of collections under their care.

At the Field Museum, Chicago, Jonathan Haas helped arrange our visit in 2007, and Gordon Ambrosino efficiently helped us with our examination of North American collections. Our thanks also go to Christine Giannoni, the Field Museum's proficient librarian, for assisting us with archives research.

Kay Fowler, Barbara Malinky, and Ted Goebel at the University of Nevada, Reno, most helpfully accommodated our study of bipointed stones from the Royel's Collection, Pyramid Lake, Nevada, and the Mount Hebron Paleoarchaic Site, California.

Special thanks go to the Nevada State Museum, Carson City, for being one of our supporting institutions. We especially thank our good friends and colleagues at the NSM, Gene Hattori, Maggie Brown, and Alanah Woody (tragically now deceased), who helped us with many aspects of our project.

In 2004 Alanah Woody put us in touch with A. K. "Sandy" Rogers of the Maturango Museum, Ridgecrest, California, about a very rare petroglyph that possibly portrayed a slinger. The glyph had been observed by Sandy and photographed by Mark Pahuta, also of Ridgecrest, at nearby Little Petroglyph Canyon on the China Lake Naval Air Weapons Station. Excitedly we contacted Sandy, Mr. Pahuta, and later Russell Kaldenberg, the China Lake Navy Station archaeologist, to gain further information and arrange a visit to the site. We thank them all for most willingly sharing their knowledge and hosting us in 2005.

At the Phoebe Hearst Museum of Anthropology, University of California, Berkeley, Natasha Johnson graciously assisted us in setting up our May 2008 visit and showing us collections relevant to the West Coast and Great Basin provinces of North America.

We wish to thank Susan Hector of ASM Affiliates, Carlsbad, California; Mim Roeder and Liz Black of the California Historical Resources Information System; and Mark Henderson and Doug Linn, USDI Bureau of Land Management archaeologists in Nevada and Oregon, for furnishing us with information of importance to our California and Great Basin research.

Special thanks goes to Pat McMillan of the Favell Museum and Todd Keppel and Lynn Jeche of the Klamath County Museum, both located in Klamath Falls, Oregon. They not only helped us with our study of significant collections held by their museums, but they displayed data related to our research and jointly hosted a public presentation of our data in 2009.

We also thank Gerald Skelton, the Klamath Tribes Culture and Heritage director, Chiloquin, Oregon, and Judith Hassen, former curator at the Klamath County Museum. They were our first Klamath Basin contacts in 2004–05, and they made us aware that bipointed stones that would be of high interest to us were prevalent throughout the Klamath Basin of Oregon and California.

Special thanks go to another of our sponsoring institutions, the Frison Institute of Archaeology and Anthropology at the University of Wyoming, Laramie. Marcel Kornfeld and Robert Kelly were especially helpful in securing our appointments as fellows and supporting our project in many valuable ways, from offering comments on manuscript drafts to arranging speaking venues.

Chris Harrison of Slinging.org gets our appreciation for maintaining a website that was of considerable value to us, particularly for finding comparative data on ballistics and on the use of slings in the Old World. Chris also supplied helpful comments on an early draft of our manuscript.

We wish to express our gratitude to Susan de Castro McCann. Susan afforded us our first opportunity to get some of our ideas into print in the early days of our research by inviting us to write an article on Marianas slingstones for her Lyons, Colorado, newspaper, the *Redstone Review*.

To our wonderful friend and colleague Mary Hopkins and her family, we extend grateful thanks for all their kindnesses, from supplying a Wyoming retreat to assistance with varied and sundry tasks. Very special thanks we reserve for Tom Baker, a most generous friend and colleague for many years. We could always depend on Tom for enthusiastic support and good advice on virtually all aspects of manuscript preparation, from drawing maps to finding a publisher.

Along that line, we most sincerely thank our publisher, the Kent State University Press, for bringing our work to fruition. We particularly express our appreciation to Joyce Harrison and Mary Young for their patience and assistance in guiding us through what to us was the arcane world of publishing.

To all our friends and families, especially to son Toby Maloney, who kindly provided accommodations in New York City and Chicago, we declare our deepest appreciation for your forbearance and for suffering us over this protracted endeavor.

Lastly, we express our gratitude for this occupation which feeds our curiosity and promotes contact with those fellow travelers bitten by the same bug.

Abbreviations

AMNH	American Museum of Natural History, New York, NY
BAE	Bureau of American Ethnology
B.C.	province of British Columbia, Canada
BCO	Baked Clay Objects, associated with northern California archaeological sites
CNMI	Commonwealth of the Northern Mariana Islands
CNMI Museum	Northern Mariana Islands Museum of History and Culture, Saipan
GS/OAS	General Secretariat, Organization of American States
NM	national monument
NMAI	National Museum of the American Indian, Smithsonian Institution, Washington, DC
NMNH	National Museum of Natural History, Smithsonian Institution, Washington, DC
NSM	Nevada State Museum, Carson City
PAHMA	Phoebe A. Hearst Museum of Anthropology, University of California, Berkeley
PPO	Poverty Point Objects: baked clay objects associated with U.S. Gulf Coast archaeology sites
UCB	University of California, Berkeley
UNR	University of Nevada, Reno
SAM	South Australian Museum, Adelaide
T-M	Thompson-Marianas Slingstones Classification System
YA	years ago, before calendar year 2000

PART 1

Setting the Stage

Introduction

THE SLING AND ITS AMMUNITION

Across the pre-European Pacific and the Americas, slings varied widely in such characteristics as materials, workmanship, dimensions, and decoration. But—and this is what is of the most interest here—mechanically one type of sling was overwhelmingly favored for use: the flexible, one-hand, missile-firing sling—David's weapon. Coincidentally (or was it?), it was the sling of choice in the Old World (Harrison 2006; Korfmann 1973). Feest's (1980, 73) succinct description is generally applicable: "The sling itself is a simple device consisting of a string [more often a thick cord or strap] with a pouch holding the sling-stone near its centre. Rotating the sling launches the missile."

There were few variations on the theme. One exception was the staff or stick sling (Korfmann 1973, 37–39). Where these exceptions exist, we will note them. What we will *not* be considering is the modern slingshot. Mechanically, the modern Y-shaped, elastic-band slingshot is more akin to the bow than the sling—being a tension rather than a centrifugal force weapon. Though the modern slingshot only dates to the mid–nineteenth century (with the vulcanization of rubber), its roots can be traced to the rare pellet bow (Knight 1880, 295; Métraux 1949, 244).

We offer little more in the way of descriptive information in the remainder of this work concerning actual slings. To some extent this is because slings have been made of perishable materials and thus relatively few have survived from ancient times to the present day (with important exceptions, such as in Peru). Of those, even fewer have been recovered from archaeological context. Our primary concern will be with what usually remains of this weapon system, its ammunition—that is, missiles made of relatively imperishable materials, usually stone and fired or sun-baked clay.

OUR GAME RULES (TERMINOLOGY, DATING RULES, ETC.)

In describing sling missiles, or probable sling missiles, we often use imprecise terms such as "hand-size," "egg-shape," "diamond-shape," "football-shape" (specifically in reference to American and/or rugby footballs). In part we do this because that is about as much information as many reports supply. We believe these terms are helpful because they place in the mind's eye clear word pictures that facilitate ready comprehension and comparison. For a little more precision, the reader may assume that hand-size spheroids/subspheroids (e.g., "balls" and "eggs") range in diameter from 3 to 9 cm. Hand-size biconical ("diamond-shape") and bipointed ovoids ("footballs") range in their midline or widest diameter from 2 to 6 cm and in length from 2.5 to 10 cm.

For ease of comparison, dates are, with the exception of known calendar dates, expressed as "years ago" (YA) before the modern era, loosely counting back from the base year of AD 2000. In this respect, we have gone against archaeological convention and chosen not to use BP (Before Present), as this term is specifically associated with radiocarbon dating, which uses a base year of AD 1950. This allows for control of time sufficient for general comparison of data without getting into the complexity and confusion of calibrated versus uncalibrated radiocarbon dates and the discussion of the merits of various other dating techniques. We caution the reader, however, to take our prehistoric dates with a grain of salt, as radiocarbon dates, on which our estimates are primarily based, are being continually revised in light of recent advances in the field. For example, as new area-specific calibration curves are worked out, in many cases "old" (ca. 10,000+ YA) New World radiocarbon dates are proving to be as much as 2,000 years too young (Largent 2007).

We will refer often to Austronesian speakers. This is because there is a strong correlation of sling use with speakers of Austronesian languages in Oceania. Admittedly, with the exception of Melanesia, virtually all the languages of Oceania are members of the Austronesian family. Interestingly, or confusingly, no languages belonging to the Austronesian family or phylum were spoken in Australia (Goodenough 1996, 1–5); nor was the sling present there.

If we fail to mention a geopolitical region that falls within our areas of interest, the reader may assume we found no information regarding use of the sling. *No information* means just that and must not be translated to mean the sling was or was not used.

CHAPTER 1

Time Out, or a Brief Try at Locating the World's First Slings and Slingstones

The early history—actually the entire history—of the sling is frustratingly hard to trace. This is partly due to a lack of preservation or graphic depictions of early slings (e.g., in rock art). But it has even more to do with a pervasive disinterest in the subject by archaeologists since about 1960. By contrast, a paucity of actual spears, darts, atlatls, and bows has hardly kept archaeologists from exhaustively studying and inferring the use of these artifacts from stone projectile points.

To rephrase and scale-up complaints filed more than fifty years ago by the noted American Southwest archaeologist Richard Woodbury (1954, 171, 172), the few archaeologists who bother to disclose that "stone spheroids"—that just might be sling missiles—often constitute a significant part of the lithics at archaeological sites then immediately drop the ball. That is, they fail to furnish even Archaeology 101 information about such finds for comparative studies—such as discovery context, sourcing data, sample numbers, weights (possibly the most informative piece of information), measurements, and technology (a high level of technical sophistication is often involved in sling missile manufacture) that may provide vital clues in interpreting artifact and site function(s). (Relative to this issue, perhaps times are changing; Collins's [1997] study of the stone balls at Monte Verde, Chile, Topic's [1989] examination of the Ostra Site, Peru, and Brown Vega and Craig's [2009] distance experiments with sling-hurled projectiles in the Andes are hopeful signs.) Regardless, we have gathered sufficient data to permit us to engage in some fairly solid speculation.

It is likely that one of the first things early hominids would do with a rock—besides pound something with it, like a finger—would be to throw it, as modern-day human infants are prone to do. (To further explore the tie between human bioevolution and throwing of stones, see Cannell [2002] and Isaac [1987].) First tosses perhaps were untargeted, made only for fun. But it wasn't long before a strongly thrown, well-aimed stone could be effective in the hunt, in driving away competing predators, or in combat. If the hurled stone did not outright kill small to medium-sized prey (not recommended for elephants) or an enemy, it would have enough stunning power to give the hunter or warrior time to close in for the kill with other weapons, such as clubs, spears, or swords (Keeley 1996, 51, 52). The David versus Goliath strategy.

Undoubtedly, stones were first thrown using arm strength alone (Cannell 2002). One would intuit that it was likely not long (in geological and biological/cultural evolution terms, maybe several thousand years) before some bright light came up with the idea for a sling device that would greatly increase range, velocity, and lethality, as the invention of the spear thrower (known in the New World as the atlatl and in Australia as the woomera) did presumably later for the spear/javelin (see figure 1).

SURVEY OF SOME VERY EARLY OLD WORLD SITES (CA. 40,000 TO 1 MILLION+ YA)

The world's first stone missiles and, however unlikely perhaps, slings may be associated with pre–*Homo sapien* hominids and be over one million years old (Isaac 1987). From the African fossil man site at Olduvai Gorge, Tanzania, Mary Leakey (1971, 265–67) described "significant numbers" of generally hand-size and larger, intentionally shaped and smoothed stone "spheroids [balls] and subspheroids." She speculated that they were "missiles or bolas stones." Her speculation that they were missile stones recently received advocacy in a *Lithic Technology* article by the Simon Fraser University archaeologist Brian Hayden (2008, 113–24). Hayden argued that functions others have suggested for these spherical artifacts (such as hammerstones or spent lithic reduction cores) are not plausible. We assume he rejected out of hand Leakey's thought that they were bola stones since he does not consider the possibility.

Oakley (1950, 43–45) mentions comparable "chipped stone balls" in apparent association with Acheulean cleavers and hand axes and the "broken bones of baboons, wild pigs and zebra" from Olorgesailie, Kenya. This material dates to around 400,000 YA (Isaac 1977, 27).

Similar stone spheroids have been reported for Pleistocene sites in northern China (including Zhoukoudian) and Java, Indonesia, dating from 200,000 to possibly in the neighborhood of one million years ago (Bellwood 1985, 60–67; Jacob 1978, 13–15; Senshui 1985, 165). However, Bellwood (1987, 186) cautions that the Java dates are not certain, and these supposed very early tools may relate to later *Homo sapien* populations and date to less than 50,000 YA.

Skipping right along to ca. 40,000 YA, Zhonglang (1985, 201) noted that over a thousand stone spheroids associated with early *Homo sapiens* were recovered from the Xujiayao site, northern China, ranging in weight from less than 100 grams to 1,500 grams, and Zhonglang speculated that "although the function of these finely made, symmetrical spheroids is not yet known, it is thought that they may have been employed as missile stones or bolas." (As we will argue, it is a good possibility that those weighing plus or minus 100 grams were slingstones and those weighing more than 300 grams were hand-hurled missiles.) Yuping and Olsen (1985, 246, 247) commented on similar stone spheroids of comparable antiquity from Mongolia.

Oakley (1950, 56, 76, 77) mentioned similar stone balls of comparable antiquity to the northern China and Mongolian finds recovered from the African and European sites at Broken Hill Caves, Zimbabwe, and La Quina Cave, France.

ARE THEY SLINGSTONES?

For now we cannot move beyond speculation relative to the function of these very early stone spheroids, although it appears to be a safe bet that many, if not all, served as hand-hurled missiles. We have no evidence, in the way of actual bolas or slings or graphic depictions of them (e.g., in rock art), preserved at these Old World sites that would support the use of one or both of these devices. However, we offer the following thoughts as conjectural food.

Where you have large quantities or caches of such stones, as reported for the Xujiayao Site, it is more likely they were missiles—either hand-, sling-hurled, or both—rather than bolas. That is, given what we do know about the historical use of bolas (Métraux 1949, 253, 254; Wood 1870, 528–530), it is more likely that these devices will be retrieved, and thus we would expect to find only a few bola weights in mostly work or domestic settings, whereas historical and archaeological data indicate that sling missiles, particularly when stockpiled for possible combat use, are often found in large quantities or spread over wide areas, such as ancient battle grounds (LeBlanc 2003, 63, 142).

It is also probable that the first bola stones (or similar artifacts, such as fish net weights or club heads) were grooved for direct tether attachment (Bird 1988, 32, 33, 48–55; Coon 1971, 97; Lavallée 2000, 83, 164; Métraux 1949, 253, 254). None of the above descriptions note that these very early stone spheroids were grooved, perforated, or otherwise modified for attachment. Enclosing bola stones in leather or fabric pouches, which negates the need for attachment modification, appears to have come much later in time and may have been unique to South America (Métraux 1949, 253, 254).

WEIGHT MATTERS

Another important clue for determining the function of early stone spheroids (and later sling missile candidates) is their weight. Cannell's (2002) experiments with hand-hurled stones indicated that 200 grams (and stones of this weight were selected only by small children) is the minimal weight for telling impact on a possible predator or enemy at a distance of approximately 10 meters. The optimum and mean weight selected by physically fit males was around 500 grams and by females 330 grams.

In comparison, 200 grams is toward the upper end of the scale for sling ammunition. Korfmann (1973, 39) gave the average weight for sling missiles from the Mediterranean area, dating to ca. 2300–7000 YA, regardless of material used (i.e., stone, clay, or lead), as 20–50 grams. He did, however, comment that Balearic Islanders possibly used sling missiles that may have weighed as much as 330 grams, which, he noted, "probably represents the outside limit for sling missiles made of stone." (There are cases where the outside limit was probably much higher [see Harrison 2006].)

Based on our examination from 1998–2002 of some 150 slingstones in the Northern Mariana Islands Museum collections and a review of archaeological reports (Hunter-Anderson 1994, 5.71; Weaver 1988, 268), Marianas slingstones rarely exceeded 120 grams, with the mode being 40–80 grams. Takayama and Intoh (1978, 25, 26) showed a similar weight curve for some 156 slingstones they examined from Truk (Chuuk). These weight ranges generally hold true for slingstones worldwide—with some significant exceptions, such as the 1 kilogram naval slingstones reportedly used in Tahiti (Hauser-Schäublin & Krüger 1998, 296).

Here we are most interested in using weight to help identify sling missiles in ancient archaeological contexts. But once we are confident that we are dealing with sling missiles, weight has high potential for helping to determine much more. For example, as Korfmann (1973, 41) noted, in a battle setting—specifically the 348 BC siege of Olynthus, northern Greece—missile weights proved most helpful in discriminating between attacking Macedonians, who used lead missiles with a narrow weight range of 30–35.8 grams, and defending Olynthians, who used lighter lead missiles with a weight range of 19.5–33.4 grams.

JUMPING TO THE NEW WORLD (CA. 10,000–13,000 YA)

Jumping forward in time and to the other side of the planet, Collins (1997, 403–470) described 121 "culturally modified" spherical and subspherical, generally hand-size stones from the Monte Verde site in Chile dating, conservatively, to ca. 12,500 years ago. These spheroids/subspheroids ranged in weight from 10.4 grams (only one of the two grooved stones weighed this little) to 606 grams (one example). Most weighed 60–80 grams. Collins opined, "We [including, we assume, Monte Verde principal archaeologist Tom D. Dillehay] believe these to be *sling* [emphasis added] or *bolas* stones" (438). Since only two of these stones were grooved, we like the slingstone interpretation for all of the rest, with the possible exception of the 606 gram spheroid. Actually, from a later publication it appears that Dillehay (2000, 94, 95) would support our interpretation, or at least he would probably not argue strongly against it.

Staying in the Americas but moving north, subspherical stones similar to the Monte Verde finds, but often with a characteristic dimple at one end, have been found in apparent unique association with Florida Paleo sites dating to 10,000–12,300 YA. In the southeastern United States these stones are generally termed "egg stones" and are thought by many of the region's archaeologists to be bolas or club heads (Milanich 1994, 51, 52; Purdy 1981, 30; Simpson 1948, 14). We, of course, recommend they examine the possibility that many, if not all, functioned as sling- or hand-hurled missiles. A colleague suggested that perhaps the dimple was where a ribbon or streamer was attached (with some kind of mastic?) to track the stone's flight.

In 2004, while examining bipointed stones from Pyramid Lake at the University of Nevada, Reno, noted paleoarchaeologist Ted Goebel asked that we examine similar artifacts of undetermined function that had been recovered from the Mount Hebron Paleoarchaic Site in northern California (see figure 3 and map 12). This should mean that these artifacts were manufactured no later than 8,000 YA and could date to as early as 13,000 YA (personal communications 2004 and 2009). To us, they were strikingly similar to certain types of Oceania slingstones. If they were in fact slingstones, which we believe they were, and they should date to as early as 13,000 YA, they would be the earliest known examples of intentionally modified sling missiles of this design in the world and demonstrate that the earliest Americans possessed the sling.

DEFINITE SLING MISSILES BY 10,000 YA
AND TECHNOLOGICAL IMPROVEMENTS

Obviously, our assessment here failed to discover the world's first sling. However, by ca. 10,000 YA the sling was in wide use throughout the Mediterranean area, particularly in the Near and Middle East (Ferrill 1985, 24, 25; Korfmann 1973; Mellaart 1967, 217, 220).

To ca. 8,000 YA, with quite possibly the exception of the Mount Hebron, California, bipointed stones, naturally occurring or little modified spherical/ subspherical stones served as sling missiles. In the Near and Middle East, 8,000–6,000 YA, and on the other side of the globe in northern California/ southern Oregon and possibly the Caribbean, we see the next and essentially the last major improvements in sling missile technology: biconical and bipointed ovoid-type missiles and missiles made of clay (Ferrill 1985, 24, 25; Korfmann 1973; Mellaart 1967, 217; Rodden 1976, 155).

Biconical/bipointed ovoid (diamond, lemon, and Rugby or American mini-football) missiles were an improvement relative to accuracy, velocity, and hence lethality (Harrison 2006, 76). Besides occurring in the Near and Middle East, probable slingstones of similar shape and size (granted, in the cited reports they are classified precariously as "charmstones," "bola stones," or, safely by Sampson [1985, 235], "bipointed stones") dating to roughly the same time were recovered from the Borax Lake and Nightfire Island sites in northern California (Harrington 1948, 95–97, Plate 25b; Howe 1979, 25–29, 42–46, 59–61; Sampson 1985, 105, 235, 236) and, as cited above, from the Mount Hebron Site (see figures 3 and 4 and map 12).

In the Caribbean, bipointed slingstones show up on Venezuela's northeast coast between 4,200 and 7,000 YA on the Peninsula de Araya and the nearby islands of Margarita and Cubagua. What is particularly puzzling is that though hand-size stone spheroids (probable slingstones or bola balls) are archaeologically ubiquitous throughout the Caribbean and well beyond (literally surrounding the Peninsula de Araya), this presumably most effective of slingstone designs appears to be isolated in this small corner of South America and the Caribbean. This will remain the case throughout the area's prehistory (Cruxent & Rouse 1958, 43–55, 240–42; 1959, 13, Plates 2, 4, 5, 8, 41; Keegan 1994, 265–69 and personal communication 2004; Rouse 1960, 1964, 395–97; Rouse & Cruxent 1963, 43–47). (See figure 33a and map 7.)

Biconical (diamond-shape)/bipointed (American or Rugby football) ovoid missiles were developed specifically for use with the sling. These designs were never improved on. Thus, they are the only designs that we can place with some confidence as definitive for sling missiles. That is, without substantial supporting evidence, it can be argued plausibly (and it constantly is) that spheroids/sub-spheroids were hand-hurled or functioned in other ways (e.g., as bola weights, club heads, and game pieces). In forensic terms, the evidence threshold for demonstrating that biconical/bipointed ovoid artifacts of requisite size and weight and lacking attachment modifications (grooves, drilled holes, etc.) functioned as sling missiles is significantly lower than for spheroid artifacts.

Fashioning missiles out of clay was accomplished in different places for different reasons (e.g., as a substitute for stone). But largely it appears it was in the interest of standardization and mass production (Harrison 2006, 75, 76; Hassig 1992, 31). Later the Greeks and Romans would make one last significant innovation, the casting of lead sling bullets. These changes, particularly the last, were primarily made to improve the sling's effectiveness as a combat weapon (Harrison 2006, 75, 76; Korfmann 1973, 38–40; Onasander 1923, 449 [which will have you rethinking the origin of the phrase "eat hot lead"]).

Meanwhile, back in the Far East, we may have a puzzling data gap between the possible north China/Mongolian (and Java?) spherical slingstones of some 40,000 years ago and the appearance around 3,100 YA of highly modified Lapita "football" slingstones in the Reef-Santa Cruz Group of the Solomon Islands (see chapter 3). How much of this break is real or is a strawman based on an incorrect assumption (i.e., that the 40,000 YA spheroidal stones in fact are slingstones) or is due to lack of archaeological knowledge we cannot say.

Figure 1. Linus demonstrates the advantages of the sling. Used with permission, *Peanuts* © United Features Syndicate, Inc.

Figure 2. Roman lead sling bullets acquired by the Smithsonian in 1918. Gift of Mrs. E. M. Chapman. Smithsonian-NMNH Catalog No. A303515. Used with permission, Department of Anthropology, Smithsonian-NMNH.

Figure 3. Four probable Paleoarchaic (ca. 8–13,000 ya) slingstones from the Mt. Hebron Archaeological Site, Butte Valley, northern California. University of Nevada, Reno (UNR), Anthropology Department Catalog Nos. (left to right) top: 96-3-84 and 3202; bottom: 96-3-51 and 3196. Used with permission, Department of Anthropology, UNR.

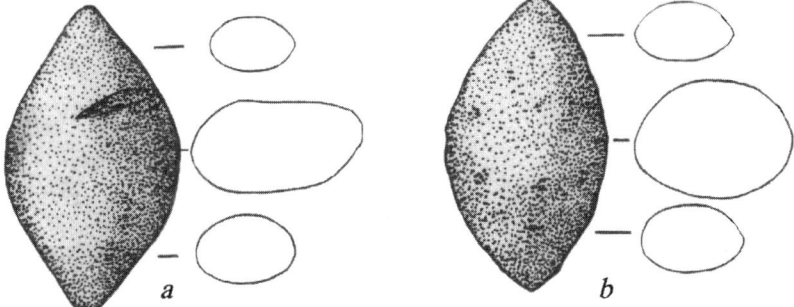

Figure 4. Bipointed stones from the Nightfire Island Site, Klamath Basin, northern California. The stones measure ca. 6 cm x 3 cm midline; weights not given (Sampson 1985, figs. 10–25a&b). T-M Types 1 and 2 correlates (see figure 7). Used with permission, Department of Anthropology, University of Oregon, Eugene.

PART 2

Oceania/The Islands of the Central Pacific

Introduction

The sling was well-known in pre-European Oceania (with the notable exception of Australia), where it primarily functioned as a combat weapon and a tool for bird hunting. Most scholars have assumed that the sling was particularly effective and largely restricted in use (for obvious reasons) to open terrain, including open seas (Feest 1980, 70–73; Korfmann 1973; Oliver 1989, 437–57; Parkinson 1999, 56; Thilenius 1936, 358). Doubt, however, is cast on this supposition by the accounts of explorers and ethnographers that report on sling use in thickly vegetated environs (Linton 1933, 241, 242; Linton 1943, 73; Porter 1815, 387).

To date, the earliest definite evidence for slings in Oceania (and possibly Southeast Asia) are bipointed ovoid, or mini-football-type, slingstones recovered from Lapita context in the Reef-Santa Cruz Group of the Solomon Islands, dated to ca. 3,100 YA (Moira Doherty, personal communication 2004; Green 1979, 39, 1991b). Although for the next 2,000 years archaeological sightings of sling missiles will be rare events in Oceania, approximately 1,000 years ago the reverse is true.

The following survey of the historical and archaeological evidence regarding use of the sling in the Pacific is unavoidably uneven. For the Mariana Islands of Micronesia there is a great deal of information concerning use of the sling. But in many areas of Oceania there is little to none. To some extent, as expressed or implied throughout this work, this reflects the worldwide situation (dramatically so for the Americas) when it comes to the lack of scholarly attention paid to this important artifact. To reinforce our introductory caveat, if we fail to mention an island or islands group the reader may assume we found no information regarding use of the sling. We stress again, "no information" means only that.

Figure 5. French sailor Jean
Baptiste Cabri, "gone native"
in the Marquesas, ca. 1800,
demonstrates a use of the
sling (Feest 1980, fig. 78).

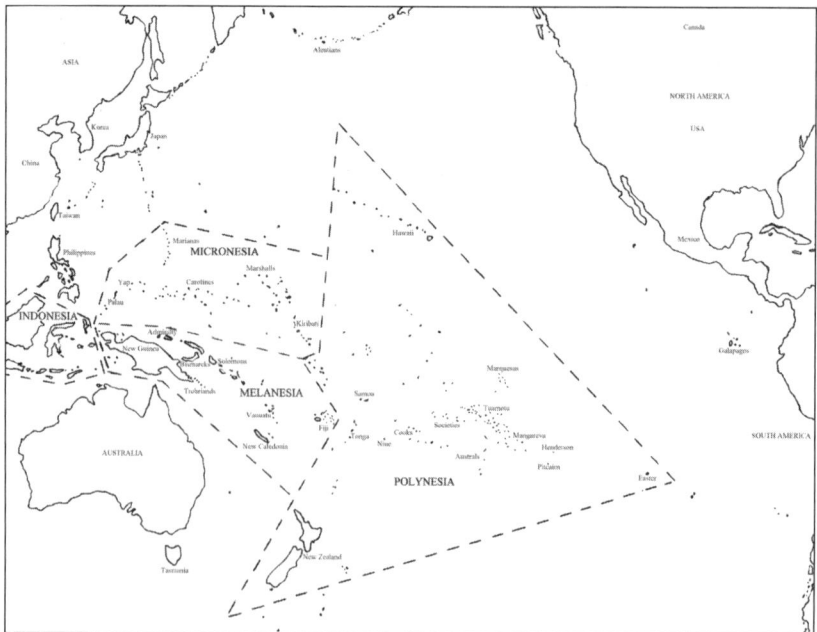

Map 2. Oceania

CHAPTER 2

Micronesia

WESTERN MICRONESIA

The Mariana Islands

The Marianas received their first human visitors, if not permanent settlers, some 3,500 years ago (Kirch 2000, 172, 173; Spriggs 2003, 63), quite possibly making the Marianas the first islands of Remote Oceania (defined as the islands of Micronesia, Polynesia, and Melanesia to the north, east, and southeast of the Solomons [Green 1991a; Kirch 2000]) to be visited by man.

Archaeologically, the sites of these early Marianas Islanders, or Pre-Latte Phase peoples, are largely identified by the presence of well-made, sometimes decorated pottery conventionally and for convenience lumped here under the term "Marianas Redware." Shell ornaments (e.g., beads, bracelets), adzes, fish-hooks, and expedient chipped-stone tools often are found associated with this pottery but little else. In time and look, this artifact assemblage is rather similar to the better-known Lapita Complex of Melanesia and western Polynesia. Although both Lapita pottery and Marianas Redware are most likely branches of the same ancient Island Southeast Asia ceramic tradition tree, currently Marianas Redware is thought to have its immediate origins in the Philippines or Taiwan rather than the Lapita Melanesian (or Near Oceania) incubator (e.g., Bellwood 1985; Butler & Harris 1995; Hunter-Anderson & Butler 1995; Kirch 1984, 2000; Moore, Hunter-Anderson, Amesbury, & Wells 1992; Oliver 1989; Russell 1998; Spoehr 1957; Spriggs 2003, 63).

At least that is what has become the orthodox—albeit far too simple—view about Marianas—and by extension Pacific—settlement. There are other views and numerous data problems (Allen 1996; Irwin 1992, 117–32; Spriggs 2003). One problem that has not been considered except briefly by Heyerdahl (1974, 223) is that ca. 7,000–2,000 years ago, the period of most interest relative to Pacific settlement, there is little to no evidence of sling technology in the Southeast Asia world, including the most likely donor areas of Malay-Indonesia, the Philippines,

Taiwan, Coastal China, Korea, and Japan. The bow and arrow and the spear thrower (atlatl or woomera) were the projectile weapons extant in the region during this period (Aikens & Higuchi 1982; Allen 1996; Blust 1996, 31, 32; Chang 1969; Chang & Goodenough 1996; Choe & Bale 2002; Robert Elston, personal communication 2004; Kim 1978; Kirch 1997, 47–49; Kiyotari 1987; Nelson 1993; Peterson 1974; Van De Velde 1984).

Given these data, one would assume that the atlatl and/or bow and arrow would be part of the Lapita assemblage—though there is only scant and ambivalent evidence for this (e.g., Bellwood 1978, 29; Ewins 1995, 55–57)—but not the sling. The sling, or more accurately well-accepted evidence for the sling in the form of definite human-modified "football type" slingstones, seems to materialize in Lapita context in Melanesia's Reef-Santa Cruz Islands around 3,100 years ago, seemingly out of nowhere.

Slingstones appear not to be part of Early Pre-Latte assemblages. The earliest known Marianas slingstones (and only a few) were recovered from Intermediate/Transitional Pre-Latte contexts on Guam and Rota dating to ca. 2,000 YA. Overwhelmingly, Marianas slingstones are associated with the Latte Phase beginning around 800 to 1,000 YA (Ray 1981; Russell 1998, 209; Weaver 1988, 270, 273). The Latte Phase is named for its hallmark feature, latte stones, which consisted of columns topped by coffee cup–like capstones, much like great inverted mushrooms. Latte stones were sometimes megalithic, weighing several tons and exceeding 16 feet in height, as seen at the House of Taga on Tinian and in the As Nieves Quarry on Rota (Morgan 1989, 116–49; Spoehr 1957). Nearly a thousand years later, the latte stone was adopted as the official symbol of the U.S. Commonwealth of the Northern Mariana Islands (CNMI). The bipointed ovoid slingstone serves the same purpose for the largest and most southern island of the archipelago, the U.S. Territory of Guam, the only political entity in the world where the slingstone is thus honored.

Thousands of complete and broken slingstones have been recovered, and continue to be recovered, from Latte Phase sites. The marked proliferation of slingstones during the Latte Phase is usually and reasonably interpreted as signaling the advent of warfare in the Marianas (Butler & Harris 1995, 256, 267; Hunter-Anderson 1994, 4.33, 5.66–5.77; Spoehr 1957, 137–40; Thompson 1932, 49–51; Weaver 1988, 255, 256, 268, 270–73, 277). Marianas sling missiles were laboriously manufactured from locally available materials, including coral, limestone, basalts, clay, and at least once out of shell, as represented by a *Tridacna* sling missile from Guam in the Smithsonian Museum collections (Smithsonian NMNH Cat. No. A382059). The raw materials were chipped and abraded into a variety of aerodynamic shapes or, when clay was used for slingstones, rolled and sun-baked or fired.

Most favored was the bipointed ovoid style, or more definitively Thompson's Types 1 and 2. Others were made into more diamond and egg shapes, or Thompson's Types 3 and 4 (see figures 7 and 8). Finish quality varied, but many Marianas slingstones, particularly those made of a red-streaked marblelike (argillaceous and indurated) coral limestone, were ground and polished, truly works of art.

The vast majority of Marianas slingstones are hand-size (or the size of a hen's egg), weighing 40–80 grams, though a rare few ones are the size of regulation American footballs and exceed 1 kilogram. These are thought to have been ceremonial, but perhaps some served utilitarian purposes, such as roof or canoe breakers, as seen in Tahiti and Hawaii.

As is often the case where the sling is the favored projectile weapon, the ancient Mariana Islanders (the Chamorros) either did not know of or only marginally used the bow and arrow. The latter is more likely, as the bow and arrow was known to other peoples of Oceania and Island Southeast Asia, so the Chamorros assuredly had some contact with it. Spoehr (1957, 164) describes a bone point recovered from Saipan that is probably "a fish spear point," but he notes its similarity to Hawaiian arrow points, hinting that the bow and arrow might have been known in the Marianas at one time though "unknown at the time of first contact [Magellan AD 1521]."

Sling missiles have been recovered from nearly all of the islands of the Marianas archipelago and from virtually all environmental zones, though mostly from shoreline areas (however, this may simply be sampling bias). They have been found cached, as surface scatter, and with burials. It appears there is no type of Latte Phase site that lacks sling missiles, even locales that appear primarily devoted to food processing and other domestic activities (Hunter-Anderson 1994, 5.74). As Spoehr (1957, 137) observed, "Slingstones are to the Marianas as projectile points are to the United States." That is, they are numerous, ubiquitous, stylistically variable, and possibly time and culturally sensitive. The latter two categories remain the most promising research areas that have received only passing attention since Laura Thompson's (1932) pioneering work with the 4,700-plus slingstones in the Hornbostel Collection. Among other things, she defined four distinct types based on shape and cautiously associated different materials and types with different islands (49–52).

One of Thompson's (1932, 52) propositions was "the study of the distribution of the limited number of slingstones in the collection points . . . to local differentiation of forms and materials. This seems to indicate less inter-island contact than might be expected in such a small archipelago." The Hornbostel Collection, however, contained slingstones only from the southern, relatively geologically complex high islands of Guam, Rota, Tinian, and Saipan. The islands north of Saipan were not included. According to Oda (1981, 122), in 1940 Ichiro Yawata of Tokyo University collected slingstones from the volcanic northern islands of Alamagan, Pagan, Agrihan, and Asuncion. He reported that they were all of limestone presumably from Saipan or possibly some of the other southern islands, as only igneous rock was available in the northern islands. Yawata's finding was supported by thirteen slingstones of coral limestone from Alamagan obtained by Peace Corps volunteer James Moses in the 1970s (Northern Mariana Islands Museum Accession/Catalog Records Group 1998.60). Slingstones of local igneous rock have yet to be recovered from the northern islands.

What apparently have not survived from the ancient times are slings. This largely appears due to the perishable nature of sling materials combined with the generally poor, tropical preservation conditions of the Marianas. It is possible that an early historic period Marianas sling, collected by one or more of the many European or Japanese explorers/occupiers, survives in some museum or other collection. It remains a remote possibility that a sling will yet be recovered archaeologically—say from a dry cave.

Saipan artist Curt Klemstein (2001, 10) is in possession of a fiber (coconut or pandanus) sling recently made by a "local woman who learned to make it from her father in 1912. Though we can't say with certainty that this is a true Marianas sling, its design is consistent with early historic writings as well as a drawing that was produced in 1819 [Freycinet Expedition]" (see figure 8).

If sixteenth- and seventeenth-century European testimonials are reliable, the ancient Chamorros were the Balearic Islanders of the Pacific (Korfmann 1973; Hornbostel 1924), the unsurpassed sling masters of Oceania (albeit slingers from Chuuk and from some of the Melanesian and Polynesian islands might have contested the point).

> They are very skilled at using the sling for which they fashion marble slingstones that fly as though bewitched. These resemble very large acorns that are flung from their slings in such a way and with such force that it is as though they were fired from an harquebus. They always hit the target with the point of the slingstone and strikes with such force that, if it hits the head or the body, it will penetrate. From the time they are very young, the boys from a given *camarin* [canoe house] or from a given village will challenge each other. Their slingstones are made of mud. (Driver 1989, 19)

> They can throw stones from a sling with such dexterity and strength that they are able to drive them into the trunk of a tree. (Higgins 1968, 46)

Their offensive weapons . . . include the sling, which they aim very skillfully at the head. Out of small ropes they weave a sort of net-bag, in which to carry stones with an oblong shape, some formed out of marble stone, and others of clay, hardened in either the sun or fire. They whirl and shoot those so violently, should it make an impact upon a more delicate part, like the heart, or the head, the man is flattened on the spot. (Lévesque 2000, 39)

A recent archaeological find on Guam provides dramatic corroboration for these European testimonials. This was the recovery of a human skull that showed perimortem trauma of such severity that the bones were shattered. A bipointed slingstone was embedded at the center of the splintered bone, leaving little doubt as to the cause of this fatal injury (Dave DeFant, personal communication 2005).

Palau (Belau) and Yap

Slingstones have not been recovered, or at least not recognized as such and/or reported on, from Palauan archaeological sites (Hunter-Anderson 2000; Osborne 1966). Osborne (1966, 31) does state that "the sling was known but not widely used." The negative archaeological findings, which are supported by historical data, appear to more than confirm this statement. It is possible that Palauan sling missiles might not be archaeologically detectable if the ancient Palauans were simply making use of unmodified coral chunks, as reported for the Marshalls, or of pebbles, as reported for Pohnpei. Unlike for those islands, early historical accounts do not indicate sling use on Palau, much less use of these types of sling ammunition (Lessa 1975, 97, 98).

The lack of sling use on Palau is of interest, given that Palau is otherwise viewed as being the most related of the Micronesian island groups to the Marianas in the areas of language, genetics, and settlement/cultural history. Albeit much of this is still being argued, particularly original settlement date, which currently is placed at ca. 3,000–3,400 YA, again comparable to the Marianas (Irwin 1992, 126; Kirch 2000, 167–73; Spriggs 2003, 63; Welch 2000).

The data situation for Yap and neighboring atolls (Ulithi and Ngulu) parallels that of Palau. Müller (1917, 330–35), in connection with the 1909 Thilenius Ethnographic Expedition, reported on and illustrated coconut fiber slings and spheroidal sling missiles (though bipointed types are also known for Yap): "[The sling] has likewise [in reference to Palau] fallen out of use on Yap, although this form has been retained in the small northern places, to which more frequent contact with the people of Uogoy might have contributed." Müller also relayed information of interest gained from Yapese on former warfare. His informants stated that battlefields could still be distinguished by "great stone walls." Battles were also carried out on the water between canoes manned by up to forty men and started with a "hail of stones."

Slings and slingstones have not been archaeologically reported for Yap or neighboring atolls (Cordy 1982; Craib 1984; Gifford & Gifford 1959; Hunter-Anderson 1982, 1983; Intoh 1984). Tentatively we interpret the negative archaeology in much the same way as for Palau. If battles employing sling missiles were mostly carried out at sea, they may be lying on the ocean floor. To our knowledge, this possibility remains to be archaeologically investigated. One would think, though, that stashes of such missiles should have been discovered on land if the sling had figured significantly in ancient Yapese warfare or hunting.

Müller (1917, 335) observed the bow and arrow on Yap but noted that it functioned only as a toy. As with the sling, the longevity of the bow—or if it ever functioned as more than a toy on Yap—is unknown. So far there is no archaeological evidence for the existence of the bow and arrow.

CENTRAL/EASTERN CAROLINES (CHUUK, POHNPEI, AND KOSRAE)

The high islands of the Central and Eastern Carolines—Chuuk (formerly Truk), Pohnpei (formerly Ponape), and Kosrae—appear to have been settled first around 2,000 to 2,500 years ago. The current archaeological consensus is that the Central Carolines show more affinity to Late Lapita than do the islands of western Micronesia and were likely settled from the east and south, from eastern Melanesia/Polynesia. Slingstones do not show up in the Central Carolines' archaeological record prior to ca. 800 YA (Irwin 1992, 128; Kirch 2000, 165–70; Parker & King 1984; Rainbird 1996).

In the Central Carolines, only on Chuuk and its neighboring atolls do historical and archaeological data come together to support the prevalence and variety of slingstones that rivals the Marianas (LeBar 1964; Rainbird 1996; Takayama & Intoh 1978, 25–28; Takayama & Shutler 1978, 7). Both biconical/bipointed ovoid and subspheroid slingstones were manufactured of "basalt . . . [and] sometimes made by molding with the hands a mixture of breadfruit sap and a reddish kind of soil" (LeBar 1964, 70). Takayama and Intoh's (1978, 25) excavations verify that basalt was preferred, but they also add sandstone slingstones to the inventory. Historically the Chuukese particularly prized coconut fiber slings from the Nama and Losap atolls (LeBar 1964).

Dam (1935) noted that the bow and arrow was only known as a toy on Satawal Atoll. Presumably this would have been the case for all the islands of the greater Chuuk region.

From various historical accounts, it is safe to conclude that the sling was an important weapon on pre-European Pohnpei. According to Christian (1899, 136), it was "the favourite missile-weapon of the Ponapeans before the introduction of fire-arms." Christian adds, "Amongst the Ponapeans, there is no more favourite passage in the Old Testament than the famous duel of David and Goliath, the translation of which is particularly spirited and happy in the missionary vernacular. The incidents of the encounter are peculiarly in accord with native fashion in every way and the name David (*Tepit*) is very common amongst the Protestant folk on the south-west coast."

According to Hambruch and Eilers (1936, 357–59), the Pohnpeian sling was mostly employed in sea battles and was still employed for hunting birds into the twentieth century. Further, they note and illustrate that both intentionally shaped "elliptically chipped stones or merely suitably shaped broad pebbles" were used as slingstones. Pohnpei is one of the few Micronesian islands—along with Kosrae, Guam, and Saipan—where stream-rounded pebbles and cobbles would have been readily available for use as sling ammunition.

Spheroid slingstones have been discovered in archaeological contexts on Pohnpei (Bath 1984; Morgan 1988, 76), though not in the quantities one would expect given the above historic information. To our knowledge, football-shaped slingstones have not been recovered archaeologically. The thin corroborating archaeological evidence at Pohnpei may be due to problems of a similar nature as those suggested for Yap, compounded by probable primary use of naturally occurring stream-rounded rocks.

The bow and arrow was long out of use, if ever used, by the time of Christian's visit in 1895. However, it may have been known to pre-European Pohnpeians, as implied in origin tales as relayed by Christian (1899, 111, 137): "The bow was used by the *Chokalai* or dwarf aborigines." The Chokalai were believed to have been Pohnpei's original inhabitants, who were later displaced by "the *Kona* and *Li-ot,* the giants and the cannibals." Presumably the Pohnpeians—either in reality, in spirit, or both—believed they were more related to the non-bow-using Kona and Li-ot. Christian speculated that the Kona and Li-ot were settlers from Polynesia and Melanesia. His speculation conforms remarkably well with current anthropological/archaeological thinking. For now, the story of the Chokalai remains relegated to legend.

The ethnohistoric and archaeological sling database for Kosrae essentially duplicates Pohnpei, except we know even less about it (Cordy 1993).

MARSHALL ISLANDS

Use of the sling historically is well documented for the Marshall Islands (Krämer & Nevermann 1938, 201–3; Lévesque 1992, 519–23; Linton 1926, 108). However, supporting archaeological evidence in the way of slingstones or slings is lacking (Dye 1987; Weisler 2000). This is not surprising. In a way, the negative archaeology corroborates the ethnographic information. Krämer and Nevermann (1938, 201) reported that "there are no special catapult stones [slingstones]. Only small coral-limestone pieces are hurled with the slings." Even more so than for the Marianas, it is unlikely that slings would be preserved in the low-lying coralline atolls of the Marshalls. And sling ammunition that simply consisted of unmodified coral chunks would be nearly invisible to the archaeologist, unless found in circumstances (such as cached along defensible barriers) or in statistically meaningful concentrations that would signal their function (see Cannell 2002, 339). To date, neither situation has been observed or reported.

Based on current understanding of sea-level fluctuations—relative to times when the Marshall atolls would have stood above sea level—and radiocarbon dates, the archaeological consensus is that settlement of the Marshalls could not have begun before 2,000 YA (Kirch 2000, 169, 174, 175; Weisler 2000). Given the so far sling-negative archaeology, it is not possible to know if the first Marshellese had slings. But we do know from Galvão's account of Saavedra's brief visit to the Marshalls in 1529 (he possibly put in at Eniwetok) that the Marshallese were armed with slings at that time (Lévesque 1992, 519–23).

In warfare, slings were the primary projectile weapons of the Marshallese and were also used for hunting birds. As is so often the case throughout Oceania, primarily spears were used for close-in fighting. Paradoxically (or, rather, what appears paradoxical), from the various European accounts it appears that when it came to the sling, the Marshallese were at the other end of the spectrum from the Chamorros: "Chamisso noticed that they were used without skill, and they are called no dangerous weapon, as there is not enough flying force in the coral stones" (Krämer & Nevermann 1938, 201). "There came unto them from the shore a kind of boat full of these men . . . who seeing the Spaniards . . . began to skirmish with slinging of stones, but Saavedra would suffer no shot at them, because their stones were of no strength, and did no harm" (Lévesque 1992, 522, 523). These comments appear to verify that failure to use natural stones of aerodynamic shape, if any occurred, or to modify stones into more streamlined shapes (diamonds and footballs), appreciably impaired the Marshallese sling's effectiveness as a weapon. (Perhaps this result was what the Marshallese desired, but that's another story.)

Marshallese women participated in battles in a manner similar to that described for residents of the neighboring Gilberts (Koch 1986, 246), the Cook Islanders of Polynesia (Wood 1870, 374), and the Yuki peoples of northern California (Foster 1944, 189). Women formed a line behind the male front ranks to supply them with sling ammunition, first aid, and water, and they "threw stones and spears at the enemies over the heads of the warriors" (Krämer & Nevermann 1938, 203). It is unclear if women made use of the sling. This may explain why Marshallese and Gilbertese coconut fiber and wood "armor" does as much to protect the warrior's backside as his front (Koch 1986, 246). It was also a wise man who ensured that he was on good terms with his female relatives before going into combat (a nod to Saipan historian Sam McPhetres for that thought).

Again, the Marshallese apparently knew the bow and arrow, but only derisively as a "woman's or child's weapon" (Christian 1899, 136).

KIRIBATI (FORMERLY GILBERT AND KINGSMILL ISLANDS)

Little is known archaeologically about the Gilbert and Kingsmill Islands, part of the Republic of Kiribati since 1979. From ethnographic and historic accounts, this area's cultural history appears tied to the Marshalls. In many respects, the narrative for the Marshalls applies to Kiribati. However, the sling may not have figured as prominently there. Linton (1926, 108) stated that it was "little used in the Gilberts." Murdoch (1923), Sabatier (in Nixon 1977), and Koch (1986) made no mention of the sling or slingstones. The Auckland (New Zealand) Museum, however, does include a sling in its Kiribati exhibit, with the label "used in warfare."

Of special interest in the Auckland Museum's Kiribati exhibit are the worked "throwing stones." These stones were presumably hand-hurled in combat. They are relatively large, ranging 15–17 cm in length by 8 cm in max/midline diameter, and are made of coral limestone. We did not obtain their weights, but we estimate they weighed well over 300 grams.

The most interesting thing about them was their shape. They are basically shaped like American footballs, except only one end is pointed, with the opposite (presumably proximal) end flattened and rounded. The Auckland Museum also displays similar stones ("fighting stones") from the Polynesian Island of Niue.

Figure 6. Exhibit of Marianas slingstones (*acho atupat*) from the Hornbostel Collection at the Guam Museum. The two oversized specimens were probably ceremonial in purpose or perhaps were used as house/canoe busters. Used with permission, Department of Chamorro Affairs, Guam Museum, Hagatña.

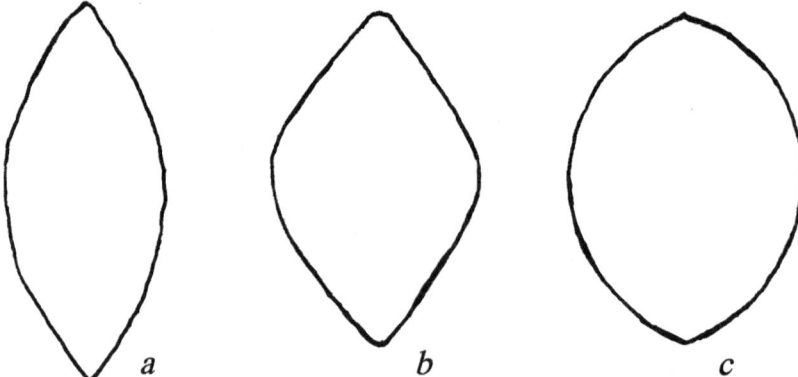

Figure 7. Revised T-M slingstones classification: (a) T-M Types 1 and 2, elongated or mini-football/almond shape, tips pointed or sometimes blunt, usually circular or ovoid in cross-section (T-M Type 1) but plano-convex and biplano forms (T-M Type 2) are also observed; (b) T-M Type 3, biconical or diamond shape, tips blunt or pointed, cross-sections vary from ovoid to biplano; (c) T-M Type 4, ovoid, egg or lemon shape. Based on Thompson (1932, fig. 22) and recent study by the authors of Marianas slingstones at the CNMI Museum.

Figure 8. Chamorro sling (*atupat*) replica and T-M Slingstone Types 1, 3, and 4. Used with permission, CNMI Museum.

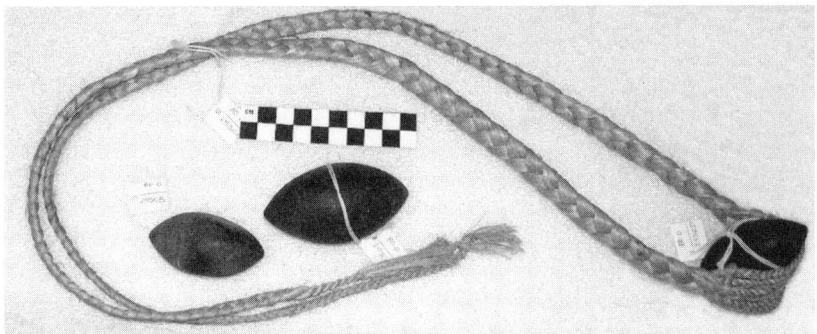

Figure 9. Chuuk (Truk) sling and three slingstones of a dense, mafic volcanic rock. Acquired from Eugene Schroeder in 1909 by the AMNH. AMNH Pacific Ethnology Collections Catalog No. 80.0/2950 A-D. Used with permission, Division of Anthropology, AMNH.

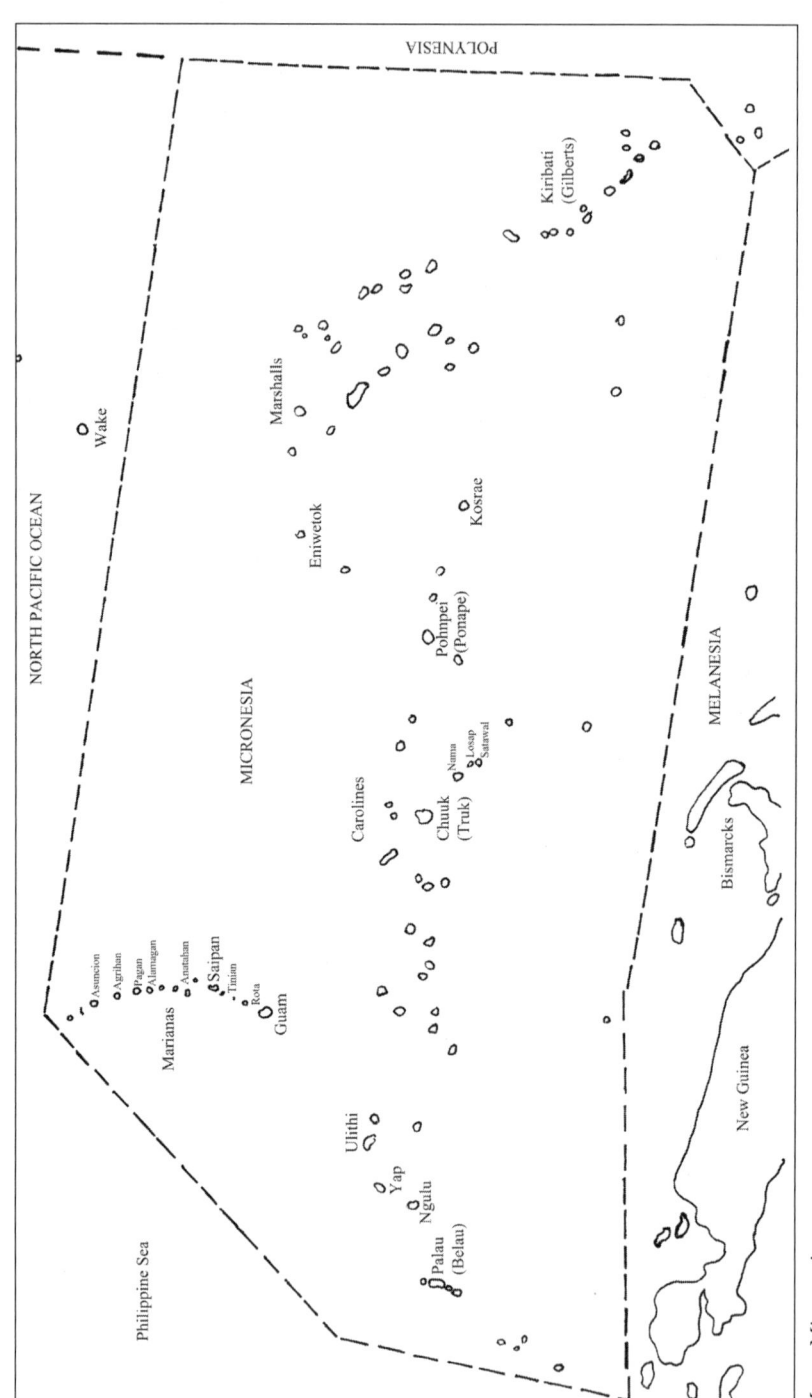

Map 3. Micronesia

CHAPTER 3

Melanesia

NEW GUINEA AND THE TROBRIAND ISLANDS

Humankind has had a foothold in New Guinea for more than 40,000 years. To date, neither slings nor recognizable sling missiles have been identified in datable archaeological context (Allen 1972; Kirch 2000, 63–84; White & O'Connell 1982).

The vast majority of historical and ethnological accounts report use only of the spear thrower and bow and arrow as projectile weapons in New Guinea (Oliver 1989, 437–39; Tregear 1892; Wood 1870, 225). However most of these accounts— and most of the archaeology to date—appear biased by data collected from the New Guinea Highlands, an area of New Guinea populated by non-sling-using Papuan speakers.

Based on data collected by the 1904 Daniels Ethnological Expedition, we know the sling was historically used by Austronesian speakers of the southern tail, southeast, and northeast coasts of New Guinea and nearby islands, including the Trobriands (Seligmann 1910, 15). Seligmann also states that these groups did not use the bow and arrow.

The 1890 Edge-Partington Album illustrates slings held in the British Museum collections from the southern end of New Guinea (Part 1, artifacts 5 and 6) and the Trobriand Islands (Part 2:157, artifact 6). In the course of our research and travels, we either located or were informed about slings and slingstones originating from the southern end of New Guinea in the ethnographic collections of the Auckland (N.Z.) Museum; South Australian Museum in Adelaide (Barry Craig, personal communication 2005; see figure 10); the University of Queensland Anthropology Museum in St. Lucia, Brisbane; and the American Museum of Natural History (AMNH) in New York City. The slingstones held by these institutions are mostly bipointed ovoids (T-M Types 1 and 2) made of a dense, mafic volcanic stone, ground and polished, ranging from 6 to 8.5 cm long by 3–4 cm max/midline diameter. While we did not manage to obtain the weights of these slingstones, they did seem heavy for their size, and our estimate is that they ranged in weight from 45 to 90 grams. The Reverend Henry Newton (1914, 76) judged the weight range of New Guinea slingstones, which he observed in the late nineteenth and early twentieth centuries, to be a quarter- to half-pound, or around 112–225 grams.

Among the AMNH slingstones are spheroids about the size of golf balls (ca. 4 cm in diameter). All are made of what appears to be the same type of dense, mafic volcanic rock, ground and polished. The AMNH Catalog Record (S-885) indicates these spheroid slingstones were purchased from Otto Finsch, the former curator of ornithology at the Rijks Museum, Amsterdam. Finsch acquired these slingstones sometime between 1879 and 1885 from the Port Moresby area on the southeast coast of New Guinea.

BISMARCK ARCHIPELAGO AND THE ADMIRALTY ISLANDS (MANUS GROUP)

Archaeological excavations conducted in the 1980s and 1990s on New Britain and New Ireland, the largest islands of the Bismarck Archipelago, revealed a surprisingly long human occupancy record of some 35,000 years (Kirch 2000, 74–78)—surprising because moving out to the Bismarcks, most likely from New Guinea, would have required an ocean crossing. Up to this time, most archaeologists were highly skeptical that humans at such an early date had the necessary skills and watercraft to accomplish such a feat. But the first settlers of Sahul (the geographical name for the New Guinea and Australia land mass prior to their separation by rising waters) would have had to cross open ocean from Southeast Asia some 40,000–60,000 years ago (Kirch 2000, 63–76; Spriggs 1997, 1–42). Additionally, Morwood and colleagues (1999) presented a compelling and largely ignored case for *Homo erectus* having this ability an astonishing 840,000 years ago.

Over 2,000 years ago, and possibly as early as 2,400 YA, the first identifiable slingstones show up in the Bismarck's archaeological record in Late Lapita Transitional context (Bellwood 1979, 249; Garling 2003, 221, 222, 229–31; Green & Anson 2000, 184, 185; White & Downie 1980, 196, 197, 202–4, 214, 215). Interestingly, in time and cultural patterns (undergoing "transition") this compares favorably to the situation described for the first appearance of slingstones in Micronesia on Guam and Rota, the southernmost islands of the Marianas archipelago.

W. R. Dickinson's personal communication to Stephanie Garling (2003, 221) concerning a biconical slingstone recovered from the Angkitkita Site, located on Lif Island of the Tanga Group off of New Ireland, has dramatic implications concerning the potential lethality of this particular missile and such missiles generally: "Made of barite, with a specific gravity of 4.5, it is probably the prehistoric equivalent of a spent uranium bullet." Arguably ethnographer Richard Parkinson's (1999, 48–50, 55, 56, 73, 99, 126, 127, 359) 1907 description of the sling, its ammunition, and its use in the Bismarcks remains the most illuminating for Oceania:

> Slingshots and stones are still used everywhere in the southern half of New Ireland and also on the offshore islands. However, they had a far greater spread in earlier times, since during road construction in areas near the northern end of New Ireland, numerous carefully worked slingshot stones have been found, different in shape from the missiles that are still used in the south. During his voyage along the east coast of New Ireland, Dampier [in 1700] found slingshots [an understatement, as Parkinson later notes that Dampier's ship was prevented from anchoring by natives attacking with slingstones from their canoes; also see Mulvaney 1978, 154] in an area where they no longer exist today, which he named Slinger's Bay. The slingshot stones found are on average 5 centimeters long and 2.5 centimeters in diameter at their thickest part. The ends are tapered [sounds like he is describing classic T-M Type slingstones; Mulvaney 1978, 152–54; figure 12 this volume]. Because of a lack of suitably shaped gravel, they worked a dense, almost crystalline coral stone into slingshot stones. In the south, streambeds and beach yield satisfactory, readily available material in the form of rounded stones, and these are used just as nature provided them, as is also the case on New Britain.

Of great interest is Parkinson's (1999, 48–50) detailed description of trepanning surgery. On the Gazelle Peninsula of New Britain, trepanning was practiced as a specific remedy, with reportedly remarkable success, for slingshot inflicted head wounds. (Graham Martin [2003, 339] claims a 75 percent survival rate for New Britain, compared to 78 percent trepanning mortality rate at London hospitals in the 1870s.) Parkinson's observation that trepanning was largely performed as a remedy for slingstone injuries confirms missionary J. A. Crump's (1901, 167–72) earlier report.

Parkinson (1999, 96) states that the bow and arrow was never observed in the western part of New Britain; nor does he acknowledge its existence in New Ireland. Earlier chroniclers, such as Dupperey in 1823, depicted use of the bow by warriors on New Ireland (Brosse 1983, 151). Parkinson (1999, 96) did observe that the blowpipe (blowgun) was used in the South Cape area of New Britain exclusively for the hunting of birds. He found it exceptionally interesting to encounter "this Indonesian instrument" in the "South Sea islands."

Humankind has been in the Admiralty and other small islands of Melanesia east and north of the Bismarck Archipelago for well over 13,000 years. There is no historic or archaeological evidence that indicates the sling was ever used in these islands. The bow and arrow was the projectile weapon of the Admiralties, at least for the historic period, and was strictly used for hunting. Clubs and spears were the exclusive weapons of warfare (Kirch 2000, 63–116; Spriggs 1997; Parkinson 1999, 158).

SOLOMONS/REEF-SANTA CRUZ-DUFF ISLANDS

There is little ethnohistoric support for use of the sling on the major islands of the Solomons: Buka, Bougainville, Choiseul, Santa Isabel, New Georgia, Guadalcanal, Malaita, San Cristobal. Historical accounts generally indicate use only of the bow and arrow as a projectile weapon in the Solomons (Parkinson 1999, 201, 202, 218–21; Wood 1870, 300), though Codrington (1891, 305, 306) is unclear on this point. These accounts show that the bow and arrow functioned in much the same way as noted for the Admiralties, with spears and clubs being the major, if not the exclusive, weapons of war.

To date, Solomons archaeology appears to support the sling-negative historical information, but as Kirch (2000, 131), echoed by others (e.g., Spriggs 2003, 63), warns: "Put bluntly, this vast archipelago has not enjoyed sufficient archaeological work—even of a reconnaissance nature—to begin to flesh out its prehistory." The Solomons picture, then, is subject to substantial change as more information is acquired on the archipelago's prehistory and more attention is paid to identifying slingstones in existing collections. For example, in the AMNH Ethnographic Collections, we located an artifact, golf ball in size and shape, made of a tufflike volcanic rock (Cat No. 85–366) and a biconical artifact, 6 cm long by 3.1 cm max/midline diameter, of a similar volcanic stone (Cat No. 85–365). The AMNH records indicate that these artifacts came from New Georgia, Solomon Islands. The records advance some guesses as to function (biconical drill) but state that the function of the artifacts is unknown. We suspect they are slingstones. Artifact 85–365 would pass in the Marianas for a T-M Type 3 slingstone (see figures 7 and 8). Also a slingstone from Malaita is included in the ethnohistoric collections of the South Australian Museum (Cat. No. A42250), and there two slings (Cat. Nos. A49182 and A49183) are shown as coming from the Solomon Islands (Barry Craig, personal communication 2005; see figure 13).

According to Kirch (2000, 95), among others, for more than 30,000 years the southeastern end of the Solomons proper (defined by the southeast tip of San Cristobal and excluding the Reef-Santa Cruz and Duff groups) "marked the limits of human existence in the Pacific." Then, ca. 3,200 YA, Lapita peoples began their epic push into Remote Oceania. First sailing eastward, presumably from the main Solomons (and/or Bismarcks?), to settle the remote southeastern islands of the Reef-Santa Cruz and Duff groups (Kirch 2000, 93–95).

As previously noted, the earliest slingstones of definite human manufacture (bipointed ovoids) in Oceania, dating to ca. 3,100 YA, were recovered from a Lapita context in the Reef-Santa Cruz Islands. Most of these are of basalt. It is of particular interest that one was fashioned from *Tridacna* shell (giant clam) (Moira Doherty, personal communication 2004; Green 1979, 39; 1991b). At the Otago Museum, Dunedin, New Zealand, we observed a bipointed *Tridacna* "slingstone" (not actually identified as such) of unknown date but apparently of recent age (though it may be an heirloom) in their Santa Cruz Islands exhibit (see figure 14). Along with the *Tridacna* slingstone from the Marianas, these are the only slingstones we know of that were manufactured from shell in Oceania, or elsewhere, for that matter.

It was more than another thousand years, or ca. AD 250, before slingstones became common in Reef-Santa Cruz and Duff islands archaeological assemblages. These later slingstones were mostly made of basalt and various grades of coral limestone (Moira Doherty, personal communication 2004; Buckley 2000, 135, 139; Edge-Partington 1890, 1:163, artifacts 6, 7). Possibly some "special purpose" slingstones were made of *Tridacna,* or they were heirlooms. Combat and hunting use of the sling and bipointed slingstones persisted into recent times on these islands (Buckley 2000, 135, 139).

The bow served along with the sling as a projectile weapon for hunting and combat in the Santa Cruz Group (Codrington 1891, 308–13). Such equivalent co-use of these weapons, as noted, was unusual for Oceania and not seen in Polynesia (except maybe in Tonga) or Micronesia, but it appears to be relatively common in Melanesia. Closer examination—and beyond the scope of this work— may indicate that preference for these weapons in Melanesia breaks down along language family lines. That is, the sling was preferred by Austronesian speakers and the bow and arrow by Papuan speakers, as substantively is the case for New Guinea. The reason for the sling being used to the virtual exclusion of the bow in pre-European Polynesia and Micronesia may be this simple: This vast area of Oceania was the exclusive domain of Austronesian speakers. But it is just not that simple. If this correlation should prove correct, it hardly answers the question of why the Austronesians preferred the sling to the exclusion of other projectile weapons. (We expand on this conundrum—Tregear's Conundrum—in our section on Tahiti and the Marquesas in chapter 4.)

VANUATU (FORMERLY NEW HEBRIDES)

Vanuatu's first human settlers were Lapita colonists who arrived in the archipelago some 3,000 years ago (Bedford, Spriggs, & Regenvanu 1998, 189). Slingstones have not been discovered, or more likely have not been recognized as such, in archaeological context (Bedford et al. 1998; Shutler & Shutler 1966). An exception is a solitary "New Caledonian type" (presumably an ovoid) probable slingstone that was recovered by the Shutlers from the Tanna Rockshelter. This artifact was recently reexamined by Andrew Hoffmann (personal communication 2004), the Vanuatu Cultural Center archaeologist, who reports that it is no more than 300 years old, postdating European contact.

From various historic accounts we know that at European contact (ca. AD 1605), the sling was a widely used hunting and combat weapon in the New Hebrides (Codrington 1891, 306; Deacon 1934, 213, 216, 217; Speiser 1996, 185, 209–13, Plate 61). However, by the time of Captain Cook's visit in 1774, the sling's use in warfare appears to be restricted to the island of Tanna at the southern end of the archi-pelago (Forster 1777, 515, 516, 534). By the time of Speiser's observations, 1910–12, the sling functioned only as a toy. According to Speiser (1996, 209), "The stones cast with slings were about the size of a nut, preferably pebbles. . . . There were no specially shaped stones such as found in New Caledonia. Bags for slingstones were also unknown." However, the Auckland Museum had on exhibit a slingstone carrying bag with several worked, bipointed/ovoid, slingstones of coral limestone, ranging from 5 to 8 cm in length by 3–4 cm max/midline diameter, labeled as being from the New Hebrides. Also, N. G. Seaman (1967, 201) mentions seeing bipointed stones, apparently identical to the Auckland Museum specimens, at a Portland, Oregon, museum, marked "sling stones from New Hebrides." It is pos-sible that the Auckland and Oregon museums misidentified the origin of their slingstones. Our bet is that Speiser was mistaken—or manufacture, or possibly import from New Caledonia, of such "specially shaped stones" and carrying bags had ceased by the time of his observation.

The bow and arrow functioned as a hunting and war projectile weapon through-out the New Hebrides (Codrington 1891, 304–13; Deacon 1934, 213; Forster 1777, 479–516; Speiser 1996, 185, 189–200, 212). More restricted in use was the rather unique thong-propelled javelin (Forster 1777, 515, 516, 568; Speiser 1996, 188, 189). Use of this weapon, along with the continuing use of the sling on Tanna, implies a strong connection between the southern islands of Vanuatu and New Caledonia.

NEW CALEDONIA AND THE LOYALTY ISLANDS

New Caledonia and the Loyalty Islands were first settled by Lapita colonists at approximately the same time as the New Hebrides, ca. 3,000 years ago (Sand 2001, 75–77; Sand, Bolé, & Ouetcho 2002).

Definite T-M Type 1 slingstones show up in these islands' archaeological record around 1,400 YA/AD 600 (Gifford & Shutler 1956, 69, 89, 135; Sand 2001, 81, 87). Presumably, these bipointed stones represent first use of the sling in New Caledonia. It is possible that unmodified rocks served as sling ammunition prior to 1,400 YA. For now, the archaeology is silent on this possibility.

Gifford and Shutler (1956, 69), among others, noted that New Caledonian slingstones were made of local basalts and steatites. They gave the weight range of ten complete "gift specimens" they received as 25.8 to 71.6 grams. They recovered two fragmentary slingstones from excavations but did not list their weights. Brigham (1902, 345) gave the average length and weight of New Caledonian slingstones in the Bishop Museum's collections as 1.75 inches, or approximately 4.6 cm and 1.56 ounces (ca. 45 grams). Further, he claimed New Caledonian slingstones were the "lightest and most acute" used in the Pacific. His claim remains untested through modern statistical analysis of (presumably) more definitive data sets that are now available.

There is a voluminous ethnohistoric record on use of the flexible hand sling in New Caledonia and the Loyalty Islands (Douglas 1998, 125, 143; Forster 1777, 568, 570; Knight 1880, 231, 232; Oliver 1989, 448; Wood 1870, 204, 205). When a major museum includes slingstones and sling gear (carrying bags) from Oceania in its collections, they are often New Caledonian (Bishop Museum Collections 1921, Book 6:29, 30; Edge-Partington 1890, 1:134, artifacts 6, 7, 8; Hauser-Schäublin & Krüger 1998, 296, 337; Wissler 1909, 339, 340; see figure 15). From these data we know that the sling was used for bird hunting and warfare, as is true for most of Oceania.

We located no information to indicate that the bow and arrow was used in New Caledonia. Spears, besides being used for close combat, functioned as projectile weapons along with the sling, which is not unusual in Oceania. What is of particular interest is that spears were often launched with the aid of a coconut fiber sling or thong (Howe 1977, 136; Knight 1880, 277; Wood 1870, 204, 205), which in the Pacific may have been unique to New Caledonia, some islands in the New Hebrides (Forster 1777, 515, 516, 568; Speiser 1996, 188, 189), and Fiji (Clunie 1977). Knight (1880, 277) describes a similar Roman device.

As in New Britain and New Ireland, trepanning was practiced in New Caledonia, at least in part, as a specific remedy for slingstone-inflicted head wounds (Martin 2003, 340; Stewart 1958, 473, 480, 484).

FIJI

Fiji was pioneered by peoples with Lapita pottery who arrived in these islands around 2,800–3,100 years ago (Hunt & Lipo 2006, 1603; Kirch 2000, 94, 155).

Slingstones either have not been discovered or not reported archaeologically (Frost 1974; Gifford 1951). As is likely evident by now, negative evidence for slingstones is not unusual, but in Fiji's case the lack of archaeologically reported slingstones seems odd. Pre-European Fiji had clear ties with New Caledonia, and much of the archaeology so far conducted has expressly dealt with "fortified sites" (Frost 1974). Given the rich historical record, particularly on Fijian combat use of the sling (Clunie 1977, 71, fig. 33; Knight 1880, 231; Wood 1870, chap. 4), we think that slingstones are there but have to date gone unrecognized.

Clunie (1977) is a comprehensive source of ethnohistoric information on the sling as well as other Fijian weapons. He states that the sling was a popular weapon into the latter half of the nineteenth century, and its use for sport continued into the early twentieth century. With obvious implications for archaeological identification, Clunie (1977, 71) states: "I have never seen a definite Fijian sling stone so cannot confirm whether they were simply rounded river stones or were pointed oval in shape. I suspect that the round stones of about tennis ball size found lying about in old forts, while definitely hurled by hand from hill forts, may well have been cast from slings on occasion."

Through Clunie (1977, 71) we have yet another testimonial on the destructiveness of a well-fired slingstone, attributed to the Reverend Thomas Williams in ca. 1858:

> I have been led to think that the natives [Fijians] throw stones and other missiles with extraordinary force. I am confirmed in this opinion by a musket which stands at my elbow. It was used by a Tonguese in the late attack on Koro na Yasaca. During the conflict a stone struck the barrel of this musket . . . shattered the lighter part of the stock; made an indentation in the barrel ⅛ of an inch in depth, and . . . drove the barrel ⁷/₁₆ of an inch out of the straight line. I have since learned that this stone was thrown from a sling.

The Fijians at one time or another seem to have made use of about every projectile weapon they could lay their hands on. Besides the sling, the bow and arrow was used along with the thong-propelled spear/javelin—in the Pacific a device apparently shared only with the New Caledonians and some peoples of the New Hebrides (Clunie 1977; Forster 1777, 515, 516, 568; Speiser 1996, 188, 189; Wood 1870, 204, 205).

Though the data are anemic, trepanning possibly was practiced in Fiji as a remedy for slingstone-inflicted cranial trauma (Heyerdahl 1953, 657).

Left: Figure 10. Sling and slingstone from Port Moresby area, Central Province, Papua New Guinea. South Australian Museum (SAM) Collections No. A10861. Image courtesy of SAM.

Below: Figure 11. New Ireland warriors. Note the sling. From Duperrey Expedition records, 1823, Bibliotheque Nationale Collections, Paris.

Figure 12. Nine New Ireland slingstones. SAM Collections No. A10960. Image courtesy of SAM.

Figure 13. Possible jagged-edged or unfinished slingstone from Malaita, Solomon Islands. SAM Collections No. A42250. Image courtesy of SAM.

Figure 14. Three probable slingstones from the Santa Cruz Islands, Solomons. Two are made of basalt and one (the white one) is of *Tridacna* shell. They were presented as being "heirlooms," or ceremonial in purpose, in the Otago Museum exhibit. Used with permission, Otago Museum, Dunedin, New Zealand.

Above: Figure 15. Eleven slingstones and a carrying bag from New Caledonia. SAM Collections No. A52449. Image courtesy of SAM.

Left: Figure 16. Fiji sling. SAM Collections No. A7283. Image courtesy of SAM.

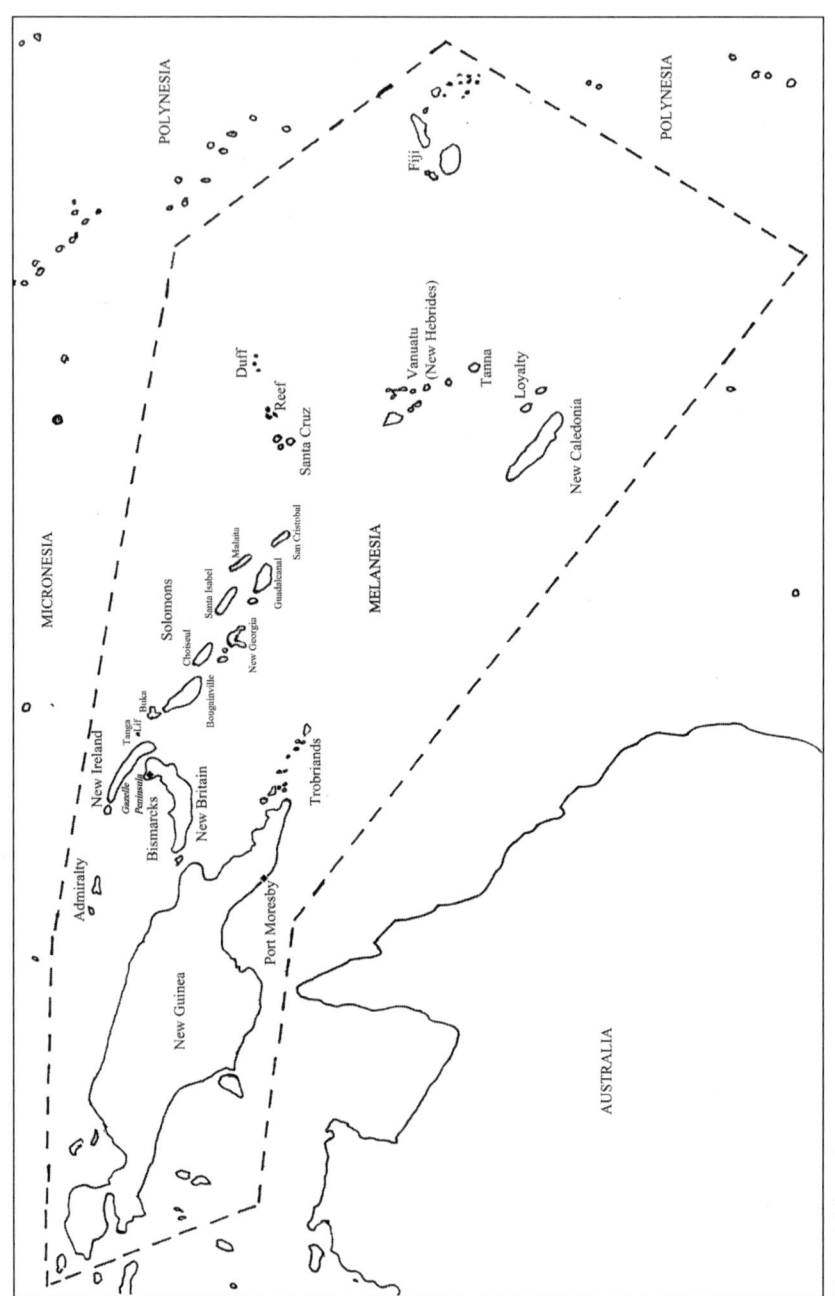

Map 4. Melanesia

CHAPTER 4

Polynesia

Let us say then that the Samoa-Tonga area was Hawaiki for the entirety of the Polynesian triangle, the source to which all island settlements must ultimately be traced.
—Robert C. Suggs, *The Island Civilizations of Polynesia* (1960)

The Tonga archipelago was first settled by Lapita colonists who landed on these islands at about the same time they reached Fiji and Samoa, ca. 2,800–3,100 YA (Hunt & Lipo 2006, 1603; Kirch 2000, 210). The peoples of Fiji, Tonga, and Samoa interacted with each other intermittently throughout their prehistory and history. These interactions varied from friendly trade and societal intercourse to lethal hostilities (Burley 1998; Ferdon 1987; Kirch 1984, 71, 217–42; Suggs 1960, 86–101).

Slingstones had not been discovered, or were not recognized as such, at Tongan archaeological sites until recently (Burley 1998; Poulsen 1987). Moira Doherty (personal communication 2004) said that she received information from David Burley concerning a probable "mini football" type of quartz slingstone recovered from the Kauvai 2 Site on Tongatapu (Tonga's largest island). It was apparently found in Lapita context dating to 2,600–3,000 YA. However, these data are as yet unconfirmed.

Although early European accounts testify that Tongans hand-hurled stones in combat with telling effect, Ferdon (1987, 235, 261, 262) notes that there is no record of sling use in Tonga prior to the nineteenth century. Further, he suggests that Tongans were "introduced" (we think more likely reintroduced) to the sling as a combat weapon in battles with Fijians. If this should prove to be the case, from Williams's account, it looks as if Fijian slingers could take great, though hurtful, pride in their Tongan students.

It is clear that the bow and arrow functioned as a warfare weapon in Tonga during the nineteenth century, apparently introduced from Fiji (Ferdon 1987, 261; Linton 1926, 108; Tregear 1892, 56, 57). It is unlikely that it functioned as a warfare weapon when the first Europeans, Le Maire and Schouten, visited Tonga in 1615 (Brosse 1983, 217). To our knowledge there is no archaeological, and little historic, support for this position. Tasman in 1643 observed "no weapons" of any type (Sharp 1968, 156), and Forster, from his stay in 1773, described the Tongan bow (replaced in the nineteenth century by an improved Fijian model), though he did not witness it being used as a weapon. In fact Forster (1777, 238–40) found it peculiar that the Tongans possessed what he assumed to be "weapons," since he was not sure they engaged in warfare at all (thus Captain Cook's reference to Tonga as the Friendly Islands).

The sling was in use in Samoa at the time of European contact in the 1700s (Brosse 1983, 83; see figure 17). Stair (1897, 244) recorded that the sling was still in use ca. 1838–45. The implications of the following statement by Stair are of special interest regarding expanding the types of injuries that may be attributed to slingstones: "The sling was always considered a very formidable weapon, and old warriors have repeatedly assured me that a wound from a stone hurled from a sling and thrown with force was often much worse than one received from a musket ball. If a stone struck the arm or leg, it was difficult to heal, since the bone was usually smashed to pieces, and caused much suffering."

This claim was quite possibly exaggerated. Although we are not familiar with Samoan slingstones, we have observed very large pocketed Cook Islands slings loaded with grapefruit-size slingstones, both spheroids and bipointed, at the Auckland and Otago museums in New Zealand. One easily could imagine them capable of inflicting this kind of horrific injury. The Samoan claim gains further independent support from accounts of such slingstone injuries suffered by combatants in early Mediterranean-area warfare (Ferrill 1985, 25) and from Captain Porter's (1815, 387) journal entry concerning such an injury sustained by one of his officers in the Marquesas in 1813.

It is safe to assume that the sling was in use prior to European contact in Samoa, but for how long is not known. To date, neither slings nor slingstones have been reported for pre-European Samoan archaeological sites. This is perplexing. Samoan archaeology, as was previously noted for Fiji, has often been concerned with survey and excavation of supposed defensive/fortified sites (e.g., Clark & Herdrich 1993; Green & Davidson 1969, 1974). Again, we strongly suspect that the primary reason for the so far sling-negative archaeology parallels the Fiji situation: Slingstones are there, but to date they simply have not been recognized as such and/or considered by archaeologists. Tregear (1892, 57) stated that the Samoans did not use the bow, "the sling being the missile weapon."

NIUE

Lonely Niue is located south of Samoa, northeast of Tonga, and west of the Southern Cooks. Niue missed the Lapita boat, not being settled until ca. 2,000 YA (from Tonga?). We know little of Niue's prehistory (Walter & Anderson 2004).

Niue is of particular interest in the study of the sling because it is one of a very few Polynesian islands where it appears not to have been used, at least historically. Niuans did, however, use specially shaped throwing or fighting stones, which they hand-hurled at enemies with damaging effect. These stones (*Tridacna* shell was also used) were worked into at least two forms: a generalized ovoid shape with the distal end pointed and the proximal end rounded, as described previously for Kiribati, and a bipointed, slingstone-like lemon-shaped missile (Isaac 1987, 9–11; Loeb 1926a, 129, Plate 8; Wood 1870, 395). Loeb (1926a, 129) mentions that a "string" was tied to some of these stones. Unfortunately, he does not elaborate on the purpose of the string. Was it a nondetachable sling or a one cord bola?

Regarding the bow and arrow, Niue is equally interesting, for it is one of a very few Polynesian islands, along with Mangareva, maybe Tonga, and possibly one of the islands in the Marquesas (Hiroa 1938, 193; Kirch & Green 2001, 192; Linton 1926, 108; Quiros 1595, 23; Tregear 1892, 56, 57), where it possibly functioned as a combat weapon at European contact. But as with Tonga, Mangareva, and the Marquesas, this issue is hardly settled. Loeb (1926a, 129) states that there is "no evidence that the sling or the bow and arrow was used in bird hunting or warfare." Wood (1870, 395) claims that the bow was part of the Niuan arsenal. Forster's (1777, 407) account of his brief visit during Cook's second voyage in 1774 mentions "a long bow, like those of Tonga-Tabboo," carried by one Niuan warrior. Perhaps significantly, Forster did not witness the bow being used. What he did witness was that this same young man, instead of firing an arrow, hurled "a very large stone, with so much accuracy, as to hit Dr. Sparrman's arm a violent blow, at the distance of forty yards."

THE SOCIETY (TAHITI) AND MARQUESAS ISLANDS

Among Pacific archaeologists, the original settlement dates for the Society and Marquesas archipelagos are a matter of considerable debate. Depending on whose archaeological arguments you find persuasive (Allen 2004; Kirch 2000, 230–34), these islands may have first been settled, most likely by Samoan and/ or Tongan pioneers, more than 2,200 years ago (ca. 200 BC) or less than 1,400 years ago (ca. AD 600).

Whatever the longevity of human occupation of the Society and Marquesas archipelagos finally proves to be, sling-wise, and in many other respects, the peoples of these islands are closely related. Of course, that statement is generally applicable to all of Polynesia, but some islands are closer than others in time, space, culture, and language, with the Society and Marquesas being two such examples. We have a voluminous ethnohistoric record documenting similar use of the sling for both archipelagos, but the archaeological record is skimpy.

The earliest identifiable slingstones so far archaeologically recovered, dating to around 1,100–1,200 YA (ca. AD 800), are from the 'Opunoho Valley, Mo'orea, in the Society Islands (Emory 1979, 204, 205). We suspect these are the mini-football type, since this is the form usually equated with slingstones in the Pacific, but we were unable to locate confirmatory descriptions or illustrations.

For the Society Islands we have numerous ethnohistoric records related to sling use (Ferdon 1981, 124, 262; Hauser-Schäublin & Krüger 1998, 296; Kaeppler 1978, 52, 53, 80, 120–23; Linton 1926, 108, 110; Oliver 1974, 134, 279, 281, 319, 376–408, 993, 1282; Oliver 1989, 443, 454; Ratzel 1896, 213; Tregear 1892, 57; Wilson 1799, ix–c, 368–70, 397). From these accounts and more, one must conclude that at European contact the sling was the premier combat projectile weapon (not a substitute for but preferred over the bow and arrow) on land and sea not only in ancient Tahiti but throughout Oceania. Oliver (1974, 392) quotes the following statement, attributed to the Reverend William Ellis (1827), which succinctly tells us much about the Tahitian sling, slingstones, techniques, and the esteem in which warriors skilled with this weapon were held.

> During the engagement, the parties often retreated, so that there was a considerable space between the ranks in these seasons, as when advancing to the onset. The slingers were then employed, and they often advanced in front of the ranks to which they belonged, and with boasting threats warned their enemies to fly or fall. The most dangerous missile was the *uriti* or stone, from the *ma* or sling. The latter was prepared with great care, and made with finely braided fibres of cocoa-nut husk, or filaments of the native flax, having a loop to fasten it to the hand at one end, and a wide receptacle [pocket] for the stone in the centre. The sling was held in the right hand, and, armed with the stone, was hung over the right shoulder, and caught by the left hand on the left side of the back. When thrown, the sling, after being stretched across the back, was whirled round over the head, and the stone discharged with great force.
>
> The most expert slingers were celebrated through the islands, as well as the most renowned among the warriors: and when one of these presented himself, a cry ran through the opposite ranks. Beware, or be

vigilant, *e ofai mau o mea*—an adhering stone is such a one; or *e ofai tano e ofai buai*—a sure or a powerful stone is such a one. The stones, which were usually about the size of a hen's egg, were either smooth, being polished by friction in the bed of a river, or sharp, angular, and rugged; these were called *ofai ara*—faced or edged stones. When thrown with any degree of elevation, they were seen and avoided, but they were generally thrown horizontally four or five feet from the ground, when they were with difficulty seen, and often did much execution. The slingers were powerful and expert marksmen.

From early European accounts of Tahiti we gain an idea of the effective range of sling-hurled missiles that fills a data gap from previously cited Spanish testimonials for the Mariana Islands. European observers in Tahiti noted it was common to see embedded in the bark of trees slingstones that had been hurled from a distance of some 200 yards (182 meters) (Ferdon 1981, 124; Wilson 1799, 370). These observations conform well to the reported effective range of Old World slingers (Ferrill 1985, 25; Lindblom 1940, 11). Harrison (2006, 76) suggested, based in part on modern ballistics testing, that skilled slingers could have been effective at even greater distances.

The following account concerning the role of Tahitian slingers in a naval battle was told to Robert Thomson of the London Missionary Society ca. 1835. Although use of slings in sea battles, particularly in Micronesia and Polynesia, is often mentioned in historic narratives, this is one of the very few accounts of sufficient specificity to be instructive to archaeologists and military historians.

> All arrangements being complete the spear men took their position in lines along the front of the platform which was laid over the double canoes, the slingers behind them each with his heap of stones and bore down before the wind upon the enemies' line; as they approached the slingers began the action on both sides and stones of considerable weight [up to 1 kilogram, if certain early European observations are believable; Hauser-Schäublin & Krüger 1998, 296; Kaeppler 1978, 123] were hurled with great power upon the canoes of the warriors. (Oliver 1974, 406)

This account is substantially the same as Captain Wilson's (1799, 397) earlier description, except that Wilson added that paddlers of war canoes were also armed with slings.

Society Islands data on the function and antiquity of the bow and arrow relative to the sling is of particular interest. At the time of European contact (AD 1767), the bow and arrow was not used as a weapon of war (Oliver 1974, 320), which, as previously stated, was the norm throughout Micronesia and Polynesia. The Tahitians may have employed the bow for bird hunting, along with what was apparently the preferred method of hand-hurling stones at perched birds (Oliver 1974, 279, 281), but what appears unique to Tahiti was their archery contest, or maybe more accurately their archery ritual. These contests were conducted in special garments accompanied by much ceremony. Archers shot their arrows from specially constructed stone platforms. The objective was to achieve great distance rather than hit a target. This appears to have been largely a male sport, but there is at least one account that indicates women also participated, though separately (Oliver 1974, 320–22; Tregear 1892, 57).

Concerning antiquity of the bow in the Society Islands, a piece of a bow and seven wooden arrow points were recovered from the Vaito'otia and Fa'ahia sites on Huahine, which dated to ca. AD 650, or around 1,400 years ago (Sinoto 1988, 121, 127). No slings or slingstones were recovered from these sites.

Returning to the Marquesas, we are again fortunate to have a voluminous ethnohistoric record concerning sling use (Ferdon 1993, 67, 75, 113, 121; Heyerdahl 1974, 171, 223; Knight 1880, 231; Linton 1923, 130, 389, 390; Porter 1815, 306–99; Ratzel 1896, 213; Wood 1870, 390). This record leaves no doubt that the sling was in use at European contact (AD 1595). Again, unfortunately, we could not find that slingstones, much less slings, have been recovered from dated archaeological contexts from which longevity of use could be established (Allen 2004; Rolett & Conte 1995; Sinoto 1979). Importing what little sling-relevant archaeological data we have from the Society Islands, it is reasonable to assume comparable antiquity for the Marquesas: sling use dating at least to AD 800, or 1,100–1,200 YA. If it turns out that the first human settlers arrived in the Marquesas no earlier than AD 700, as many archaeologists are now persuaded (Allen 2004, 186; Green & Weisler 2002, 235), then we would guess that the sling and slingstones were brought to these islands (physically and/or conceptually) by those first Marquesans.

The U.S. Navy frigate *Essex*, under Captain David A. Porter's command, visited the Marquesas in 1813. Porter's (1815) journal entries from that stay concerning use of the sling, slingstones, and trepanning surgery are particularly instructive, as they are some of the very few relatively detailed accounts we have by someone actually facing the sling in battle (1815, 323, 324).

Their slings are made of the fibres of the bark of the cocoa-nut tree [probably coconut husk and/or hibiscus bark], and are executed with a degree of neatness and skill not to be excelled. The stones thrown from them are of an oval shape, of about half a pound weight [ca. 225 grams, on the heavy side for slingstones], and are all highly polished, by rubbing against the bark of a tree; they are worn in a net suspended about the waist, and are thrown with such a degree of velocity and accuracy, as to render them also equal to musketry—wherever they strike they produce effect; and the numerous scars, broken limbs, and fractured skulls of the natives, proves that. It is no uncommon thing to see a warrior bearing about him the wounds of many spears . . . some bear several wounds occasioned by stones; and I have seen several with their skulls so indented, as that the whole hand might have been laid in the cavity, and yet the wounds were perfectly healed, and appeared to give no pain [many of these injuries were likely club inflicted]. While on the subject of fractured skulls, [I] mention a practice which is pursued by them. Whenever the skull is cracked, the bone is laid bare, and the fracture traced to its end, and there a small hole is drilled through the skull to prevent the crack from going further. This practice is pursued wherever the fracture branches off in rays. If there are any loose pieces of bone, they are carefully laid in their places, the wound is bound up with certain herbs.

These are also some comments from Porter's journal (1815, 327–399) relating to combat with "Happahs" and "Typees" (Marquesan groups).

Mr. Downes [one of Porter's officers] to rush up the hill; at that instant a stone struck him on the belly and laid him breathless on the ground.

We had two wounded, and one of the Indians [Marquesan allies] had his jaw broke with a stone.

We entered the bushes and were at every instant assailed by spears and stones. We could hear the snapping of the slings, the whistling of the stones . . . but we could not perceive from whom they came.

From the thicket . . . we were assailed with a shower of stones, when lieutenant Downes received a blow which shattered the bone of his left leg, and he fell.

Three of the men remaining with me were knocked down with stones. The wounded entreated me to permit the others to carry them to the beach.

And our allies pursued in turn, and knocked over with a stone one of
the Typee warriors, whose body they triumphantly bore off.

For long-range fighting the Marquesans employed "elaborate" slings that
often measured more than 1.5 meters in length (Knight 1880, 231; Linton 1923,
389; Wood 1870, 390). Linton added that "specially prepared slingstones were
used." These "stones were oval or double conical [T-M Types 1–3] and *sometimes*
[emphasis added] weighed as much as half a pound." Linton does not contradict
Porter but does imply that "half a pound," or around 225 grams, is near the upper
limit for Marquesan slingstones. Linton also mentions that these stones "were
made of heavy close grained rock [probably basalt] and the specimens seen were
symmetrically pecked but unground." Modified and unmodified rounded or egg-
shaped stones, largely gathered from the ocean floor and thus requiring a dive
of several meters, were used as well (Ferdon 1993, 113; Linton 1923, 389). In this
endeavor, most likely some recycling was involved—that is, many of these stones
were probably previously used slingstones expended during naval battles.

Linton (1923, 389, 390) mentions that at close range, at distances of less than
45 meters, stones were often hand-hurled rather than slung at the enemy. Also,
when going into battle, the Marquesan warrior wrapped his sling around his
hand, but on nonhostile, festive occasions he wore it as a headband.

As is often seen in Oceania, Marquesan women occasionally participated in
land battles, at least to the extent of supplying slingstones to the male warriors
(Ferdon 1993, 121).

Again, as with the Tahitians, the Marquesans fought battles at sea. And again
the sling was the long-distance projectile weapon used to initiate these engagements (Linton 1923, 389).

In the Marquesas the sling may have been strictly a warfare weapon. We found
no mention of it functioning in another way (such as for bird hunting)—unless
you consider doubling as a headband on festive occasions a "use." But even at
these times, if the mood of the "partygoers" should turn ugly, it was readily
available for use in combat (Ferdon 1993, 67). Trepanning was practiced in both
the Society and Marquesas islands as a remedy for slingstone-inflicted cranial
trauma (Heyerdahl 1974, 224–26; Martin 2003, 340, 341; Porter 1815, 323, 324).

Concerning the bow and arrow, one account indicates that at initial Spanish contact in 1595, at least on one island of the Marquesas, the bow and arrow
may have functioned as a warfare weapon along with the sling (Ferdon 1993,
113; Quiros 1595, 23). By the 1700s, however, the bow was merely a "toy" and for
shooting rats (Heyerdahl 1974, 223; Linton 1923, 389; Wood 1870, 390).

The foregoing raises the distinct possibility that the bow antedates the sling in

Tahiti and maybe the Marquesas. Depending on how far you want to push these data, possibly the bow preceded the sling across Polynesia or even all of Oceania. Consider, for example, the implications of the Pohnpeian legend of the Chokalai. A correlate of what we suggest Pacific archaeologists should frame as a working hypothesis would be that these data as well indicate that the sling replaced the bow as a functional weapon in the Marquesas and Tahiti and perhaps beyond, as suggested by Ferdon (1993, 113).

This proposition goes against what many military historians and archaeologists accept as the "normal" evolution of these weapons systems based on the supposed superiority of the bow. Albeit there are countering arguments. See, for example, Harrison (2006) and Lindblom (1940, 9) as well as Onasander's (1923, 445, 449) ca. AD 59 advice to Roman field commanders on the deployment of light troops armed with slings. That view, of course, assumes that at some point in Tahiti's prehistory the bow functioned as a combat weapon, an assumption tenuously supported by a Spaniard's account of initial contact with one group of Marquesans (Quiros 1595, 23) and a linguistic reconstruction (Bellwood 1978, 29). It also assumes that the current chronology will hold up (most unlikely) as future archaeological excavations are accomplished yielding more reliable radiocarbon dates and, among other things, slingstones.

What all this does suggest is that we need more scholarly attention (particularly from archaeologists, anthropologists, and military historians) paid to the Austronesian bow versus the sling, or Tregear's Conundrum.

Edward Tregear (1892, 56), in his article on the Polynesian bow in the *Journal of the Polynesian Society,* first posed the question: "Perhaps one of the most puzzling problems known to anthropologists is to account for the apparent dislike shown by the fair Polynesians [which we propose should now be expanded to include all of Oceania's Austronesian speakers] for the use of the bow and arrow." The unstated half of Tregear's puzzle concerns Polynesians' preference for the sling. Some 119 years later, Tregear's question remains to be answered, even though Emory (1965, 234, 235) and Ferdon (1993, 113) took stabs at doing so. We, too, have some thoughts on the matter, which we will share in our concluding remarks.

SOUTHERN COOK (HERVEY) ISLANDS

The Southern Cooks lie southwest of the Society Islands. By AD 900, or ca. 1,100 YA, Polynesian settlements were well established in the Southern Cooks. Although they left few traces, many archaeologists suspect that humans first arrived in these islands much earlier. As is still too often the case in Oceania, dates for original human entry into the Southern Cooks remain to be fixed (Kirch 2000, 232–34).

Once more we will need to rely on ethnohistoric sources and museum collections for our information on use of the sling and slingstones in the Southern Cooks, as it appears these artifacts have not been found in archaeological context. Or this is what we must assume since we could find no discussion of the sling or slingstones in relevant archaeological literature (Allen & Schubel 1990; Kirch 2000, 250–57).

The sling was in use at the time of European contact in 1775. We suspect its use dates at least to AD 900, based on Polynesian settlement data and linguistic reconstructions (Kirch & Green 2001, 190, 191; Osmond 1998, 227). But again, for more definitive knowledge of its pre-European longevity and use(s) in the Southern Cooks, sling-relevant archaeology is needed.

In many respects the history and use of the sling in the Southern Cooks is comparable to that described for Tahiti and the Marquesas; and there was some connection, particularly with Tahiti. One major exception was that we found no reference indicating that the Cook Islanders used the sling in naval battles—understandable, for it appears they did not engage in such battles. According to an early nineteenth-century missionary, John Williams, battles were fought in an organized fashion on the Southern Cook island of Mangaia. Opposing armies would meet in open terrain and form themselves into four ranks. The first row consisted of warriors armed with long, thrusting spears followed by a second row of warriors with clubs. The third row was the slingers backed by a fourth row of women who furnished the slingers with ammunition and carried other spare weapons and supplies. Occasionally women more actively participated by hurling stones at adversaries who were placing their husbands in mortal danger (Wood 1870, 374, 375).

The sling may have functioned strictly as a warfare weapon in the Southern Cooks. As noted for the Marquesas, we found no mention of it being used for other purposes (Hiroa 1927, 351–54; Wood 1870, 374, 375). Hiroa (1927, 352, 353) illustrated and described two types of slings (exhibited at the Auckland Museum) from Rarotonga, the largest island in the Southern Cooks. One is a "small sling" with a stone-holding pouch measuring approximately 12 cm by 3 cm. The overall length of the small sling still exceeds 1.5 meters. The "longer sling" exceeds 2 meters in length with a pouch approximately twice the size of that of the small sling. Hiroa illustrated and described spherical slingstones, of an unidentified type of volcanic rock, that range from golf-ball size (3–4+ cm in diameter) to softball or grapefruit-size (9+ cm in diameter). It is probably safe to assume that the smaller shot was used with the small sling and the larger shot was hurled with the longer sling.

In 2005 we observed these slings with their ammunition at the Auckland Museum. Hiroa did not mention bipointed ovoid slingstones. But we observed this form displayed in the Rarotonga exhibit at the Otago Museum in Dunedin, New

Zealand. The museum examples appeared to have been fashioned from both lime-stone and basalt and ranged in size from 5–10 cm long by 3–5+ cm in max/midline diameter. We did not have the opportunity to record the weights of these slingstones but estimate that they ranged from 45 to 300 grams (see figure 20). According to Hiroa (1927, 351) the bow and arrow was only used by "children in play."

AUSTRAL (TUBUAI) ISLANDS

Kirch (2000, 349) noted that the "Austral Islands represent a major gap in our knowledge of Eastern Polynesian archaeology." This presents another unfortunate situation, as the Australs may hold the key(s) to answering many questions rela-tive to use/nonuse of the sling as well as the bow and arrow on the southeastern fringe of Polynesia.

Rapa Iti, or simply Rapa, the remote southern island of the Australs group, provides the most (though still little) information relative to the sling and other weapons. Rapa appears to have first been colonized by Polynesians less than 1,000 years ago, or sometime between AD 1,000–1,300 (Green & Weisler 2002, 236, 237; Kennett, Anderson, Prebble, Conte, & Southon 2006, 343, 350).

Numbered among the artifacts recovered by the 1956 Norwegian Archaeologi-cal Expedition from the Rapa hill fort of Morongo Uta were two "elliptical beach pebbles of fine grained basalt" (Mulloy 1965, 52). Measuring 6.3 and 6.6 cm in diameter (no other measurements were given), they were identified as probable slingstones. Mulloy thought these stones were not modified by man but expressed uncertainty on this point. According to Mulloy (1965, 23, 58), support for this iden-tification comes from Stokes's 1921 manuscript filed with the Bishop Museum in Honolulu, where he noted that two types of slings were used on Rapa Iti, one with a "hand pocket" and one with a split pocket. He also mentioned that slingstones were simply "picked up from the beach," implying, we assume, that these were formed by nature only. Mulloy (1965, 58) also mentions that Stokes was of the opinion that the bow and arrow may have been used as a weapon of war on Rapa Iti. However, we could find no archaeological or historic basis for such conjecture.

POLYNESIA'S SOUTHEASTERN FRONTIER:
MANGAREVA (GAMBIER), HENDERSON, PITCAIRN,
AND EASTER (RAPA NUI) ISLANDS

Original settlement dates for these islands remain conjectural, but it appears that Mangareva, Henderson, and Pitcairn were first colonized by Polynesians (from the Marquesas?) ca. 1,000–1,300 years ago, or AD 700–1,000 (Anderson, Conte, Kirch, & Weisler 2003; Green & Weisler 2002, 233–37; Weisler 1994). Easter Island appears to have been colonized (from the Marquesas via Mangareva?) some 800 years ago, or ca. AD 1,200 (Green & Weisler 2002, 234–37; Hunt & Lipo 2006; Kirch 2000, 271).

The weight of available information from various fields of inquiry (archaeology, ethnology, linguistics, history) argues for the sling having been known at one time in these islands but dispensed with, at least as a weapon of war, by the time of early European contacts in the eighteenth and nineteenth centuries. At times on Mangareva, possibly both the sling and the bow and arrow were used as combat weapons. One of Hiroa's informants stated that specially shaped basalt slingstones were used. However, Hiroa noted that the first Europeans to land on Mangareva, the Beechey party in 1825, were opposed by locals armed with only the spear and unmodified hand-thrown stones of "suitable size." He noted as well that slings were not collected from Mangareva by the early European explorers. Possibly significantly, Hiroa (1938, 193) did not interpret this collection failure as meaning they were not present but, rather, that they were "not important." We have no idea what he meant by "not important." To our knowledge, to date, slingstones have not been recovered archaeologically from Mangareva (Emory 1939).

Pitcairn lay long abandoned by Polynesians by the time the *Bounty* mutineers landed there in 1790. According to Heyerdahl and Skjölsvold (1965, 3), included among the Polynesian artifacts found by the mutineers and their descendants were "sling stones." Unfortunately, we have no way to verify this identification, since no more information was provided. Slingstones were not included in Emory's description of Captain Brisson's (1928) collection of stone artifacts from Pitcairn in 1920, but this was a highly biased collection since it consisted almost entirely of adzes.

Henderson Island, like its neighbor Pitcairn, had long been abandoned by Polynesians by the time of the first European landings in the eighteenth century. To our knowledge, no evidence (archaeological or otherwise) of the sling—or of other kinds of weapons, for that matter—have been reported for Henderson (Emory 1939, 7; Kirch 1984, 90–92; Weisler 1994).

When it comes to information about the sling, Easter Island presents us with a mixed bag. Ethnographic and historic accounts indicate the sling was unknown at the time of European discovery in 1722. By that time fights were initiated, and sometimes finished, with apparently unmodified hand-hurled stones and obsidian-tipped javelins. Use of these weapons for hunting was not indicated (Geiseler 1995, 72; Métraux 1940, 165, 354). Métraux's (1940, 165) informants stated the sling was a recent, post-European introduction from Tahiti. Geiseler's (1995) 1882 report, among others, does not support Métraux's information in that he made no mention of the sling. However, there is support from historical linguistics for the sling having been known to Easter Islanders prior to the late

Tahitian introduction or reintroduction, if Roussel's 1869 translation of the Easter Island word *hura* for sling was correct (Métraux 1940, 165; Smith 1961, 390).

The only physical evidence for pre-European existence of the sling appears traceable to the 1955–56 Norwegian Archaeological Expedition's excavation of the Poike Ditch feature, reported by Carlyle Smith (1961, 385–91). Smith labeled as slingstones three objects of vesicular basalt recovered from the Poike Ditch. He described two of these objects as cylindrical with shallow depressions at one end. His narrative implied that these specimens were human modified, although he is not clear on this point. The third object he described as "oblately spheroidal," which "may owe its form to modification by man or to wave action." None of these objects was illustrated.

Smith (1961, 390) did, however, supply some curious measurements. They are curious in that they do not conform to standard measurements for known Oceania slingstones. Measurements for the two cylindrical artifacts he gave as 6.5 cm in diameter by 5.3 cm in "height" (*height?*) and 6.2 cm in diameter by 3.6 cm in height. Measurements for the "oblately spheroidal" specimen were 7.4 cm in diameter by 5.5 cm in "thickness." He did not list weights. His descriptions and odd measurements, particularly when not supported by illustrations for comparison, do not instill confidence that these artifacts were classified correctly.

These possible slingstones date to Easter Island's Middle or Ahu Moai Period, ca. AD 1,100–1,500 (Ferdon 1961, 529–31; Kirch 2000, 272). McCoy (1979, 150) and Van Tilburg (1994, 107) only incidentally mentioned slingstones. We suspect, however, that they were alluding to Smith's three questionable slingstones as they supplied no amplifying data. (McCoy confirmed this suspicion via personal communication in September 2005, adding that he never saw a "shaped slingstone" during his 1968 survey of Easter Island.)

There is no support from any relevant discipline for the bow and arrow having any great antiquity on Easter Island. It appears to have been introduced as a toy from Tahiti probably by Father Roussel in ca. 1869 (Heyerdahl 1961, 49; Métraux 1940, 354). This probability is reinforced by use of the Tahitian word *fana* for the bow and arrow (Métraux 1940, 354).

NEW ZEALAND AND THE CHATHAMS: THE SOUTHWESTERN
POINT OF THE POLYNESIAN TRIANGLE

It is possible that the sling (or the bow and arrow, for that matter) was not used in New Zealand, although it is likely that it was known to the Maoris given the relatively recent settlement of New Zealand by Polynesians (from the Southern Cooks?) in approximately AD 1,200, or 800 YA (Hunt & Lipo 2006, 1603). New Zealand data on the subject are skimpy and inconclusive (Davidson 1987; Fagan 1995, 309; Hamilton 1911, 103; Honoi 1918, 226; Knight 1880, 232; Skinner 1918, 96).

We do know that at least hand-hurled stones were used in defense of *pa*, fortified settlements, similar to British Iron Age hillforts, which were specifically designed to defend against slingstone barrages and in turn facilitate use of slings and hand-hurled stones by defenders (Avery 1986; Brice 1985, 26–32, 132, 133; Fox 1976, 28, 29). One Maori informant claimed that slings were used in attacking a pa "to throw red-hot stones into it" (Honoi 1918, 226).

NORTH TO THE HAWAIIAN ISLANDS

The Hawaiian Islands were likely first settled by pioneers from the Marquesas and maybe Tahiti about 1,300 years ago, AD 700–900 (Allen 2004, 181). The first identifiable slingstones date to 800–1,000 YA (Kirch & Green 2001, 190). Much of our previous discussion relative to sling use in the Societies and the Marquesas fits Hawaii, with some important differences.

Again, we have a voluminous ethnohistoric record documenting principal use of the sling on land and sea as a weapon of war. Additionally, the Hawaiian ethnohistoric record, supplemented by a little archaeology, gives us a fuller description of the types of slings and slingstones used there (Bishop Museum 1917, 236–38; Brigham 1902, 344–46; Ellis 1827, 110–16; Emory 1924, 22, 75, 82; Emory 1965, 234–38; Hiroa 1957, 461, 463; Kamakau 1961; Kane 1997, 43, 48, 95; Kirch 1984, 213, 215; Oliver 1989, 443; Tregear 1892, 57).

Hawaiian slings were fashioned from coconut and pandanus fiber and human hair. References indicate that they were rather crude when compared to the finely braided slings made in the Caroline Islands (most likely Chuukese). Both modified stones and unmodified water-worn stones, primarily basalt, were used as sling ammunition. All of Thompson's (1932, 50) four major types of slingstones are represented in Hawaiian collections (see figures 7, 8, and 22), though lemon or egg shapes, or Thompson's Type 4, seem to have been the preferred style. As in the Marianas and elsewhere, Hawaiian slingstones varied in finish quality, with many of them meticulously shaped and polished.

Brigham (1902, 13) gave the average length and weight of some thirty-six lemon-shaped Hawaiian slingstones in the Bishop Museum's collections as 2.65 inches (ca. 7 cm) and 4.73 ounces (ca. 140 grams). He noted that the lightest slingstone in the collection weighed 2.7 ounces (ca. 80 grams) and the heaviest 10 ounces (ca. 300 grams). Further, he claimed that Hawaiian slingstones were the "largest and heaviest" in the Pacific. This claim might not withstand a modern-day challenge from several other Pacific locations—the Southern Cooks, the Societies, and the Marquesas immediately come to mind.

Over much of Oceania, warriors wore no protective gear to defend themselves against slingstones and other weaponry. They depended solely on their agility to dodge the missiles. The coconut fiber and wood armor worn in the Gilberts and the Marshalls is one exception; another is the unique gourd helmet worn by Hawaiian canoemen (Emory 1965, 236; see figure 21). Trepanning was apparently not practiced in Hawaii. At European contact, the bow and arrow functioned only as a toy and for shooting rats (Kirch & Green 2001, 192).

Now here is the odd thing. As noted, there is a little archaeology incorporated into the foregoing data synthesis—but we would expect much more, given Hawaii's battle-laden history documenting the important role slingers played in combat. Captain Cook may have been felled by a slingstone (Laut 1905, 204, 205). In 1783, Kiwala'o, in his losing battle with the forces of Kamehameha at the Battle of Moku'ohai, was felled by a slingstone (Kane 1997, 42, 43). And there is the account by Samuel Kamakau (1961, 29) of a battle that likely took place ca. AD 1,600 in which a canoe landing force from the Island of Hawaii was repelled by slingers on the beaches of Maui: "Ho'olae-makua fought with those who slung the solid *'ala* stones of Kawaipapa, the skilled throwers of the smooth pebbles of Waika-'ahiki, the expert stone tossers of Waikiu and Honokalani, and the quick stone slinging lads of Ka'eleku. These men used their skill with stones, and the Hawaiian warriors were sent helter skelter. Some of the canoes were broken."

Over most of Oceania, the most likely explanation for sling-lean archaeology is a serious lack of field investigations and/or sampling error. In Hawaii's case, these explanations seem insufficient. Certainly as much, and probably more, documented archaeology has been accomplished in the Hawaiian Islands as in the Mariana Islands of Micronesia. Slingstones have been found at almost all Marianas archaeological sites dating to ca. 1,000 YA and later. So perhaps the explanation lies in some fundamental differences in how the sling functioned in these societies—an issue that to date has not been explored. Culin (1899, 242) described *Huna Pohaku,* a Hawaiian guessing game that featured the use of slingstones in a nonstandard way: "A number of players stand in a row with their closed hands outstretched, and another endeavors to guess in which hand a stone (*po-ha-ku-maa,* "slingstone") is concealed, slapping the hand he selects. If he guesses correctly, the one who had the stone takes his place."

It is a simple game, variations of which are played all over the world. Culin (1899, 1907) describes many variations that were played by native Polynesians and North Americans. What is unique to the Hawaiian game is the use of slingstones as the objects to discover. But perhaps this was not uniquely Hawaiian. A remarkably similar game, down to featuring the use of probable bipointed slingstones, was played by certain native peoples in North America's West Coast and Great Basin provinces.

MADAGASCAR—OFF THE CHART BUT RELEVANT

Before departing Oceania, we need to say something about Madagascar. Madagascar is not located in the Central Pacific Basin, or Oceania. It is a great distance off, at the western edge of the Indian Ocean along Africa's southeast coast. We include it here, however, since it must be included in any discussion concerning use of the sling and colonization of oceanic islands by Austronesian speakers.

An understanding of Madagascar's human prehistory is elementary, and many questions remain to be answered. Surprisingly, it appears that this great island located so near the putative birth place of humankind in East Africa has had human occupants for less than 2,000 years, possibly less than 1,300 years. Again surprisingly, the current scholarly consensus, based largely on linguistics, is that the first occupants were not Africans but Austronesian speakers from Indonesia (e.g., Brown 1979, 10–19; Dewar & Wright 1993; Horridge 1995, 137; Linton 1943, 72–80).

Madagascar's similarities with the Pacific islands hardly end with the Austronesian language family tie. There is, for example, the shared use of the outrigger canoe (Brown 1979, 15; Dewar & Wright 1993, 419). And, of most interest here, the sling was the islanders' projectile weapon of choice, with the bow and arrow largely relegated to "toy" status (Lindblom 1940, 26, 28; Linton 1933, 241–43, 258; Linton 1943, 74–78).

Linton (1933, 242) recorded that only stream-rounded stones were used in Madagascar for sling ammunition. Regarding slings, however, he made a provocative observation: "In about 50 percent of Tanala slings one cord is of plaited and the other twisted fiber. The natives could give no reason for this except that it was an ancient practice. Slings from the Marquesas and Society Islands show the same peculiarity." It remains for future research to determine if this was more than merely a "peculiarity" and was in fact unique to the slings of the Tanala of Madagascar, the Marquesas, and Society Islanders.

We must mention that K. G. Lindblom (1940, 26, 28), one of the few anthropologists who studied sling phenomena to any extent, voiced his feeling that this feature of Tanala, Marquesas, and Society Islands slings was unlikely to be either peculiar or unique, despite his admission that "I have not studied this detail at all." This is where the matter stands, with no follow-up comparative studies completed to settle the issue. Lindblom's admission reinforces the principal tenant of this work: Slings and slingstones have been remarkably understudied, particularly by anthropologists and archaeologists.

Figure 17. Samoan (Tutuila) slingers battle LaPerouse's men, 11 December 1787. From a lithograph by N. Ozanne, *Atlas of the Voyage de La Perouse,* Musee de la Marine, Paris.

Figure 18. Tahitian slingers engage the HMS *Dolphin* in Matavai Bay, 1767. From an anonymous watercolor in the Nan Kivell Collection, National Library of Australia, Canberra.

Figure 19. Two probable basalt slingstones from the Marquesas. AMNH Pacific Ethnology Collections No. 85-1232. Used with permission, Division of Anthropology, AMNH.

Figure 20. Display of slingstones from Rarotonga, the Cook Islands. Used with permission, Otago Museum, Dunedin, New Zealand.

Figure 21. *Masked Man of the Sandwich Islands,* an 1785 engraving by R. Benard. Bibliotheque Nationale, Paris. Emory (1965, 236) thought that these gourd masks were worn by Hawaiian canoemen "as protection against slingstones."

Figure 22. Three Hawaiian slingstones. Smithsonian–National Museum of Natural History (NMNH), Dept. of Anthropology Catalog Nos. (left to right) E258007, E405687, and E258068. Used with permission, Department of Anthropology, Smithsonian-NMNH.

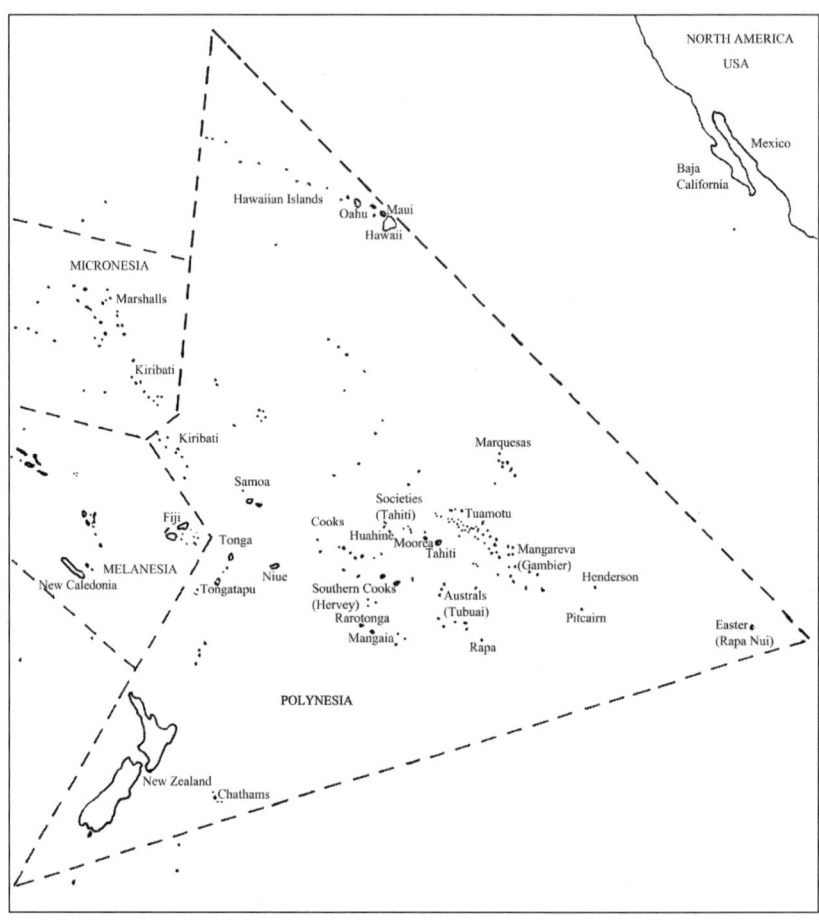

Map 5. Polynesia

CHAPTER 5

Oceania Summary

TREGEAR'S CONUNDRUM BRIEFLY REVISITED

Kenneth P. Emory (1965, 234, 235) proposed that "the sling took the place of the bow in Polynesian warfare, not because of ignorance of the bow, but because the sling had certain great advantages over the bow in their method of warfare. It could, for instance, be tucked in the belt during hand-to-hand fighting and the missiles could usually be secured on the spot."

Edwin Ferdon (1993, 113) said much the same thing, with a concluding thought that many readers may find surprising: "Although this is purely hypothetical, the demise of bows and arrows as weapons of war in eastern Polynesia could have been caused by the introduction of the less cumbersome sling, which may have proved more effective as a long range offensive weapon."

The long-range attributes of the sling may be surprising for many archaeologists and laymen who have assumed the bow and arrow outranged the sling. If such were the case, Ferdon's idea that the sling was adopted because it "may have proved more effective as a long range offensive weapon" would be without merit. However, Ferrill (1985, 24, 25), Harrison (2006), and Korfmann (1973, 36, 37), among others, furnish data that show the sling actually was a more effective long-distance weapon than the bow, giving ballistics credibility to Ferdon's conjecture. It remains, however, to be demonstrated that this was a reason for the Polynesians and other Pacific Islanders to favor the sling over the bow.

We would add to the "less cumbersome" theme that a possible reason for the sling being the projectile weapon of choice in Oceania was that sling gear would require far less space than bow and arrow equipment in the relatively small seagoing vessels used by the peoples of the Pacific.

Central to both Emory's and Ferdon's rationales is the concept that the Pacific Islanders preferred close-quarters hand-to-hand combat (also see Kaeppler 2005) and that the sling facilitated this method of warfare. But is it not true that well into the nineteenth century ultimately this was the goal of *all* battles fought worldwide—that is, to close with and defeat the enemy in hand-to-hand combat, an enemy that had hopefully first been weakened by long-distance weaponry, such as javelins, bows, cannons, and/or sling-hurled missiles (Harrison 2006; Lindblom 1940, 10; Onasander 1923, 445–51)?

We suspect that the real reason(s) for preference of the sling in Oceania may be far less tangible. The truth may lie more in cultural concepts concerning manliness, as captured by Christian's (1899, 136) quote from a Marshall Islands male that the bow and arrow was viewed derisively as a "woman's or child's weapon." In 1936 a Marquesan Islander expressed much the same sentiment to Thor Heyerdahl (1974, 223): "Arrows were beneath the dignity of a Marquesan warrior." And military historian Martin H. Brice (1985, 26, 27) offered a similar explanation for why Iron Age Britains (ca. 1,000 BC–AD 43) were scornful of and relegated the bow to the hunt, exclusively employing the sling as their combat projectile weapon.

We know that competent use of the sling required far more skill and practice than did mastery of the bow (Harrison 2006, 77, 78; Lindblom 1940, 9–11; Warner 1988, 13). Such qualities may have been more valued by Pacific Islanders than mere weapon effectiveness, perhaps functioning to reinforce the status and value of a warrior class analogous to the Japanese Samurai and their long resistance to the use of firearms.

Then again, quite the opposite, or, more accurately, a variation on the machismo theme that would still serve to reinforce the position of a warrior class, might prove to be true—at least in the Society Islands. That is, Pacific archaeologists usually dismiss the Tahitian bow and arrow as mere sporting equipment. But their archery contests, on which the standard interpretation is based, are impressively ceremonial in nature. These contests are perhaps better seen as rituals. This interpretation could lead to a quite different understanding of the function of the bow in ancient Tahitian society. At one time in the Tahitian past, the bow may have functioned as a warfare weapon. There is some archaeological support for this proposition. Perhaps, however, it was deemed an "unfair" weapon—too easily mastered, too lethal at a distance, too threatening to the established power structure for the kind of personal combat the Tahitians wished to wage. By the time of European contact, though, the bow had been dropped from the Tahitian arsenal. It may have been venerated still as a sacred and dangerous relic, only to be used with appropriate ceremony in the Tahitian archery contest.

Before departing Tregear's Conundrum, we must mention that Kirch and Green (2001, 192) obliquely weighed in by stating their belief that the bow and arrow never was an important weapon of war in Polynesia. Although their "belief" does not address the core question, if it should prove true, it would counter

Ferdon's assumption that the sling replaced the bow as a combat weapon, at least in Polynesia.

Not until determined scholars complete well-designed studies that tackle Tregear's Conundrum will Emory's, Ferdon's, Kirch's, Green's, and our thoughts escape the realm of speculation and conjecture. Surely, inert is not the realm where they should stay.

CONCLUDING THOUGHTS

There is essentially nothing we have presented here that shouldn't be challenged. Much of our information, particularly sling-negative data, has necessarily been gleaned from popular and semi-popular, secondary, and century-old archaeology publications. For example, our Marianas Islands archaeology discussion statement, "that circa 7,000–2,000 years ago . . . there is little to no evidence of sling technology in the Southeast Asia world," is largely supported by negative sling data provided by the artifact inventories found in these kinds of references. To echo another of Woodbury's (1954, 171) complaints, in the course of our research we have learned to become distrustful of such negative data. For when we have had the luxury to go beyond generalizing type publications and gain firsthand knowledge (such as in the case of New Guinea), we have found that slingstones often are present in archaeological or museum collections, yet these publications made no mention of their existence.

As with the attention paid fishhooks, ceramics, and adzes, slings and slingstones merit the serious attention of Pacific archaeologists. To date, this has not been the case. If we had relied on published syntheses of Pacific archaeology, we would barely be aware of the presence of slingstones—much less their significance.

We believe we have posed enough questions to keep interested scholars busy for many years. We think it astounding that so little is known about the premier projectile weapon of pre-European Oceania. Our primary intent is to show that study of the sling and slingstones in Oceania has much to offer on a range of important archaeological/anthropological topics, particularly in the areas of settlement of the Pacific, warfare, creation and retention of power, technology transfer (reasons for acceptance or rejection), and pre-Columbian Austronesian contacts with the Americas.

Through this work we are, in essence, reissuing Korfmann's (1973, 42) challenge to archaeologists to recognize the importance of the sling and slingstones and diligently pursue their study—a challenge that was universally ignored, if it even registered with the field at all.

Table 1
Selected slingstone data for Oceania

Area	Pre-European Use	Modified Slingstones	Use	Remarks
MICRONESIA				
Marianas	+	+	Combat/Bird hunting (?)/ Ceremonial (?)	Earliest modified slingstones date to ca. 2000 YA. Commonly associated with Latte Period sites (ca. 300–1,000 YA). One of only two locations (other is Chuuk) in Pacific where clay sling missiles were produced. Numbers and types of slingstones found in the Marianas is striking—only comparable Oceania locations are Chuuk, the Bismarck Archipelago, and maybe Hawaii.
Palau	?	o	?	No recorded historic use. Possible pre-European use, but to date the archaeology is slingstone negative.
Yap	?	+	Combat (land & sea)	Documented historic use. Antiquity unknown. To date, slingstone-negative archaeology.
Chuuk	+	+	Combat (?)	Earliest modified slingstones date to ca. 800 YA. Rivals Marianas in numbers and types of missiles, including use of clay. Arguably, Oceania's highest-quality slings were manufactured in Chuuk.
Pohnpei	+	+	Combat (land & sea)/Bird hunting	Documented historic use. Antiquity unknown. Few reported archaeological finds.
Kosrae	?	?	?	Little relevant data. Sling history probably comparable to Pohnpei.

Area	Pre-European Use	Modified Slingstones	Use	Remarks
Marshalls	+	o	Combat (land & sea?)/Bird hunting	In use at European contact (ca. 470 YA). Antiquity unknown. To date, slingstone-negative archaeology.
Kiribati	?	?	Combat (?)	Little relevant data.
MELANESIA				
New Guinea/Trobriands	?	+	Combat (?)	Historic use by Austronesian speakers. Antiquity unknown. To date, slingstone-negative archaeology.
Bismarks	+	+	Combat	First modified slingstones date to ca. 2,000–2,400 YA. The "Marianas of Melanesia," except clay slingstones not reported. Trepanning practiced as a remedy for slingstone-inflicted cranial trauma on New Britain and New Ireland.
Admiralties	o	o	o	Sling-negative ethnohistory and, to date, archaeology.
Solomons	?	?	?	Slings and possible slingstones discovered in museum collections. Little ethnohistoric support for sling use. What little archaeology has been accomplished is slingstone negative.
Reef–Santa Cruz–Duff Islands	+	+	Combat/Hunting (unidentified prey)	Earliest modified slingstones in Oceania (and Island SE Asia?), found in Lapita context, dated to ca. 3,100 YA. Not common in archaeological assemblages until ca. 1,700 YA. Includes slingstones manufactured from coral limestone, basalt, and Tridacna—shell slingstones are exceedingly rare and appear to only occur here and in the Marianas.

Area	Pre-European Use	Modified Slingstones	Use	Remarks
Vanuatu (New Hebrides)	+	+	Combat/Hunting (unidentified prey)/"Toy"	In use at European contact (ca. 400 YA). Antiquity, and a lot more, unknown. Serious lack of archaeological data.
New Caledonia	+	+	Combat/Bird hunting	Earliest modified slingstones date to ca. 1,400 YA. Trepanning practiced as a remedy for slingstone-inflicted cranial trauma.
Fiji	?	?	Combat/"Sport"	Historic use well-documented. Antiquity unknown. Puzzling slingstone-negative archaeology, as Fiji archaeology has been focused on excavation of "fortified sites." Trepanning possibly practiced.
POLYNESIA				
Tonga	?	?	Combat	Late (19th c.) historic use documented. Antiquity unknown; but the recent, tentative, identification of a "mini-football" type slingstone found in Lapita context, dated 2,600–3,000 YA, if confirmed, would fill this data void dramatically.
Samoa	+	?	Combat	In use at European contact (ca. 300 YA). Antiquity unknown. Puzzling slingstone-negative archaeology parallels the Fiji situation.
Niue	?	?	?	Possible pre-European sling use. Modified "football-like" stones hand-hurled in combat at European contact (ca. 240 YA). To date, slingstone-negative archaeology.
Society Islands (Tahiti)	+	+	Combat (land & sea)/"Sport"	Earliest modified slingstones date 1,100–1,200 YA. Voluminous ethnohistoric record, but slingstones rarely reported archaeologically. Trepanning practiced as remedy for slingstone-inflicted cranial trauma.

Area	Pre-European Use	Modified Slingstones	Use	Remarks
Marquesas	+	+	Combat (land & sea)	In use at European contact (ca. 400 YA). Antiquity unknown; probably parallels Societies. Voluminous ethnohistoric record on sling use. To date, puzzling slingstone-negative archaeology. Trepanning practiced as remedy for slingstone-inflicted cranial trauma.
Southern Cooks	+	+	Combat	In use at European contact (ca. 225 YA). Antiquity unknown; best guess, dates to ca. 1,100 YA. To date, apparently, slingstone-negative archaeology.
Austral Islands	+	?	Combat	Little known.
Mangareva	?	?	?	Essentially Niue remarks apply.
Pitcairn and Henderson Islands	?	?	?	Little known. Slingstones possibly collected from Pitcairn by Bounty mutineers (1790).
Easter Island	?	?	?	Only recent use of the sling as a "toy" is certain. Questionable archaeological data suggests the sling may have functioned as a weapon of war ca. 500–900 YA. Historically only hand-hurled, unmodified rocks observed being used in combat.
New Zealand	?	o	?	Sling used apparently little or not used historically. Historically hand-hurled rocks only (?) used in combat. It is not plausible that N.Z.'s Polynesian pioneers (ca. 800 YA) did not bring at least knowledge of the sling. But to date there is little ethhnohistoric and no archaeology support for this probability.
Hawaii	+	+	Combat (land & sea)	Earliest modified slingstones date to 800–1,000 YA. Voluminous ethnohistoric record. In comparison, strikingly lean archaeology record. Of high interest is the Hawaiian stone hiding game, Huna Pohaku, that expressly used slingstones as the objects to be discovered. A remarkably comparable game, down to featuring use of probable slingstones, was played by peoples of North America's West Coast and Great Basin.

Note: + indicates well supported by archaeology and/or ethnohistoric data; o no evidence; and ? uncertain/unknown.

PART 3

The Americas

Introduction

The sling was widely known in the pre-European Americas. Harold Driver and William Massey (1957, 349) listed the sling as one of the principal weapons of North America's native peoples. Driver (1969, 85) later noted that the sling "is reported for about half the North American tribes." This proved to be underestimated. Driver and James Coffin (1975, 72–108), in their follow-up to the Driver and Massey study, showed that 164 out of 244 North American Indian tribes surveyed claimed functional knowledge of the sling, and we have added to their total. The sling's antiquity possibly goes back to the first Americans. It was, in fact, considered equal to or even preferred over the bow and arrow as a projectile weapon by the so-called high cultures of South and Mesoamerica and, intriguingly, perhaps by many North American peoples.

Never more than a blip, the sling in the Americas dropped off the archaeology radar screen in about 1960. Presumably this happened because there were few actual slings to study (the Lovelock and Humboldt Cave examples may be the only preserved pre-Columbian slings north of Mexico), and it was believed that sling missiles, if subject to human modification at all, were hard to identify as such and changed little, if at all, over time. (Actually, this loss of interest can be attributed as much to changing trends in the profession away from the study of warfare and diffusionism with which the sling was linked.) Study of more time- and culturally sensitive artifacts, particularly pottery and stone projectile points (spear, dart, arrow tips), was believed to be more productive. Such studies remain dominant in the archaeology of the Americas. Even in Andean South America, where it is questionable, stone-tipped projectile weapons were more important weapons of the hunt or combat (Bennett 1946, 23, 56; Cooper 1917, 209, 212; Cooper 1944, 439; Mason 1968, 195; Métraux 1949, 229, 230).

The following survey reflects these a priori archaeology assumptions regarding the sling and, in particular, slingstones. These assumptions have worked to mask the existence of a parallel universe of weaponry that there can be little doubt played a role of paramount importance in the affairs of the peoples of the Americas, from the earliest to recent times.

CHAPTER 6

South America and Mesoamerica

After the Sun [in the Inca pantheon], ranked Thunder, God of Weather, to whom prayers for rain were addressed. He was pictured as a man in the sky, and identified with a constellation. He held a war club in one hand and a sling in the other, and wore shining garments. The thunder was the crack of his sling, the lightning the flash of his garments as he turned, and the lightning bolt was his slingstone.

—John H. Rowe, "Inca Culture at the Time of the Spanish Conquest" (1946)

From the epigraph, the reader might well assume that much of the remainder of this work would be devoted to South America—particularly Andean South America, where for thousands of years the sling was not only the standard projectile weapon of warfare but an instrument of the gods. If so, the reader's expectation will not be met, for our interest lies in slingstones, particularly worked slingstones. In this regard, South America—except for the unlikely locations of Caribbean Venezuela, Argentina, and Uruguay—surprisingly, but most interestingly, disappoints . . . maybe.

When it comes to the sling and its sister artifact the bola, South America stands out. On no other continent do we see such long-term, widespread, and diverse use of these artifacts for hunting and combat, for sport, for control and protection of livestock and crops, and as sacred objects (Arkush & Stanish 2005, 13, 22; Bird & Hyslop 1985, 214; Bram 1941, 55, 56; Coon 1971, 96, 97; Cooper 1917, 184, 191, 208, 209, 214–16; Dillehay 2000, 94, 95, 164, photo 5.10, 206, 213, 218; Engel 1963, 57; Kidder 1964, 455; Lanning 1967, 63, 168; Lau 2004, 167, fig. 3, 171, fig. 7.3, 172, 176; Mason 1968, 195; Means 1920; Métraux 1949, 229, 230, 248, 252–54; Owen 1995, 3; Rowe 1946; Stirling 1938, 79; Tschopik Jr. 1951, 214, 246; Wood 1870, 517, 518, 528–33).

The world's oldest surviving slings, dating to more than 4,000 YA, were recovered from Peruvian Preceramic sites (Bird & Hyslop 1985, 53, 214; Burger 1992, 27, 37, 230; Engel 1963, 10, 57, 85, 86, 100). The most elaborate, colorful, decorative, and largest slings in the world were and still are made in Peru and Bolivia, although some Tibetan yak herders might argue the point (Bennett 1946, 138; Means 1920; O'Neale & Kroeber 1930, 31–33; Rowe 1946, 275; and examination by the authors of sling collections at the AMNH and Smithsonian-NMNH in 2004 and 2006). Yet, supposedly with only a few exceptions, sling missiles were universally unworked stream- or wave-rounded stones (John Topic, personal communications 2000, 2005).

In no respect does this mean that archaeologists can ignore South American slingstones simply because, for the most part, they were not strictly artifacts. There is much to be learned from their study, as John Topic and Theresa Topic admirably demonstrated at Ostra and other Andean sites. One would hope that archaeologists would attend more to the Topics' lead. Perhaps then we would gain more knowledge about sling use and, by extension, larger human society issues (e.g., hunting and warfare longevity and techniques) not only in South America but in places like Madagascar and the Marshall Islands, where unworked slingstones appear to have been used exclusively.

At the 5,000-plus-year-old cliff-top site of Ostra on the Peruvian coast, the Topics recorded fifty-three piles of human-transported pebbles, or manuports, that they convincingly argued were most likely caches of slingstones. Observing, among other things, that the pebbles were relatively uniform in size (hand-size, approximately 10 cm in diameter) and the piles were spaced two to three meters apart—the usual spacing between Andean slingers—this led to the most plausible interpretation of the site's function as a fortified defensive position, ultimately showing that warfare was a fact of life on South America's west coast far earlier than most archaeologists then believed (Topic & Topic 1987; Topic 1989).

A question that immediately comes to mind is why did the warring Andean states pay so much attention to the sling and so little to its ammunition? The obvious answer would seem to be that stream-tumbled stones of suitable shape, weight, and size were readily available throughout the continent, so South Americans generally saw no need to manufacture sling missiles. This must be part of the answer. It certainly meets the parsimony test of Occam's razor. However, there are vexing comparative data issues that disallow uncritical acceptance of this explanation:

- As mentioned in Part 1, worked, spheroidal stones—many of which, if not all, were quite likely slingstones—were manufactured ca. 13,000 YA at the

Monte Verde Site in Chile. Why would production of such stones later be abandoned as use of the sling grew?

- Wood (1870, 528) relates that Patagonian women (presumably Tehuelche and/ or Puelche) would devote as much as a day to "cut and grind" bola stones. The Indians of Patagonia were said to have been "expert" in use of the sling (Cooper 1946, 162). So why did slingstones not merit comparable effort? We suspect that they did, that besides bola stones, the Patagonian women were "cutting and grinding" slingstones. Wood, as with many New World archaeologists up to the present day, may have knowingly or unknowingly subsumed slingstones under the term "bola." He may have simply been using the term to mean "round or globular" rather than implying specific use. Some support for our speculation is provided by this observation of the Guarani of Paraguay by Jesuits ca. 1754 as they prepared for war with Spanish and Portuguese forces: "The women had busied themselves rounding stones for slings" (Caraman 1975, 245).

- Worldwide, many peoples had access to and used suitable naturally shaped slingstones, yet they saw a need to manufacture their own deadlier models (Harrison 2006, 75, 76). This appears to have been universally the case with military states, with the supposed exception of the Andean states.

- Because the subject has been understudied, we are quite possibly operating on an erroneous assumption. For example, this obscure passage from *The Conquest and Settlement of Venezuela,* written ca. 1723 by Don José de Oviedo Y Baños (Varner 1987, 467), regarding a battle fought in 1537 between Spaniards and Indians in the border area of present-day southwest Venezuela with eastern Columbia, causes us to question the validity of the extant database: "The barbarians had a strong asset in a group of stonecutters who, with snapping slings and hurling rocks, so frightened the horses that neither bit nor spur could compel them to enter the battle." Under other circumstances we would assume that "stonecutters" alluded to masons or quarriers, but in this context the Spaniard may have meant specialists who made slingstones.

Our suspicion is reinforced by the presence of worked, nonstandard, lenticular, disc, and domed (biconical) types of slingstones in collections from Uruguay and Argentina (see figures 31 and 32). These slingstones were largely (or solely?) manufactured by the Charrua (Evans 1897, 418; Serrano 1946, 194; and examination by the authors of Smithsonian-NMNH examples, 2006).

Serrano (1946, 194) opined that "the so-called slingstones—carefully shaped lenticular stones—appear really to be a special type of bolas stone." It is unclear why Serrano adds this remark when John Evans (1897, 418) expressed no such reservation. Perhaps Serrano did not witness these lenticular stones being used with slings. But from his wording we assume he did not witness them being used as bola weights either. The example Serrano illustrates (we photographed a virtually identical one at the NMNH; see figure 31) is more suited to sling use than as a bola weight; it displays sharp edges that would render it unsuitable for sealing in a bola pouch, and it shows no modification (grooves, perforations, etc.) that would facilitate direct attachment of cords.

Again, though, as suggested above in connection with Wood's information, Serrano may have been using "bolas" in a generic sense, and by "special type" he may have implied use in a different way—perhaps as slingstones.

In Andean South America, trepanation was commonly practiced for quite possibly more than 4,000 years. The pre-Inca and Inca peoples employed trepanation as a surgical remedy for blunt force, very much including slingstone-inflicted cranial trauma, as testified to by the more than 2,500 trepanned skulls recovered archaeologically. This number by far represents more such finds than the combined total for the rest of the world (Engel 1963, fig. 184; Muñiz & McGee 1897; Rose 2003, 349; Stewart 1958, 474, 475, 480–85; Verano 2003, 223–36; Von Hagen 1963, 105, 106).

CARIBBEAN VENEZUELA

Unexpectedly, the one area in South America where modified, bipointed slingstones (T-M Types 2–4) have been identified archaeologically is on Venezuela's Peninsula de Araya and the nearby Caribbean islands of Margarita and Cubagua.

Archaeologists J. M. Cruxent and Irving Rouse described these slingstones in several publications, along with bone points and conch shell "gouges" (adzes), as definitive artifacts of the maritime pre-Columbian Manicuaroid Series or peoples (Rouse 1958, 43–56, 240–42; Cruxent & Rouse 1959, 13, Plates 2, 4, 5, 8, 41; Rouse 1960, 8–10; Rouse 1964, 395–97; Rouse & Cruxent 1963, 43–47). Bipointed slingstones occur in the lowest or earliest stratigraphic levels of the Series, the Cubagua Complex, which dates to at least 4,200 YA but possibly dates to as early as 7,000 YA (see the above references and also Keegan 1994, 265–69). Bipointed slingstones continued in use through the succeeding Manicuare and Punta Gorda complexes, or to ca. AD 300, or 1,700 YA. Manufacture and use of bipointed slingstones in Caribbean Venezuela and, by extension, Latin America apparently ends at this time.

The Manicuaroid slingstones are a curiosity in the archaeology of the Americas, as, for that matter, is the maritime Manicuaroid Series itself in that it features an assemblage of artifacts akin to those of Oceania but with no clear local antecedents (Cruxent & Rouse 1958, 49; Sanoja & Vargas 1983, 210). As Cruxent and Rouse (1958, 49) recognized, the only other area in the New World where virtually identical bipointed slingstones occurred was on the West Coast and in the Great Basin provinces of North America—and those "slingstones" are not generally accepted by American archaeologists as such. It is curious that no other South American, Caribbean, or Mesoamerican slingers seem to have ever made use of bipointed missiles—from the ballistics viewpoint the most effective of slingstone designs (Harrison 2006).

MESOAMERICA (CENTRAL AMERICA AND MEXICO)

The sling has a long history of use in Mesoamerica, comparable to that in South America. It was a projectile weapon—possibly the earliest—in the arsenals of all the high cultures of Mesoamerica. Many peoples (e.g., the Tarahumara and Tepehuan of northern Mexico) continue to use it to this day for such purposes as hunting small game and protection of cornfields from avian and terrestrial fauna (Bancroft 1874, 627, 628, 655; Bancroft 1875, 408, 409, 743, 744; Di Peso, Rinaldo, & Fenner 1974, 31, 32; Driver & Coffin 1975, 72, 108; Driver & Massey 1957, map 142; Gorenstein 1973, 15; Hassig 1988, 80, 81; Hassig 1992; Joyce 1916, 72, 98; Maudslay 1928; Means 1920, 317, 318; Pennington 1963, 56, 93, 195, 233–37; Pennington 1969, 123, 124, 131, 347, 349; Vaillant 1931, 412; Webster 1999, 343; Webster 2000, 66, 79, 102).

Anthropologist Ross Hassig (1992, 28, 29, 189) accepts as the earliest evidence of sling use in Mesoamerica the discovery of "solid, fired clay spheres ranging from 2 to 4.2 centimeters in diameter" that date to ca. 3,000 YA at the Olmec Site of San Lorenzo Tenochtitlan.

Slings may not have originated with the Olmecs, but the distribution of slingstones at Olmec-influenced sites during the La Venta period, including Tehuacan, Chalcatzingo, Zacatenco, Ticoman, Gualupita, El Arbolillo, and Chalchuapa, suggests that the Olmecs spread this technology. The sling's high rate of fire, great range . . . , and effectiveness gave the Olmecs both an offensive and defensive capability unmatched elsewhere at that time and permitted the expansion of their merchants into areas that had been too hazardous under previous conditions.

An apparent difference with slingstones used over much of South America (if the existing South American database proves accurate, which we have expressed reservations about) is that in Mesoamerica, besides the use of suitable naturally occurring rocks, modified stones and baked clay slingstones were used as well. Invariably these slingstones were spherical (round balls), ranging 2–6 cm in diameter with a weight range of 25–325 grams, but clustering at 25–50 grams (Hassig 1988, 80; Hassig 1992, 28–31, 189, 190, 249; Nadaillac 1884, 279), which compares favorably to the weight and size ranges of sling missiles previously given in this work.

We could discover no evidence of bipointed/biconical sling missiles, or any other shape other than spheroids, ever being used in Mesoamerica. That the spheroid design would be maintained by many different peoples for, most conservatively, more than 2,500 years seems remarkable, particularly when the neighboring Manicuaroid peoples of Caribbean Venezuela, who some peoples of Mesoamerica must have had occasional contact with, possessed what was ballistically a "better idea."

Another notable difference, particularly with the pre-Columbian Andean cultures of South America, is that trepanning was practiced comparatively little in Mesoamerica—or that is the conclusion forced by the fact that only some thirty-four trepanned crania have been reported from Mesoamerica, with seventeen of these from one location, the Classic Period (AD 250–900) ruins of Monte Alban and nearby sites located in the surrounding highland Valley of Oaxaca of southern Mexico (Casso 1936, 282; Rose 2003, 349; Stewart 1958, 478, 479; Stone & Urcid 2003, 235–49). Again, this seems peculiar since battle weapons and tactics were virtually identical, and thus the types of cranial injuries sustained were identical and would presumably call for similar remedial surgery.

Most tentatively, we draw from these data that either the Mesoamerican states were generally less concerned with survival of the injured than the Andean states or that they relied on some other, unknown, minimally to noninvasive curative methods. This, of course, could be said of any of the areas where sling-hurled missiles and clubs were the prominent or exclusive weapons of combat but there is no evidence that trepanning was practiced (e.g., Micronesia).

Although we had assumed that the bola was used in Mesoamerica given close ties to South America, we found no ethnohistorical or archaeological data to support this assumption.

Figure 23. A modern-day Andean slinger—an annual Tinku war games participant in the Canas Province, Peru. From McIntyre (1973); used with permission, G. Scott McIntyre, © Loren McIntyre Estate/www.lorenmcintyre.com.

1

2

3

Above: Figure 24. Three depictions of Inca sling use from Felipe Guamán Poma's ca. 1615 chronicle (Von Hagen 1963): (a) Inca Huayna Capac brandishes sling; (b) a *Chasqui* (courier) armed with star club and sling announces his arrival with a conch-shell trumpet; and (c) a farm boy in wolf skin and armed with a sling protects his cornfield from birds and small animals.

Left: Figure 25. An Inca wool, solid-pocket sling from the Coyungo Site, Peru. Dr. Aleš Hrdlička Collection, 1913, NMNH Catalog No. A301143. Used with permission, Department of Anthropology, Smithsonian-NMNH.

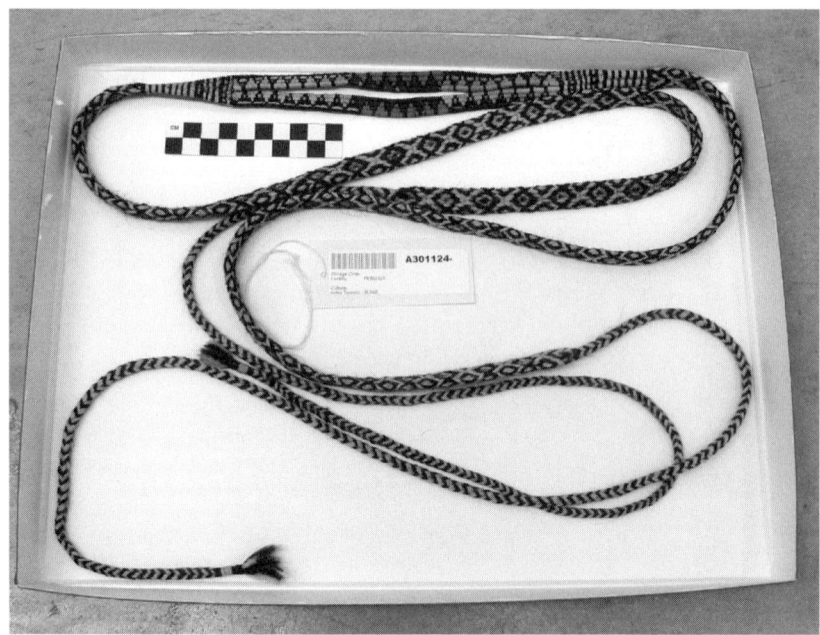

Figure 26. An Inca wool, split-pocket sling from the Coyungo Site, Peru. The split pocket allowed users to hurl "oversized" slingstones of differing shapes and diameters (8 cm+). Dr. Aleš Hrdlička Collection, 1913, NMNH Catalog No. A301124. Used with permission, Department of Anthropology, Smithsonian-NMNH.

Figure 27. Pre-Columbian (Inca?) sling-stones. These are mostly unworked, water-tumbled rocks, but a few appear to have been pecked and/or ground to achieve the desired ovoid or spheroid shape. Collected in Bolivia ca. 1900 by A. F. Bandelier. AMNH Accession No. 1900-18/Cat No. B-6879. Used with permission, Division of Anthropology, AMNH.

Figure 28. An Inca spherical slingstone that is golf ball–like both in size (4–5 cm diameter) and dimpled surface. The dimpled surface, whether natural or human made/enhanced, may have been selected to achieve longer flight distance (Fritts 2002; Scott 2005). Collected in Peru ca. 1895 by A. F. Bandelier. AMNH Accession No. 1895-14/ Cat No. B-1927. Used with permission, Division of Anthropology, AMNH.

Figure 29. An Inca wool, plaited sling from Nazca locale, Peru. Displayed in Andean weapons exhibit, AMNH. Gift from Juilliard and Gaffron, 1914. AMNH Accession No. 1914-19/ Catalog No. 41.0-1279. Used with permission, Division of Anthropology, AMNH.

Figure 30. A historic Brazilian sling from the "Raamkokamekra-Canela people—village of Sardinha, Maran-hão, Brazil." Dr. W. H. Crocker Collection, 1966. NMNH Catalog No. E405091. Used with permission, Department of Anthropology, Smithsonian-NMNH.

Figure 31. Plan (a) and side views (b) of lenticular slingstone recovered from "excavations on site of Casa del Gobierno Nacional, Federal District, Buenos Aires, Argentina." These are comparable to Charrua, Uruguay, slingstones described by Serrano (1946, 194). NMNH Catalog No. A259927. Used with permission, Department of Anthropology, Smithsonian-NMNH.

Figure 32. A "domed" or cone-shaped slingstone recovered from "excavations on site of Casa del Gobierno Nacional, Federal District, Buenos Aires, Argentina." NMNH Catalog No. A259944. Used with permission, Department of Anthropology, Smithsonian-NMNH.

Figure 33. Caribbean Venezuela Manicuaroid Series bipointed slingstones—comparable to T-M Types 2–4 (see fig. 7): (a) Cubagua Complex, ca. 4,200+ YA; (b & c) Manicuare Complex, ca. 3,000–3,500 YA; (d & e) Punta Gorda Complex, ca. 1,700+ YA. Estimated size range: 4–5 cm length by 2.5–3.5 cm midline diameter; weights not given. From Cruxent and Rouse (1959, Plates 4, 5, 8, 41); first published by GS/OAS and used under rights granted by GS/OAS.

Figure 34. A *soldato Mexicano* armed with *macana* (broadsword edged with obsidian blades), shield, and sling. From *Ixtlilxochitl Codex, Part 2* (ca. 1582).

Figure 35. This pre-Columbian Zapotec (?) spherical slingstone is large for the type at 8+ cm diameter. Collected by L. H. Ayme in 1885 from Zaachila, near Monte Alban, Oaxaca. NMNH Catalog No. A115185. Used with permission, Department of Anthropology, Smithsonian-NMNH.

Map 6. Mesoamerica and South America sling distribution. Shaded areas indicate known sling use.

Map 7. South America locales discussed.

Map 8. Mesoamerica locales discussed.

CHAPTER 7

North America

THE SOUTHWEST AND THE MYSTERY OF THE STONE BALLS

Only boys used to make and use slings. The men never used them in war as they were not powerful enough.
— Grenville Goodwin

Stones used in slings would hardly need to be as carefully shaped as are these stone balls.
— Richard Woodbury

The Southwest culture area boundaries are slippery. The area generally thought of as the American Southwest by archaeologists embraces the U.S. states of Arizona and New Mexico touching on west Texas, much of Utah, western Colorado, southeast Nevada, and the Mexican states of Sonora and Chihuahua. This is an area whose southern border overlaps with Mesoamerica and that throughout its human prehistory and history has influenced and been influenced by events in Mesoamerica (Jennings 1989, 289–327; Willey 1966, 179–245; Woodbury 1979, 22–30). We make this point because we think the Mesoamerican connection is relevant for interpreting the function of "stone balls" often found on southwestern archaeology sites and, as Woodbury (1954, 171, 172) noted, that are often overlooked.

All the Native American tribes of the Southwest knew the sling. Through interviews with various ethnographers native informants related that in the recent past the sling principally was used for killing small game and birds, for crop protection, and as a boy's toy. Ute, Navajo, Mescalero Apache, Yavapai, Hopi, Tewa (Walpi pueblo), Santa Ana, and San Ildefonso informants additionally claimed that the sling had functioned as a combat weapon (Basso 1971, 245; Driver & Coffin 1975, 72, 93, 98, 103, 108; Driver & Massey 1957, map 142; Drucker

1941, 120, 185; Forsyth 2004; Fowler & Fowler 1971, 48; Gifford 1932, 225; Gifford 1936, 288; Gifford 1940, 33, 123; Heizer & Johnson 1952, fig. 68; Pennington 1963, 56, 93, 195, 233–37; Spier 1928, 249, 256, 342, 343, 373; Stewart 1942, 269). The Yuma and Western Apache can probably be added to the combat list, based on the 1880s observations of U.S. army officer and ethnologist John G. Bourke (1890, 59). Also, as Frank Hamilton Cushing (1988, 87) observed in the 1880s, included among the armaments of the Zuni Twin War Gods were "slings and death-dealing stones carried in fiber pockets."

Driver and Massey (1957, 357) reasonably conjectured that "the tribes where the sling was only a boy's toy may well have employed it as a man's weapon in earlier times." We assume that, at this point, we have presented sufficient data to satisfy the reader of the fallacy of Grenville Goodwin's comment: Though specific to Western Apache sling use, it reflects too often the opinion held by American archaeologists. Besides being refuted by Bourke's earlier observations, Goodwin's statement was as well challenged by I. W. Forsyth's (2004) seventy-five-year-old Mescalaro Apache informant, who claimed in 1963 that slings had been used by the Mescalero for hunting animals up to the size of deer or in combat "for centuries."

The David and Goliath sling, as elsewhere, was the standard-issue sling of the Southwest, with a notable twist and one exception. The notable twist is that historical-era slings (we know of no surviving pre-European slings) of the South-western tribes appear to be substantially identical. Made of leather (although Pennington [1963, 93] states that the Tarahumara sometimes made the pouch out of Yucca or other plant fibers) and basically undecorated, they featured a diamond- or triangle-shaped pouch as a separate element attached to the cords (Basso 1971, 245; Knight 1880, 231, fig. 31; Spier 1928, 342, 343; authors' examinations of Southwestern sling collections at the AMNH and Smithsonian-NMNH, 2004 and 2006). The exception is a very simple sling device described by Forde (1931, 173) that was used by the Yuma Indians of the Lower Gila and Colorado rivers in the combat training of boys to teach them to dodge incoming missiles: "[Opposing] groups [of boys] would also sling hard mud balls at each other. The balls were stuck on the end of flexible willow sticks which were swung from the shoulder so that the balls flew out toward their opponents."

In the historic period, with the exception of the Yuma clay balls, it appears that only naturally occurring stones were used as sling ammunition. This does not mean that attention was not paid to selecting stones of suitable size and shape, as verified by Forsyth's (2004) Mescalero informant. This is not unexpected; it simply reflects the worldwide situation. As the sling lost its importance as a weapon, the need to improve on nature by fabricating more uniform and lethal shot became of little import. Of course, in some areas (the most puzzling of which may be Andean South America), only naturally occurring stones appear to have ever been used.

When it comes to slingstones in the archaeological record, a confounding thing happens as we approach and cross the U.S. border from Mexico: they disappear. This is not for lack of hand-size (3–9 cm diameter), often ground and polished stone and clay spheroids found in archaeological context (Anderson 1967; Barnett 1993, 29; Broms & Moriarty 1967; Di Peso et al. 1974, 31, 32; Fewkes 1907, 325, Plate 39e; Gunnerson 1957, 21, 23, 25; Haury 1976, 292; Hewett 1938, 128–32; Kidder 1932, 61, 62, 141; Martin 1936, 63, 388, 389; Morris 1986, 540, 541; Steward 1970, 3; Taylor 1954, 11, 49, fig. 20c; Woodbury 1954, 171–73). Boasting at least a 6,000-year-old time depth, they are as common to Southwestern sites as they are to Mesoamerican sites (Broms & Moriarty 1967, 98). Whereas in Mesoamerica such spheroids are often interpreted as slingstones, in the Southwest they almost never are. Rather, they are usually and safely interpreted as "function unknown," with "game balls" running a close second (Anderson 1967; Broms & Moriarty 1967; Fewkes 1907, 325; Woodbury 1954, 172, 173).

Only a few Southwestern archaeologists have entertained the idea that these stone and clay balls were slingstones. Among those few, Edgar Lee Hewett's (1938, 132) declaration concerning stone balls recovered in 1905 from the San Ildefonso ancestral pueblo ruins of Otowi, located on the Pajarito Plateau near Los Alamos, New Mexico, stands out: "There is a notable rarity of projectile points, stone axes, and other implements for use in war, except sling stones—small spherical balls of agate." Hewett offers no explanation for reaching his conclusion about the function of these "balls of agate." We would guess that he was influenced by such factors as their resemblance to Mesoamerican slingstones, by San Ildefonso informants who claimed the sling was used in warfare (Gifford 1940, 33), and by prominent display of the "belly-of-sling" (sling pocket) symbol in their game of *cañute* (Harrington 1912, 268–86; see figure 39 and map 10).

Richard Woodbury (1954, 171–73), though he could not have been more wrong in his rationale for eliminating the possibility that the subject stone balls were slingstones, provides more data and analysis of these artifacts than any Southwestern archaeologist had before or, it appears, since.

However, though Woodbury supplied comparative data on the seventy-nine stone balls relative to shape (more "oblate spheroids" than true spheroids), size (e.g., mean diameter 5.5 cm), and material (fifty-three are of a yellow sandstone, the rest of various other kinds of stone), he joins other Southwestern archaeologists, if they addressed the subject at all, in mentioning weight only in vague terms, like "light" and "heavy." As we have noted elsewhere in this work, reasonably accurate metric weights are essential in defining slingstones and, we assume, would be equally of value in determining or eliminating other proposed functions (for example, "game balls").

Woodbury (1954, 173) guessed that the stone balls recovered from the ancestral Hopi village ruins at Jeddito and Awatovi in northern Arizona were used in kiva ceremonies to imitate thunder and/or in kicking races and/or as club heads.

Woodbury's (1954, 172) admitted guesswork that these stone balls may have been used ceremonially to imitate thunder, based on reported practices at Zuni and Acoma, but "not . . . reported for the modern Hopi," brings to mind the symbolic connection of slings and slingstones with the Inca thunder god (Rowe 1946, 294, 295). We plant this seed for future researchers to discover if this is more than coincidence.

The following passage from Judd (1954, 258), based on various cited accounts concerning the use of hurled stones in the defense of several Southwestern pueblos, may be relevant to this discussion.

> The sample of Zuni weapons Coronado sent from Hawikuh was not quite complete. He should have added half a bushel of assorted rocks and cobblestones. For rocks were one of the chief defensive weapons of the Pueblos, as Coronado himself had ample reason to know. Twice during the assault on Hawikuh [July 1540] he was floored by rocks thrown from the housetops and was saved only by his steel helmet and the prompt action of his army master.
>
> When a company of Spaniards under Vicente de Zaldívar stormed the stairway at Acoma in January 1599, according to witness Pérez de Villagrá . . . , the defenders "sent down a shower of arrows and stones . . . a veritable deluge of stones, clubs, and arrows." Some 250 years later the inhabitants of Mishongnovi turned back a Navajo attack by identical means.

For corroboration that Judd "had it right," plus additional data relative to use of stones by the Zuni in the defense of Hawikuh and, later, by Southern Tiwa in defense of the Tiguex pueblos along the Rio Grande River in New Mexico, see Bolton (1949, 123–25, 218–21) and Flint and Flint (2005, 257).

Unfortunately, none of these accounts remark on the nature of the stones used or how they were thrown. It is generally assumed that the pueblo defenders were simply hand-hurling unmodified rocks. However, given that we have good reason to believe the sling was known to the pueblos prior to the Spanish invasions, plus the testimony of various pueblo informants that the sling was used in warfare, and, perhaps most relevant, the inclusion of the sling in the armaments of the

Zuni Twin War Gods, it is likely that at least some of these rocks, of which some or many may have been modified "stone balls," were sling-hurled.

New Mexico governor Don Diego de Vargas's account of his 1694 assault on the people of Jemez Pueblo at their mesa top redoubt of Astialakwa verifies just such use of the sling (Kessell et al. 1998, 150, 244). It is also notable that recent archaeological investigations at the ruins of Astialakwa recorded "piles of fist-sized granite cobbles stacked at trailheads which served as ammunition for the slings of Jemez warriors" (Liebmann 2010, 40).

Controversial "new" interpretations by J. J. Golio and Mike Golio (2004) of certain human figure petroglyphs located in the desert mountains in the vicinity of Phoenix, Arizona, may prove pertinent to this discussion. (In 1888, Frank Hamilton Cushing, the famous and controversial Southwestern adventurer/ethnologist/archaeologist, advanced substantially identical interpretations [Matthews 1889, 43].) The subject rock art is presumed to be associated with the Hohokam. These archaeologically defined people maintained a farming-based village life in the deserts of southern Arizona for more than a thousand years, AD 300–1450. Of all the Southwestern pre-European cultures, the Hohokam had the most Mesoamerican cast: presence of ball courts, canal irrigation, truncated pyramids, turquoise mosaics, copper bells, etc. (Gumerman & Haury 1979, 75–90; Haury 1976; Jennings 1989, 293–99).

The Golios (2004), and Cushing (Matthews 1889, 43) some 120 years earlier, proposed that the subject human figures or anthropomorphs appear to be twirling South American–type bolas and/or slings. However, this is not obvious, unlike, for example, unambiguous bow and arrow depictions in adjacent petroglyph panels. Alternative interpretations (dancers or snake handlers) are currently more in favor with Southwestern archaeologists (Bostwick 2002, personal communication 2007).

While we are sympathetic toward the Golios' interpretations—more so in respect to the possibility that some of the figures may be using slings (of course)—their arguments, particularly when it comes to the bola, fall short of convincing. Their reasoning depends on comparison with South American–type bolas of recent vintage and the possibility that many of the stone balls found on Southwestern sites may be bola stones. Essentially their arguments echo those of Carrol B. Howe (1979, 25–29) and others who ascribed a bola stone's function to bipointed stones found in the southern Oregon/northeastern California area. Accordingly, our criticism of Howe's arguments, as given in our discussion of the West Coast and Great Basin, is relevant here.

Interpreting the meaning and significance of the graphics of any age, but particularly anonymous prehistoric rock art, is a perilous enterprise. Even if the

Golios/Cushing bola interpretation of the Phoenix rock art is correct, it would only demonstrate that the Hohokam had knowledge of this device (which would be pretty exciting in itself), not that the Hohokam, without solid corroborative evidence, actually impressed the bola into service.

A cogent example, though in reverse, is that in the vast expanse of Oceania, an area of the world where there is solid evidence of widespread sling use and warfare, there is a remarkable lack of indigenous rock art or art rendered in other media depicting sling use or use of any kind of weaponry. If one only looked at the art of Oceania, one would think that little else went on than lovemaking and canoe voyaging. The point is, art is a valuable clue to our understanding of the past, but what a people express in their art does not necessarily reflect all of what they do, or do at all.

Trepanation was little practiced in the pre-European Southwest. Only two documented cases of uncertain pueblo Indian affinity are known from the Lamy, New Mexico, area. In 1897 Carl Lumholtz and Aleš Hrdlička reported on two female trepanned skulls from northern Mexico. They were apparently Tarahumara in origin and probably date to later than AD 1,500 (Stewart 1958, 476–78; Stone & Urcid 2003).

THE WEST COAST AND GREAT BASIN—
HOME OF NORTH AMERICA'S OLDEST SLING
AND MYSTERIOUS BIPOINTED STONES

This man [Kay-kay-my-alth-may] of wonderful physique was a Klamath Indian, a lone and mighty warrior for all who opposed him. . . . This warrior did not use bow and arrows, spear or shields to defend himself in his conquests, but used instead the sling and pebbles.
—Lucy Thompson, *To the American Indian* (1991)

We focus here on the area of North America that includes the U.S. states of California, Oregon, Washington, Idaho, touching on western Montana, Nevada, western Utah, southeast Alaska, and the Canadian province of British Columbia.

All the native peoples of North America's Pacific Coast and Great Basin probably knew the sling. It served as a boy's toy and often as a hunting weapon for taking small game and birds—particularly waterfowl. Many knew the sling as a combat weapon, more so than any other area of North America outside of Mexico (Bean & Shipek 1978, 552; Bean & Smith 1978, 542; Driver 1937, 72, 118; Driver 1940, 190, 191, 213, 215; Driver & Coffin 1975, 72, 83, 88, 93, 98; Driver & Massey 1957, map 142; Drucker 1950, 187, 259; Drucker 1951, 335; Drucker 1955, 91–93; DuBois 1940, 39, 125; Eells 1889, 616, 619, 632; Foster 1944, 168, 169, 189; Fowler 1989, 70; Gifford & Kroeber 1939, 142; Goldschmidt 1978, 347; Haeberlin & Gunther 1930, 26; Heizer & Johnson 1952; Kelly 1978, 418; Kroeber 1925, 845; Landberg 1965, 37; La Pena 1978, 329, 330 [fig. 6], 334, 337; McIlwraith 1948, 341, 342, 384; Olson 1936, 77; Ray 1942, 123, 153; Steward 1941, 237, 291, 338; Steward 1943, 315, 333, 383; Stewart 1941, 386, 401; Voegelin 1942, 73, 192). But even more applicable to the West Coast and Great Basin, Driver and Massey's admonition (1957, 357) is worth repeating: "The tribes where the sling was only a boy's toy may well have employed it as a man's weapon in earlier times."

Unlike the uniformity seen in Southwestern slings, West Coast and Great Basin slings varied considerably from tribe to tribe, both in style and materials used. In respect to the Pomo, there were intratribal differences, with different types of slings for war and duck hunting (Barrett 1952, 145, 188). The slings of the Hupa and Wintu of northwest California, which were similar, were of particularly complicated construction (Mason 1889, 225, fig. 83; La Pena 1978, fig. 6): "The sling of the Hupa is a very intricate affair made of buckskin. The thongs of sinew or tough cord are united to the leather [pocket] by passing through it and then coiling on themselves. The ordinary loop on one end and knot on the other are also used by them" (Mason 1889, 225).

Historically, mostly naturally occurring, rounded, hand-size stones served as sling ammunition. There were exceptions. The Eastern Pomo of the Clear Lake area in northwest California, besides using possibly modified, ca. 4–5 cm diameter, round stones, manufactured similar-sized "flattened spheroids" or discs of baked clay (Barrett 1952, 145, 146, 188, 226, 244, Plates 14.3, 23.2; Loeb 1926b, 184, 185, Plates 2, 3). According to Loud (1918, 379), the clay sling projectiles weighed 55–75 grams. Loeb tells us that the Eastern Pomo used the stone balls to harvest geese and in warfare (1926b, 184, 185). However, they "preferred clay balls to stones when shooting at ducks or mud hens because they were lighter and would skate along the water. They were said to be sometimes able to kill three or four mud hens at a shot" (see figures 54 and 55). And the Wintun, the Eastern Pomos neighbors to the east, were likewise reported to have hunted "wild fowl with a sling, using bolas [meaning spheroids, *not the* South American–type] made of hard-baked clay" (Mason 1899, 61).

Many—maybe all—of the "sling-shot pebbles" used in warfare by the Stóló of British Columbia's Fraser River Canyon were nearly perfectly round stone balls intentionally pecked and ground to shape. These balls were at the large end of the scale for slingstones, ranging 6–10+ cm in diameter (Duff 1952, 60; Schaepe

2006, 686, 687, 691, fig. 13). Duff (1952, 60) related that a Stólō man "from Yale [a village on the Fraser River] was said to have been able to split enemy canoes with stones up to 4 inches [10+ cm] in diameter."

Lovelock and Humboldt Caves, Nevada

Lovelock Cave, located in the Humboldt Sink of northern Nevada, holds an important though unrecognized place in sling research. It is the earliest pre-European site in North America from which both a sling and probable slingstones were recovered.

The Lovelock sling—or, more precisely, sling pocket—was recovered by L. L. Loud of the University of California, Berkeley, in 1912, though it was not until the 1950s that it was identified as such by Robert F. Heizer and Irmgard W. Johnson. Heizer and Johnson (1952, 139) explained:

> Loud did not describe or mention the textile [sling] though he illustrates it (Loud and Harrington 1931, Pl. 53a), and one suspects that, being reluctant to disturb the bead strands to which it was affixed, he did not recognize the specimen for what it was.
>
> The sling (Fig. 67, a), made probably of *Apocynum* [Indian Hemp], was wrapped with a compound necklace of *Olivella* shell bead strands and was found about the neck of a partially mummified child about 6 years old.

Heizer and Johnson (1952, 139) guesstimated that the Lovelock sling dated to ca. 2000+ YA, based on a loosely associated radiocarbon date of 2,482+/- BP. We can now be confident that the sling dates to 3,200+ YA, based on more recent and better associated radiocarbon determinations obtained for Loud's "Lot 26" burial, which included the subject sling (Bennyhoff & Hughes 1987, 165, 167–69; Shackley n.d.).

Equally significant are bipointed and spherical stone and clay "balls" recovered from Lovelock Cave (Loud & Harrington 1931, 109, 113, Plates 53, 57). These objects were not identified by Loud and Harrington as slingstones and remain not widely recognized as such. We have little doubt that if Loud and Harrington had not lacked critical pieces of the puzzle—if they had recognized the sling among their collections—they would have reached our conclusion, that these artifacts are most likely sling missiles.

Sling pockets were also recovered from nearby Humboldt Cave. These slings date to ca. 2,000 YA (Heizer & Krieger 1956, 62, 102–5, Plate 24; O'Neale 1947). That basically only the pockets of the slings (they did show short sections of attached cordage) were recovered from Lovelock and Humboldt caves seems curious.

This was also reported for slings of even greater antiquity made of similar materials recovered from Peruvian Preceramic sites (Bird & Hyslop 1985, 214; Engel 1963, 57). The explanation may again be provided by the Eastern Pomo of northwest California. Pomo hunters carried replacement pockets for their special waterfowl hunting slings. These sling pockets were made of cured green tule (a similar plant fiber to the *Apocynum cannabinum* of the Humboldt and Lovelock slings) and were only good for several throws before they frayed and required replacement (Barrett 1952, 146).

The Lovelock and Humboldt cave examples remain the only known prehistoric slings found north of Mexico. We can't help but wonder if among museum collections of cordage and textiles, which have often only been superficially examined and described, like the Lovelock sling, hide other pre-Columbian slings.

BIPOINTED/BICONICAL STONES

In the Trask collection from San Nicolas Island, southern California, there are about thirty objects of sandstone, 35 mm to 75 mm in length. There is much variety of form, but two or three specimens quite closely approach in shape and size some of the clay balls from Humboldt Bay. There are also sling shots from Guam, made of coral limestone, which resemble the clay balls from Humboldt Bay.
—Llewellyn L. Loud, *Ethnogeography and Archaeology of the Wiyot Territory* (1918)

I have found them [three illustrated, modified biconical ovoid stones of fine-grained basalt] in the Tualatin Plains, about ten miles west of Portland in Calapooia country. The museum at the city hall in Portland has a tray of very similarly shaped stones marked "sling stones from New Hebrides." The size, shape, and kind of stone are so much like those . . . that I doubt if I could separate them from those of a desert collection, if they were mixed.
—N. G. Seaman, *Indian Relics of the Pacific Northwest* (1967)

Shortly after starting work for the Northern Mariana Islands Museum of History and Culture in 1998, we met Will Shapiro, an archaeologist from California who was conducting investigations on Saipan. At this point we had become intrigued with Marianas slingstones and wondered if comparable artifacts occurred elsewhere. We asked Will if he had ever come across similar objects beyond Oceania. He responded, "Yes, virtually identical clay and stone artifacts are found in northern California. In California they are often called 'lemon stones' in reference to their shape but their true function remains a mystery."

Upon our return to the United States mainland we not only confirmed Will's information but greatly expanded on it. Biconical/bipointed ovoid stone and clay artifacts comparable to Pacific islands slingstones (see figures 7 and 8) have been found from southern California north to the Columbia River (possibly even through British Columbia to southeast Alaska). They are often associated with marshlands or former marshlands, with especially great numbers of these artifacts having been recovered from the Klamath Basin–Clear Lake wetlands of northeast California and southern Oregon. Although temporal parameters of manufacture and use remain to be pinned down, they conservatively date to 8,000 YA and quite possibly to as early as 13,000 YA at the Mount Hebron and Borax Lake sites in northern California. Generally, these artifacts disappear from the archaeological record between 2,500–3,000 YA (see table 2), with the significant aberration being the Humboldt Bay–Gunther Island "elliptical clay balls."

Gunther Island and Humboldt Bay are located along California's Pacific Coast some 220 miles north of San Francisco. The excavations of L. L. Loud in 1913 and those of H. H. Stuart (a Eureka, California, dentist) in the 1920s generated more than 300 "elliptical baked clay balls" that Loud compared to slingstones from Guam and similar-shaped artifacts from San Nicolas Island, California. These bipointed/biconical ovoids ranged in size from 2.3 to 5 cm in length and in weight from 29.5 to 43 grams. They were mostly recovered from burials and excavation trenches at site HUM-67 on Gunther Island and dated to 1,100 YA or somewhat later (see table 2; Elsasser 1978, 50–52; Fredrickson 1984, 484–91; figures 60 and 61).

(Curiously, you will find no mention of these "elliptical clay balls" in major published syntheses of California archaeology that include description of "Gunther Pattern" artifacts [Chartkoff & Chartkoff 1984, 194–203; Fagan 2003, 222–25; Fredrickson 1984, 484–91]. The lone exception we found is Albert Elsasser's [1978, 52] incidental reference to "clay balls" in his overview of northwest California archaeology. This parallels the previously alluded to situation relative to slingstones in Oceania; you would hardly be aware of the existence of these artifacts if you relied on secondary synthesis archaeology publications.)

Virtually every function imaginable has been proposed for these stone and clay artifacts. To us and a few others (Miles 1963, 35, 37; Shapiro, Shapiro, Bloomer, & Jackson 2002) the most supportable explanation that they were slingstones has, if proposed at all, been summarily dismissed. Even Loud (1918, 379) and Seaman (1967, 201), who explicitly noted the extraordinary resemblance of the "bipointed stones" to slingstones of Oceania, rejected the possibility of a slingstone function for no more substantial reason than "it just can't be." We suspect, though, that if Loud and Seaman had the benefit of today's database, they would have given the idea more consideration.

THE CASE FOR SLINGSTONES

If it looks like a duck, quacks like duck, walks like a duck, it's probably a duck.

Why do we think they are slingstones? Let us count the ways.

Versus the Bola Stones Interpretation

While others had suggested that the "mysterious" bipointed stones commonly found in S Oregon/NE California, particularly numerous in the Klamath Basin–Clear Lake area, were bola stones (Cressman 1956, 429), wide acceptance of the bola theory appears largely traceable to the late Carrol B. Howe of Klamath Falls, Oregon, an amateur archaeologist and prolific collector of local Indian artifacts. In his 1979 book *Ancient Modocs of California and Oregon*, Howe put forth the bola interpretation as a plausible explanation for the function of these bipointed stones (25–29). He substantially based his interpretation on comparison with South American bolas. As he noted, those made by northwest coast native peoples, the closest and presumably most appropriate bola weights for comparison, featured drilled holes at one end for direct cordage attachment (Howe 1979, 27, fig. 16), whereas South American bola stones did not show any modifications to facilitate direct cordage attachment (as they were sealed in and attached to cords by the use of leather pouches), in this respect making them comparable to the Oregon/California bipointed stones. To demonstrate this possibility, Howe (1979, 27, fig. 17) replicated a South American–style bola using the local bipointed stones for weights. So why did Howe not make a comparison to bola weights used by the local Modoc? The answer is that the Modoc did not use the bola. They did, however, historically use the sling (Heizer & Johnson 1952, fig. 68; Voegelin 1942, 50, 73).

Although we recognize bola weights and slingstones as two branches of the same technology tree (see Coon 1971, 96, 97; Dillehay 2000, 94, 218; Knight 1880, 214; Métraux 1949, 253), for the following reasons we argue that Howe's South American model was inappropriate and a slingstones interpretation is more likely to be correct:

1.   Pervasive historic period sling use by Native Americans—including the Modoc—has been well-documented for the Pacific Coast and western North America, from Baja to the Arctic (Driver & Massey 1957, 357, map 142; Heizer & Johnson 1952, fig. 68; Voegelin 1942, 50, 73)—in fact, from Tierra del Fuego to the Arctic. In contrast, bola use was relatively rare (Driver & Massey 1957, 359, 361).

2.   On the North American continent the bola was primarily employed by the Inuit and a few northwest coast tribes in hunting avifauna (Driver & Massey 1957, 359, 361). Inuit and northwest coast bola weights were quite different from South American bola weights or the West Coast/Great Basin bipointed stones of interest here. As Howe (1979, 27, fig. 16) observed, unlike South American bola weights and the subject bipointed stones, they invariably displayed bored holes for direct cordage attachment.

3.   Howe did not, however, point out that they differ in many other ways. For example, South American bola weights were nearly always spheroids—as originally implied by use of a Spanish word for round balls or globes, *bola* or *bolas*, to describe these devices (Dillehay 2000, 94; Knight 1880, 233, 234; Métraux 1949, 253, 254; Wood 1870, 528). In contrast, northwest coast and Inuit bola weights were highly varied in shape, ranging from teardrop-like to unshaped chunks, and wood, ivory, and bone were more often the materials of choice than was stone (Graburn, Lee, & Rousselot 1996, 91–94, Plates 102–13; Hughes 1984, 272, fig. 15; Knight 1880, 234; Stanford 1976, 38; examination by the authors North American bola collections at the AMNH and NMAI-Smithsonian, 2004 and 2006).

4.   As previously discussed, pre-European slings dating to as early as 3,200+ YA, along with the subject bipointed stone and clay artifacts—probable slingstones—were recovered from Lovelock and Humboldt caves in northwest Nevada. To our knowledge, *no* bolas, much less South American–style pouch bolas, have ever been recovered from a North American archaeological site. Archaeologically, then, as much as such use has been proposed in the archaeological literature, we know of no comparable, indisputable evidence to support prehistoric bola use in North America.

5.   Although not particularly relevant, as these artifacts are so dissimilar to the bipointed stones under discussion, we would be remiss in not mentioning that the dean of Oregon archaeology, L. S. Cressman (1960, 49, 59, 60, 68, 74, fig. 47a; 1977, 110, 111), argued that "girdled" (intentionally grooved around the middle) "stone balls" (otherwise unmodified pebbles) found at the Five-Mile Rapids Archaeological Site on the Columbia River were bola weights. Cressman (1977, 110, 111) even proposed that perhaps the bola was invented

here more than 9,000 years ago. However, actual bolas to support his argument were lacking. Consequently, other explanations for the function of these stones—as net weights, the explanation eminent Oregon archaeologist C. Melvin Aikens (1993, 104, fig. 3.10) favored—remain viable. Cressman's evidence, then, is hardly indisputable. Cressman (1960, 60, fig. 47b) also found "unmodified bolas" (manuported pebbles) that he suggested might be slingstones; we have no argument with this interpretation.

6. The subject bipointed stones are, in all substantive respects, identical to slingstones found in Oceania—to such an impressive degree that they could be inserted into a collection of, for example, Marianas slingstones without any native islander or Pacific archaeologist noticing anything was amiss.

7. Archaeologist C. G. Sampson (1985, 235, 236, figs. 10–25a, b, 240), in his brief analysis of bipointed stones (as well as provocative "pebble manuports") recovered from the Nightfire Island Site located in the Klamath Basin of northeast California (also included by Carrol B. Howe in his assessment), reached no conclusion about their function, though he was fairly certain they were not bola stones or atlatl weights or line sinkers. He did grant that Howe's suggestion that they might be gaming stones had merit but added that this "cannot be verified." Sampson did not consider the proposition that they were slingstones. Our guess is that he did not explore this possibility because he was unaware of their extraordinary resemblance to the slingstones of Oceania.

Versus the Gaming Stones Interpretation

The case for the gambling or gaming stones theory largely rests on two pieces of historic information. The first concerned the Klamath people of south-central Oregon, attributed to George A. Dorsey, curator of anthropology at the Field Museum, Chicago, in Stewart Culin's comprehensive study *Games of the North American Indians* (1907, 293; Strong 1969, 161):

In connection with the hand game there should be mentioned a lozenge-shaped stone . . . measuring 2¼ inches long by 1½ inches in breadth and an inch in thickness. This stone, with several others similar in shape, was found at Klamath falls, near the foot of Klamath lake, and was obtained by me [ca. 1900] from a merchant as I was leaving the reservation. The person from whom I procured the specimen said that a number of Klamath Indians had seen the stone and had unanimously declared it was formerly used in playing the hand game. It was not possible for me to verify this statement.

Dorsey's statement was substantially verified by an unnamed Klamath in the late twentieth century (Moore 1973, 163, 167).

The second piece of information relates to the Honey Lake Paiute of northeast California (Riddell 1960b, 30):

> The late Zeb Johnston and his brother Bert Hostetter came to the ranch [in the Honey Lake Valley] as children ca. 1872 and remember the Indian camps near their place and recalled them using lemon-shaped gambling stones in the hand game (Culin 1907, p. 293). These stones are commonly found archaeologically in the Honey Lake Valley region, and additionally were used ethnographically in the Madeline Plains area [Paiute and Pit River peoples historic hunting area located some forty miles northwest of Honey Lake] as gambling stones. The Wadátkuht [Honey Lake Paiute] informants, incidentally, did not recognize these stones and did not use them in the hand game.

We do not question the reliability of the Dorsey and Riddell information. But it is also relevant that we unearthed no claim by the Klamath, Paiute, or other Native Americans that these bipointed stones were made historically. Rather, it appears they were found or handed down and then made use of as gaming pieces.

Interpretations of these objects as slingstones or gaming pieces are not mutually exclusive. That is, as with many artifacts in all cultures, functions change over time. Culin's description of the comparable Hawaiian hand game of Huna pohaku that explicitly used known and substantially identical slingstones allows us to propose with some confidence that this is exactly what happened here.

As Howe (1972, 196, 197, fig. 159; 1979, 26, 27) noted—from our observations, correctly—bipointed stones are so numerous and found in so many different circumstances, particularly in the Klamath Basin–Clear Lake area, that it is hard to believe they functioned originally and solely as gaming pieces. To buy into the gambling stones theory, you would have to show that the Klamath Basin, as well as the general southern Oregon/northeastern California/northwestern Nevada area, ca. 13,000–2,500 years ago, functioned something akin to a prehistoric Las Vegas (Howe 1972, 196). Now we suppose this is possible, but we'll risk a priori dismissal of a single-use gambling stones theory.

Versus the Charmstones Interpretation
Subsuming the subject bipointed stones under the term "charmstones" has been particularly popular among California archaeologists (Elsasser & Rhode 1996; Gifford & Schenck 1926, 93–97, Plates 29, 32; Hector, Foster, Pollack, & Fenenga 2006).

Universally, based on ethnographic analogs, the term "charmstones" has been broadly applied by archaeologists to virtually any objects that have been found in contexts that strongly suggest they have been invested with magical or ceremonial properties (e.g., medicine bundles, burials). This can include about anything—from fossils, to stream-polished pebbles and quartz crystals, to projectile points. Examples include the various kinds of "strangely shaped stones" (quartz crystals, pebbles, ammonites) collected as charms by the Wintu people of the northern Sacramento Valley (Du Bois 1940, 82) or the ancient arrowheads and spear points collected by the Klamath and Modoc for use as "charms in medicine and gambling" (Barrett 1910, 253).

In California archaeology, usage of this term over the years has become more descriptive than functional, pertaining only to teardrop- or pear-shaped artifacts usually perforated at one end, presumably for suspension purposes. Some of these teardrop objects are more diamond-, football-, or lemon-like in shape and imperforated, making them virtually identical to the bipointed stones commonly found in southern Oregon/northeastern California/northwestern Nevada and to the slingstones of Oceania.

As with gaming/gambling stones, charmstones and slingstones are not mutually exclusive terms. Elsasser and Rhode (1996, 44), quoting Gerow, though not specific to slingstones, in principle lend support to this view: "There is really no conflict, and the charmstones could have both practical and sacred connotations at the same time." We have added to this the hardly novel recognition that the role of artifacts can change over time, often passing from the practical or utilitarian to the sacred or magical, as with the use of ancient projectile points as charms by the Klamath and Modoc or the more prosaic use of slingstones as game pieces by the Hawaiians (Culin 1899, 242).

Relative to Wintu use of the sling, we suspect that Cora Du Bois's (1940, 125) informants were "both right": "oblong stones with an encircling groove found archaeologically, identified by some informants as sling stones, by others as charm stones."

Another piece of evidence from Riddell (1960b, 30, 31), concerning the same lemon-shaped stones discussed under "gambling stones," is also of interest in this regard: "The Pit River [Achumawi] people, however, apparently did use these lemon-shaped stones in the ethnographic period, but as hunting charms. They apparently held the stone against their bow with their bow hand as they shot their arrows (personal communication with Dr. Louis Payen of Sacramento)." Johnson (1984, 285) relates a similar tale about an Achumawi man who carried a "bipointed rock around in his shirt pocket whenever he went fishing or hunting. This was to insure good luck."

This information prompts us to wonder if these bipointed stones were used in this way because in the remote past they functioned as slingstones in the hunt? Such past use was now, perhaps, only a dim or lost memory to the Pit River people. But these stones retained a certain power and now worked as good-luck charms in the hunt. This is, of course, pure speculation. But to us it seems a plausible explanation, as we are convinced that these lemon-shaped stones were ancient slingstones.

If it is important to our understanding of the past to get the function of artifacts right, then the definition of charmstones, particularly in California archaeology, needs to be reexamined. Certainly context needs to be brought back into the definition as Hector and colleagues (2006) have done in presenting a persuasive case for the bipointed artifact they are dealing with as being a charmstone, though quite possibly it was slingstone derivative. If this happens, we predict that many slingstones (as well as "Eskimo-type" bola weights, net weights, line sinkers, etc.) will be found hiding under this catchall term.

Versus Miscellaneous Other Interpretations

At one time or another, other possibilities have been suggested to explain the function of these bipointed stones, none of which have gained much traction with archaeologists.

The array of proposed uses has included net weights or line sinkers, hammerstones, picks, drills, atlatl weights, club heads, and cooking or boiling stones. They all suffer from many of the same weaknesses as the more widely accepted explanations. But the most damning problem they all have in common is the lack of ethnographic analogs.

In determining the function of ancient artifacts, archaeologists depend greatly on documenting how identical or very similar objects functioned historically. For example, we can be confident that generally triangular, bifacially chipped, small stone artifacts with pointed tips are most likely to have been arrowheads or other types of projectile points, as we have numerous, worldwide, historic examples—ethnographic analogs—for comparison. Of all the interpretations that have been advanced to explain the function of the subject stones, the only one well supported by ethnohistoric data is the slingstones interpretation.

Essentially there appear to be two reasons for the slingstones interpretation not being widely accepted by American archaeologists: (1) a general ignorance of the remarkable resemblance of West Coast and Great Basin bipointed stones to the slingstones of Oceania; and (2) our most compelling ethnographic analogs being from Oceania, so a residual antidiffusionism, anti-pre-European transpacific contacts bias in American archaeology works against acceptance. However, the recent publication by the Society for American Archaeology in its journal

American Antiquity of Terry L. Jones and Kathryn A. Klar's (2005, 457–84; 2006, 765–70) articles debating the possibility of an Oceania origin for the Chumash plank canoe with Atholl Anderson (2006, 759–63) may signal erosion of this long-standing bias.

Issue one we trust we are disposing of here. The second issue is not so easily dealt with. Fortunately, other than to acknowledge the presence of this "elephant in the room," we need not make it our problem here, except to say that it should be no more of an impediment to acceptance of the slingstones interpretation than understanding that projectile points are projectile points wherever they are found, though they may have also functioned as charms, etc., depending on provenience or other factors that bear on the issue.

Acceptance does not imply direct connections, as in the case of projectile points between the Americas and Europe or wherever, or in the case of sling-stones between the Americas and Oceania or the Mediterranean (Korfman 1973; LeBlanc 2003, 61). Of course, direct or indirect connections are not ruled out. Independent invention, however, remains a distinct possibility especially in light of hard-to-explain temporal disparities.

Given the fledgling state of slingstones research, nothing of significance can be contributed here to the debate between supporters of diffusionism versus independent invention. However, failure to recognize these bipointed stones as slingstones *is* a serious impediment to gaining an accurate picture about the behavior of ancient peoples in the Americas, especially with regard to warfare, hunting practices, and, yes, transpacific contacts.

NORTH OF THE COLUMBIA RIVER:
A FOCUS ON BRITISH COLUMBIA

North of the Columbia River, substantial changes in pre-European sling use and particularly in the kinds of sling missiles used seems to occur (with our standard caveat that much of this difference may not be real but rather due to insufficient archaeological data). We were struck by the apparent lack of hand-size bipointed stones so common to Oregon/northeast California/northwest Nevada, though possibly a larger version occurs in B.C. Across much of Washington State, the lack of reported modified and/or unmodified spherical rocks that might qualify as slingstones is also striking, particularly when it is likely that all the historic period native peoples of Washington knew the sling and that such phenomena are common to prehistoric and historic sites in B.C. (see table 2).

Large (+/-16 cm by 8 cm midline diameter) bipointed/biconical ground stone artifacts, many of which resemble T-M type slingstones, have been found associated with B.C. fortified sites, particularly at Prince Rupert Harbor on the northwest coast. These fortified defensive sites and the bipointed stones date to as early as 3,000 YA. They do not, however, become a common feature of the coastal B.C. landscape until ca. 1,500–1,000 YA.

Although the function of the bipointed or biconical stones (northwest archaeologists use the terms interchangeably) remains an unsettled question, many archaeologists are persuaded that they were weapons based primarily on provenience. However, they seem none too sure of how they were used except vaguely as weapons of "close-in combat" (Knut Fladmark, personal communication 2005). To date, the notion that they might have been hand- or sling-hurled projectiles (comparable to the "throwing stones" of the Pacific islands of Niue and Kiribati) seems not to have been explored. Granted, they are certainly large for slingstones, but they're not beyond the range seen in Oceania. Historically, outsized slingstones are known to have been used in British Columbia, as previously cited relative to Stólō use of 10+ cm diameter cannonball-like shot.

For now, the function of the bipointed/biconical stones is conjectural. This does not mean that we do not have good evidence of sling use in pre-European B.C. Worked and unworked rounded stones have also been found there associated with fortified sites. They are usually lumped together and functionally obscured under the term "pebbles." In at least one instance, such pebbles were recovered from former wetlands, most likely related to waterfowl hunting dating, to ca. 4,000 YA at the Pit Meadows Locality in southwest B.C. (Ryan Sagarbarria, personal communication 2008). Regional archaeologists do assume these pebbles to be slingstones (see table 2).

Trepanation was practiced in British Columbia. Stone and Urcid (2003, 237–40, 243, 247) consider B.C. to be one of only two cranial surgery centers in pre-Columbian North America; the Oaxaca Valley of Mexico is the other.

Arctic-Subarctic

The area covered by this brief discussion (dictated by a poverty of available data, not the possible importance of the sling) stretches across the top of the world, taking in nearly all of Alaska, northern Canada, and Greenland. Most all the native peoples of the Arctic (Inuit-Aleut) and Subarctic (Athabascan-Nadene groups from southern Alaska to central Canada and Algonquians in central and eastern Canada) knew the sling. In historic times it functioned mostly as a boy's toy and for hunting small game and birds (Birket-Smith 1929, 61, 146, 243, 313, 314; Burch Jr. & Forman 1988, 70; Driver & Coffin 1975, 17, 72, 78, 83; Driver & Massey 1957, 169–75, map 142; Fitzhugh 1972, 48; Graburn et al. 1996, 158, 159, Plates 424–28; Nelson 1899, 134; Osgood 1937, 92; Osgood 1940, 396; Oswalt 1967; Vanstone 1972, 50, 52; Vanstone 1980, 29, Plate 6i; Vanstone 1985, 36, 47, 54; Willey 1966, 411–15).

Again, the sling of the Arctic and Subarctic peoples was the flexible, one-hand, missile-firing type of David and Goliath fame. Most often they were made of caribou hide or seal skin (or a combination of), and they often featured split pockets.

Historically, we surmise that only naturally occurring stones served as sling ammunition. This may as well hold true for prehistory, though this is little more than guesswork based on the near-silence of the ethnohistoric record on this issue. We can be certain that the sling was used as a warfare weapon at least by the Chugach of southern Alaska (Oswalt 1967, 188), the Greenland Inuit, and peoples of Canada's east coast. In the vicinity of Godthaab (Nuuk) on Greenland's west coast, the British expedition led by John Davis in 1586 recorded being opposed by Inuit "hurling heavy stones from slings" (Oswalt 1979, 39). James Hall, sailing with a Danish expedition in 1605, experienced a similar slingstone barrage while investigating the west coast of Greenland at a cove that he aptly named Sling Road (Oswalt 1979, 42, 43). Earlier accounts attributed to Sebastian Cabot regarding the expeditions of 1494 and 1497 counted slings among the war weapons used by peoples of unidentified tribal affiliation(s) encountered in the Labrador–Newfoundland–Cape Breton area of Canada's east coast (Babcock 1913, 155, 156; Birket-Smith 1929, 146).

Based on the sling's historic ubiquity and the previously cited initial contact testimonials of European explorers, we have little doubt that the sling existed in pre-Columbian times, even though the current archaeological record offers little support for this view. Danish anthropologist Kaj Birket-Smith (1929, 61) said that this was likely due to "defective investigation." Problematic small round stones/pebbles, referred to as "spherelets" or spheroids/balls in the regional archaeology, that have been recovered particularly from Archaic sites (dating to ca. 4,000 YA) may prove to be slingstones (Fitzhugh 1975, 124, 125).

There is no clear evidence of trepanation in the Arctic-Subarctic regions. In the 1930s, Aleš Hrdlička identified a few human skulls recovered from Kodiak Island as trepanned, questionably dating to as early as 2,000 YA. Recent reexamination concluded that this was unlikely and that these skulls simply exhibit "healed depressed skull fractures" (Stone & Urcid 2003, 242, 243). From our perspective, this could be of equal interest; it would be informative to know how these injuries were sustained.

Mountains, Prairies, and Forests—North America's Interior

The immense area we will cover in this section encompasses all the interior states and provinces of the United States and Canada not considered in our other survey areas. As our title for this section implies, an amazing diversity of environments, terrains, and peoples existed and exist there. Ordinarily it would be ludicrous to consider such an area under one heading. The common denominator is, even more so than for the Arctic-Subarctic, the poverty of sling-relevant data—which Driver and Massey (1957, 357) suggested might actually reflect reality, reasoning that the supposed rarity of the sling (quite possibly a faulty assumption) on the vast prairies of the United States and Canada was "because it would have been ineffective against the buffalo, on which the entire culture hinged." Its rarity east of the Great Plains, they thought, was to some degree determined by environmental factors: "It would be less effective in dense woods, and stones would also be scarcer in the eastern woodland than west of the Rockies."

There may be some truth to their reasoning. However, smaller game was more important to Great Plains subsistence economies than they believed (Hill Jr. 2007). And, as previously noted, there are exceptions to the dense forests and scarcity of stones arguments (which in this case may simply be bogus arguments, particularly regarding the availability of suitable rock). But primarily in the absence of sling-oriented studies, it is premature to accept their conclusions.

Documented historic period examples of sling use are few, though we strongly suspect that its use was more widespread than believed based on discovery of information that shows the Winnebago (AMNH Sling, Accession No. 1910-18/ Cat. Image No. 50.1/1014), Teton Dakota (Dorsey 1891, 341), Arapaho, and Cheyenne (see figures 65 and 67) knew the sling, all groups shown as nonusers by Driver and Coffin (1975, 98). The tribes claiming knowledge indicated that the sling was used exclusively by boys in games and/or for killing birds and small animals (Dorsey 1891, 341; Driver & Coffin 1975, 72, 78, 83, 93, 98, 103; Driver & Massey 1957, map 142; Kroeber 1908, 190, 191; Vanstone 1997, 15, fig. 37d).

Again, we interpret the silence of the ethnohistoric record as indicating that mostly unmodified stones of suitable size and shape served as sling ammunition, with one notable exception. Included among the collections of the American Museum of Natural History is a Gros Ventre leather sling with a disc-/pucklike modified slingstone, 4.5 cm in diameter by 1.3 cm in thickness (AMNH Accession No. 1901-28/Cat. Image No. 50/1858 a & b). This sling and slingstone were obtained in 1901 by the Mrs. Morris K. Jessup Expedition from the Fort Belknap Reservation in northern Montana. The sling was referred to by A. L. Kroeber in his 1908 AMNH publication *Ethnology of the Gros Ventre* (190, 191), but not the slingstone. If it can be confirmed that this is a historic period Gros Ventre slingstone—and we need to state this caveat lacking Kroeber's confirmation—it would be a heretofore unrecognized type for North America, though comparable types are known for Uruguay and Argentina.

Regarding the probability that the sling existed in the pre-European period, we could virtually clone our thoughts on this matter from our Arctic-Subarctic discussion. The usual suspect stone spheroids have been recovered archaeologically from the earliest (ca. 12,000 YA) to the latest (ca. 500 YA) sites of the prehistoric period (e.g., Agogino 1962, 246; Lehmer 1971, 81), accompanied by the usual list of speculations on how these spheroids might have functioned (as bola or net weights, as club heads) but rarely, if ever, including the thought that they could have been slingstones.

Of particular interest are three granite spheroids, 6–7 cm in diameter, recovered from the Fire Heart Creek Site in North Dakota. Lehmer (1966, 40, Plate 12) described them as intentionally "pecked into rough spheres. The surfaces are roughened from the pecking process, but they show no battering which would indicate use as hammerstones." From Lehmer's images it appears that they were not grooved, bored, or otherwise modified for attachment. Use as directly attached net or bola weights, or as hafted club heads, therefore can be ruled out. Use as a pouch-sealed bola weight or club head (i.e., in a "blackjack" type club known to have been used by Plains Indians) is not likely, as intentional roughening would serve no purpose in this configuration. Instead let us look at the golf ball as an analogue.

The intentional roughening of a golf ball's surface through dimpling reduces aerodynamic drag, thereby allowing the ball to fly further than a smooth spheroid (Fritts 2002; Scott 2005). Be assured that we are not proposing that these stones were ancient golf balls, but similar surface modification of a spherical stone to be hurled with a sling would achieve the same end. Increased flight distance was/is generally desired by slingers (in other venues such as Oceania, the Old World, and far western North America this was achieved through the streamlined football, or "bullet," shape), as it is a quality that is often advantageous in hunting, war, and sport. Trepanning appears to have been little practiced. Two or three cases considered to be pre-European are known from Michigan and Illinois (Stewart 1958, 475–79; Stone & Urcid 2003, 243).

Southeast and East Coasts

The final area of our survey encompasses the southern United States along the Gulf of Mexico from Texas to Florida plus the Atlantic Coast states stretching north from Florida to Nova Scotia and New Brunswick, Canada.

Driver and Massey (1957, 358, map 142), with Driver and Coffin's (1975, 103) follow-up study, show substantially more ethnohistoric sling use for the East and southeast coasts than for the North American interior. However, as was true for the interior, they underestimated its use. We located information that indicates that at least two groups missed by Driver and Coffin, the Catawba of the Carolinas (Rudes, Blumer, & May 2004, 304) and the Seneca Iroquois of New York (figure 68), knew the sling.

The earliest known European account of sling use for the southeast coast is taken from Cabeza de Vaca's 1542 narrative of the ill-fated Narváez Expedition. Cabeza de Vaca (1999, 79) recorded that in 1528 they were attacked by "Indians hurling stones from slings" along the Gulf Coast in the vicinity of Pensacola, Florida, and Mobile Bay, Alabama (also see Miller 1962, 87; Swanton 1946, 587).

In October of 1540, De Soto's horsemen in their brutal assault on the palisaded village of Mabila, located along the Alabama River near the present-day city of Selma, Alabama, were met by "a great barrage of arrows and stones" (Hudson 1997, 240). The De Soto journals do not specify the means by which these stones were hurled. It seems a good bet that slings were to some degree involved given Mabila's location some 190 miles up the Alabama River from its mouth at Mobile Bay, where a short twelve years earlier the Narváez Expedition suffered a similar sling-delivered barrage.

Of the many hostile actions documented by de Vaca and De Soto, native use of the sling and hurled stones was only mentioned in connection with these incidents. Coupled with the widespread historic use of the sling along the Gulf Coast, it has been suggested that the Spaniards arrived when the sling was being phased out as a weapon of war in favor of the bow and arrow (Miller 1962, 89; Swanton 1946, 587).

Benjamin Hawkins, an Indian agent with the federal government, reported an incident involving the sling that occurred in Georgia in ca. 1798. A Creek boy, apparently while "playing," accidentally killed his companion with a sling-hurled stone (Swanton 1946, 587). Besides demonstrating that the sling was used by the Creek at the end of the eighteenth century, this tragedy dramatically makes the point that it was no "toy."

Once again, and for the last time, the sling of choice historically—we know of no surviving prehistoric slings—was the one-hand type, some of which were wonderfully made, like the Seneca Iroquois braided sling in the Chicago Field Museum's collections (see figure 68). An exception to the one-hand type is a stick sling attributed to the Abnaki Penobscot of Maine in the Smithsonian-NMAI collections (NMAI No. 025864.001), which was obtained by F. G. Speck in about 1910. It consists of a leather strap with an expanded area, to serve as the missile holding pouch, that is attached to a stick that served as the sling's handle. Though smaller, it is essentially identical to Old World staff slings described by Korfmann (1973, 37–39). The stick or staff sling functioned in the same manner as the one-hand type: Centrifugal force imparted by the slinger propelled the missile, as opposed to tension on which catapults, bows, and modern-type slingshots depend. Korfmann (1973, 38) notes that the stick slings did not have as long a range as the one-hand type, but they required less skill to master and could be used to hurl larger projectiles, which made them popular siege weapons during the European Middle Ages.

In the post-European period, presumably only naturally occurring stones were used for sling ammunition, based again on the near-silence of the ethnohistoric record regarding the subject. Nor have indisputable sling missiles been identified for the pre-European period, though as we move back in time, besides the usual suspect "bola stones" (Bottoms & Painter 1989), we are presented with a number of possibilities.

As discussed earlier, slingstone technology may date to the earliest chapters of human prehistory in the southeast if the problematic egg stones of the Paleoindian Period (12,000 +/- YA) prove to be such. Then there are the patella stones to consider.

Carl F. Miller (1962, 87–89) called certain bifacially worked chert discs recovered from archaeological sites along the Roanoke River in Virginia "patella stones" due to their resemblance to human kneecaps. He believed them to be Archaic or even Paleoindian in age. With little confidence, he tentatively identified them as slingstones based on favorable comparisons to certain British Iron Age slingstones described and illustrated by John Evans (1897, 419). Miller did not mention that they were also comparable to the "throwing stones" recovered from sites in the Dalles-Deschutes Region along the Columbia River in Oregon (Steward 1928; Strong, Schenck, & Steward 1930).

Additionally, Miller (1962, 89, 249, Plates 33b&c, 770) provided data on "magnetite and stone balls" recovered from Roanoke River sites. These spheroids ranged from approximately 3–5 cm in diameter. He safely labeled them as "function unknown" but did hazard a guess that they might be "bolas." We think a better guess would have been slingstones.

Regarding the magnetite balls, Miller (1962, 90) made the following provocative observation (per our previous discussion, think golf balls): "From the appearance of the surfaces of each, it can readily be seen that they received considerable attention, and whether the shallow pits upon the surfaces represent the results of pecking or just one of its many natural features is not known."

Particularly compelling are some 1,600 ceramic and stone spheroids and ovoids collected by Thomas Beckwith from archaeological sites in and around Charleston, Missouri, at the end of the nineteenth century (see map 15). Beckwith identified them as "pottery and stone sling balls" (1911, 56–60, 80, 91, 92, 122, 126, Plates 1, 6, 13, 14). However, many modern-day Southeast archaeologists have raised questions about the archaeological context and identification of these objects as sling missiles—yet another situation requiring further investigation.

POVERTY POINT OBJECTS — A SETTLED ISSUE?

Poverty Point Objects (PPOs), sometimes less than helpfully referred to as "baked clay balls," are defining artifacts of the Poverty Point Complex that thrived in the Lower Mississippi River area and along the Gulf Coast from ca. 4,000–3,200 YA. PPOs are small artifacts (3–7 cm in applicable dimensions, depending on shape) of baked earthenware. They were hand molded into a bewildering array of shapes and styles—cylinders, spheroids, melon shapes, bicones, biscuit shapes, spirals, mushroom shapes, grooved and ungrooved, etc. Many show decorative elements, such as finger impressions and sometimes painted incised lines and indentations (Ford, Phillips, & Haag 1955; Ford & Webb 1959; Gibson 2000, 2007; Moore 1913; O'Brien & Wood 1998; Sassaman & Anderson 2004; Thomas 2000; Webb 1968).

PPOs occur in various quantities on Late Archaic sites of the southeast, with truly massive amounts noted for the namesake site in Louisiana. James Ford and Clarence Webb (1959, 44) estimated that some 24 million PPOs were made at Poverty Point, and they ventured that this was probably a "minimum figure." Gibson (2000, 112) stated that "whole and broken PPOs made up ninety-seven out of every hundred artifacts found at most spots on the rings [man-made ridges], but other encampments had fewer, some considerably so. Surrounding field camps sometimes had as few as one PPO for every 150 stone objects."

Major production of PPOs ended some 3,000 years ago, though downsized Plain Bicones continued to be made into Mississippian times or until ca. AD 1,400/600 YA, though with no clear ethnohistoric referents (e.g., Ford et al. 1955, 40, 41, 51–56; O'Brien & Wood 1998, 165), leaving us to ponder the role this most important artifact played in the lives of an ancient people.

In 1913, Charles Willoughby of the Peabody Museum, Harvard, suggested to Clarence B. Moore (1913, 73, 74) that the biconical PPOs might have functioned as objects used in a game and/or as sling missiles. In his opinion, they compared favorably to similar objects used by the Paiutes of southern Utah in a hand game, as well as to Polynesian slingstones and clay pellets thought to be slingstones from the Stockton Mounds in California (also see Holmes 1902, 177, Plates 26, 27, 28a).

Later it was proposed that PPOs functioned as substitutes for cooking stones in an area that was devoid of stone—that is, the Lower Mississippi River Valley. Archaeologists Ford, Phillips, and Haag (1955, 56), in reporting on PPOs recovered from the Jaketown site in Mississippi, though they presented data largely supporting the cooking stones theory, remained open to other ideas: "We still lack the required positive evidence of the association of Poverty Point Objects in fireplaces, ash beds, etc., to prove the validity of the cooking-stone theory."

Ford and Webb (1959, 39) found this association at the Poverty Point site, closed the case, and relegated Willoughby's suggestions to the dustbin of history.

We think the case needs to be reopened. We do not dispute that many PPOs functioned as cooking stones, as supporting data appear convincing (Ford et al. 1955, 39–57; Ford & Webb 1959, 39–49; Gibson 2000, 112–16; Webb 1968, 308). The key word here is "many." Even the theory's proponents have questions about its ability to account for the full range of phenomena. For example, is it likely that cooking stones would be painted and decorated, as many PPOs are? Some archaeologists think not and have suggested the decorated forms had a different, though undetermined, function (Ford et al. 1955, 55; Gibson 2000, 117, fig. 6.3, 268).

Great effort was expended by the inhabitants of Poverty Point to import tons of stone into the site, including for cooking (Ford & Webb 1959, 39; Gibson 2000, 171–81, 218–31, 268–74; Webb 1968, 308, 311–18). If PPOs filled the need, why did they go to this trouble? There seems little basis for the explanations offered, that stone was needed to cook up "special recipes" or do things in the "old ways" (Ford & Webb 1959, 39; Gibson 2000, 116, 268).

We wonder if the purpose of at least some of the roasting pits or earth ovens was more to fire PPOs (kilns) than for cooking. This should be true at least for the decorated forms that presumably were not cooking stones. In particular, the biconical, melon, and spheroidal forms attract our attention. All could have served as sling ammunition.

Concerning the biconical PPOs, as Willoughby suggested, they are similar to some Polynesian slingstones—and, from our observations, particularly certain Hawaiian forms. Closer comparative analysis might also reveal correlates that have been incorrectly subsumed under the T-M Type 3, or biconical/diamond form (see figures 7 and 8). The differences are that T-M Type 3s are usually ovoid in their midline x-sections and significantly longer in length relative to midline diameter (often a difference of more than 2 cm), whereas the PPO bicones strike us as being bidomed lenticular objects (reminiscent of spinning toy tops) with little difference between length and midline x-section measurements. Sometimes the midline diameter even exceeds the "length." The more compelling analogs are biconical or "bidomed" slingstones found in Argentina and Uruguay. They are nearly identical to the biconical PPOs except for being executed in stone (see figures 32, 69, and 70).

As previously mentioned, small Plain Bicones continued in use long after the demise of the Poverty Point Complex and other forms of PPOs. This has led some archaeologists to entertain the idea that this form may have changed in function over time (Ford et al. 1955, 51–56). Certainly a good possibility, perhaps they were impressed into service as slingstones. Yet we submit for consideration that they may have always functioned as sling projectiles and that the small forms simply "won the preference competition" for use with the kinds of slings that continued in use.

Also dropped from archaeological purview with Ford and Webb's 1959 "cooking stones declaration" was the similarity between PPOs and Baked Clay Objects (BCOs) found in northern California. In their publication on the Jaketown Site, Ford, Phillips, and Haag (1955, 55) were so impressed with this resemblance that they were prompted to state, "It is certainly not mere coincidence; it must have some meaning." Such a pronouncement seemed to beg for a comparative study that, to our knowledge, has never been undertaken.

Many of the California BCOs were considered to be substitute cooking stones in an area that was also stone poor. However, it was clear that many were not. Ford, Phillips, and Haag (1955, 53–55) were well aware of this, but in their discussion on possible other functions ascribed to the California BCOs, they fail to mention that many were thought to be slingstones, a proposition reinforced by more recent work. Robert Heizer (1937, 36, fig. 2.4g, 41) noted that a spool-shaped BCO, a form heretofore not considered to be a slingstone, was found embedded in a human skull recovered from the Johnson Archaeological Site (or Site 6) in northern California, indicating that even this form, comparable to some of the barrel or grooved PPOs, may have served as a slingstone.

In this context, it is also of interest that the father of American archaeology, A. V. Kidder (1932, 142, 143, fig. 123), recovered "fired clay objects" from Pecos Pueblo, New Mexico, comparable to PPOs and the California BCOs. Two of these objects were bicones that Kidder considered to be identical to specimens collected at Poverty Point (see figures 69 and 70). Kidder's limited analysis failed to determine a function for these artifacts, but use as cooking stones is not probable, as such objects are not known to have been used for cooking by pueblo peoples. It may or may not prove relevant to the issue, but it is highly likely that the sling was used at Pecos Pueblo. Again, further analysis is called for.

The Poverty Point site itself figures into a theory of slingstone use. Poverty Point's most distinctive feature is a semicircular arrangement of six man-made earthen ridges arcing out from a precipitous bluff above the Bayou Maçon. Archaeologist Jon L. Gibson (2000, 228–31, 270, 271), probably the foremost living authority on Poverty Point, proposed that these ridges were built primarily to symbolically "protect" Poverty Point's residents from supernatural forces, though he hints at the possibility that "real" enemies were cause for concern. We do not disagree, but we do suggest that real or perceived human enemies loomed as large in the construction of these earthworks as supernatural forces did. Some support for this suggestion comes from studies of eastern and southeastern human burials, which show a significant jump in the number of violent deaths in the Middle and Late Archaic periods (Milner 1999, 116, 120–22).

Comparable constructions are seen at Iron Age British hillforts and New Zealand pa, as well as at "fortified temples" and defensive works found in Andean South America and Mesoamerica, plus other sites in the southeastern and eastern United States. All of these constructions combined both practical and magical protection features (Arkush & Stanish 2005; Armillas 1951; Brice 1985, 26–32, 132, 133; Fox 1976, 28, 29; Keeley, Fontana, & Quick 2007; LeBlanc 2003, 178, 183–91; Parkinson & Duffy 2007; Squier & Davis 1848). Do not all humans, to the present day, solicit aid from both worlds when confronting enemies? This thought was better captured by the Reverend William Thomas Cummings in 1942 at the Battle for Bataan, when he said, "There are no atheists in foxholes."

The "multivallate" (ringed by multiple ridges and ditches) British Iron Age hillforts were expressly designed to defend against slingstone attacks and in turn facilitate defenders' use of slings and hand-hurled stones (Avery 1986; Braidwood 1967, 163; Brice 1985, 26–32). Given that slings and/or hand-hurled stones were primary projectile weapons in South America, Mesoamerica, and New Zealand, it is probable that the comparable fortifications constructed in these locations were designed in response to use of this weaponry as well. (For particularly relevant descriptions of Andean "fortified hilltops," see Arkush [2010, 37], Rowe [1946, 278, 279], and Zorich [2010].) It is not much of a stretch to extend this reasoning to Poverty Point and later types of fortified sites in the eastern and southeastern United States.

Simply put, this model is based on the principle that similar problems prompt similar solutions. Given the incredible cultural and temporal distances involved in the development of these fortifications (ranging from ca. 3,500 YA at Poverty Point to ca. 1,100 YA for New Zealand pa), it appears safe to rule out diffusionism, unless the concepts originated in the Americas.

Lastly, archaeologists have been struck by how heavily littered Poverty Point earthworks are with projectile points (presumably spear and atlatl dart tips), arguably approaching PPO numbers. This seems strange for a site whose inhabitants, in theory, were only engaged in peaceful activities and largely reliant on aquatic and vegetative food resources (Gibson 2000). However, if Poverty Point, for at least part of its history, functioned more as an arsenal/fortification along the lines of what we see particularly in pre-Columbian Andean South America and Mesoamerica, its array of artifacts and features meets expectations. That is, as noted, we see comparable defensive works in South America and Mesoamerica along with use and stockpiling of atlatls, spears, and stone and clay sling projectiles from ca. 5,000 YA to the time of the Spanish invasions.

Regarding trepanation, we could locate information pertaining to only three known cases from Arkansas, Georgia, and Maryland (Cosgrove 1929; Stewart 1958, 476–79; Stone & Urcid 2003, 243; Wakefield & Dellinger 1936). All victims were adult males and pre-Columbian, though specific dates and cultural affiliations are uncertain. It appears, then, that trepanation was little practiced in the eastern and southeastern area of what is now the United States. T. D. Stewart's (1958, 476) remarks regarding the Maryland find, however, cast some doubt on this supposition: "This one is perhaps the most convincing example of (trephining) yet found in the northern continent. Yet as an example of primitive surgery it is singularly isolated among hundreds of skulls from this site. It would seem unreasonable to expect such a successful end result on a first attempt at cranial surgery." Once again, perhaps, the problem is inadequate study rather than reality.

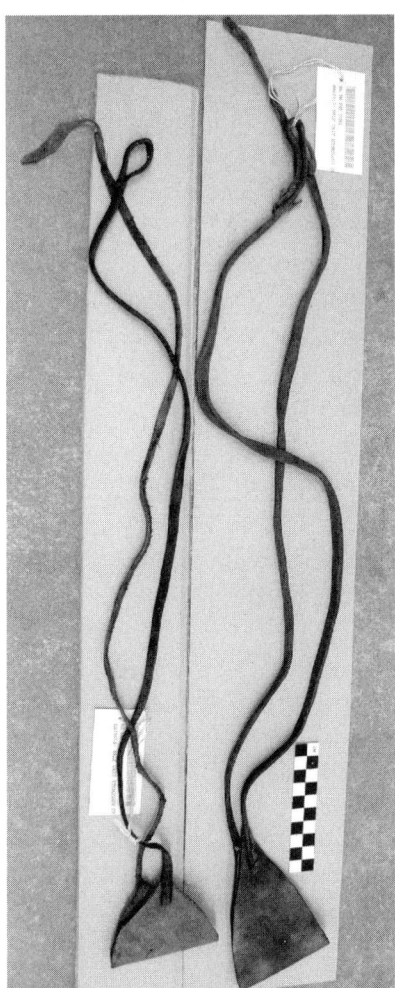
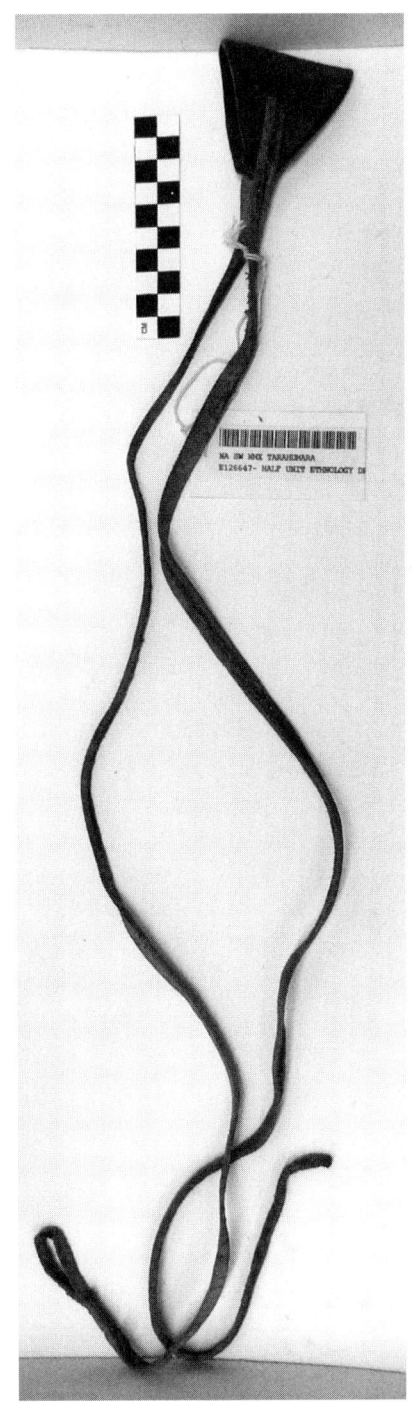

Figure 36. Two (a) Zuni Pueblo, New Mexico, and (b) Tarahumara, Mexico, leather slings. They are virtually identical and typical of historic period Southwestern slings. Bureau of American Ethnology (BAE) and Dr. Palmer Collections, 1881–1885. NMNH Catalog Nos. E069313, E075664, and E126647. Used with permission, Department of Anthropology, Smithsonian-NMNH.

Figure 37. Two typical pre-Columbian stone balls from the American Southwest, golf ball in size (3–4 cm diameter) and appearance (dimpled surface). Used with permission, El Paso (TX) Museum of Archaeology.

Figure 38. Two more typical pre-Columbian Southwest stone balls, 5–6 cm diameter. Collected from Santa Clara Mound, Saint George, Utah, by Dr. E. Palmer, ca. 1876. NMNH Catalog No. A021002. Used with permission, Department of Anthropology, Smithsonian-NMNH.

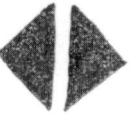 

Figure 39. Two "Belly of Sling," or sling pocket, representational designs from Tewa Pueblos, New Mexico (Harrington 1912, 268, 281).

Figure 40. "Gaming stones" from Clear Lake, Modoc County, CA. (Compare with the New Ireland, Melanesia, slingstones in figure 12.) Frank and Doris Payne Collection, Klamath County Museum. Used with permission, Klamath County Museum, Klamath Falls, OR.

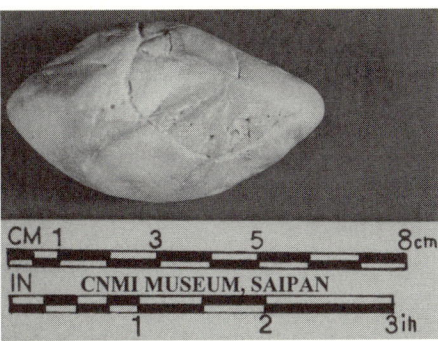

Figure 41. A T-M Type 3 (biconical/ diamond-shape) slingstone of argil- laceous coral limestone from LauLau Beach, Saipan. (Compare with figures 3 [artifact 96-3-3196], 33c, and 42.) CNMI Museum Catalog No. 1999.37.1. Used with permission, CNMI Museum.

Figure 42. A basalt, diamond-shape "charmstone" from Kramer Cave, Falcon Hill, Winnemucca Lake, NV. Nevada State Museum (NSM) Catalog No. 26WA196/1346. Used by permission, NSM, Carson City.

Figure 43. The two bipointed stones from the Stiles Ranch Site (LAS-4), Honey Lake Valley, Lassen County, CA, as recorded by F. Riddell in 1948, are actually cataloged as "slingstones"—a classification rarity in North American archaeology. Phoebe A. Hearst Museum of Anthropology (PAHMA), UC Berkeley Catalog Nos. 1-202884 (of a type of granitic igneous rock, 55.6 g); 1-202883 (basalt, 50.6 g). Used with permission, PAHMA and the Regents of the University of California.

Figure 44. Two basalt bipointed stones from Lassen County, CA. Deisher Collection, 1915. National Museum of the American Indian (NMAI) Catalog Nos. 4-2728 and 4-2729. Used with permission, Smithsonian-NMAI.

Figure 45. Two bipointed stones of unidentified rock (igneous?) from Sonoma County, CA. NMAI Catalog Nos. 04-3366 (J. B. Lewis, 1915) and 11-8239 (purchased 1923). Used with permission, Smithsonian-NMAI.

Figure 46. Seven "bipointed charms" of limestone and igneous rocks from Alpaugh vicinity, Tulare County, CA. Sam Fry and August F. Meyer Collections, 1926. NMAI Catalog Nos. (top row, left to right): 14-5787, -8220, -8226; (bottom row) -5818, -8218, -8228, -8219. Used with permission, Smithsonian-NMAI.

Figure 47. A "plummet" of unidentified stone, probably igneous, from San Miguel Island, CA. W. M. Fitzhugh Collection, 1936. NMAI Catalog No. 19-2380. Used with permission, Smithsonian-NMAI.

Figure 48. Lovelock Cave, NV, 2004.

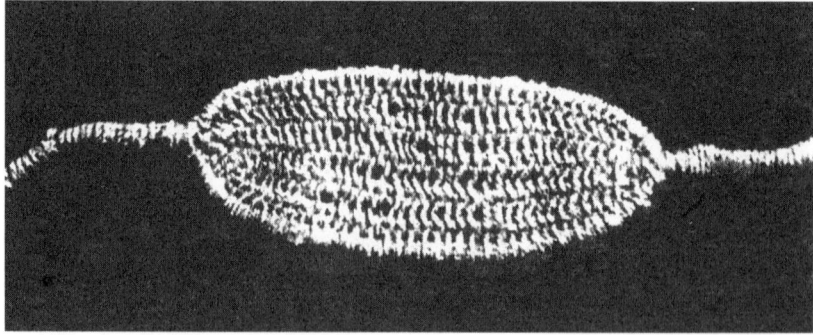

Figure 49. A sling recovered from Lovelock Cave, NV. Dating to ca. 3,200 YA, it is the oldest known surviving sling in North America. Woven of Indian hemp (*Apocynum cannabinum*), it measures 8.89 cm by 3.81 (Heizer & Johnson 1952, fig. 67a). Used with permission, Society for American Archaeology (SAA).

Figure 50. These two bipointed stones from Lovelock Cave, NV, are comparable to T-M Types 1 and 2 (see fig. 7): (a) nearly complete, smoothed, reddish-brown sandstone, 5.15 cm x 2.3 cm midline diameter, 28.5 g; (b) complete, polished, gray-white quartz, ca. 5.5 cm x 3.5 cm midline diameter, 57 g. NMAI Catalog No. 13-4786. See Loud and Harrington (1931, 113, 181, Plate 57d). Pencil drawing by G. York, 2006. Used with permission, Smithsonian-NMAI.

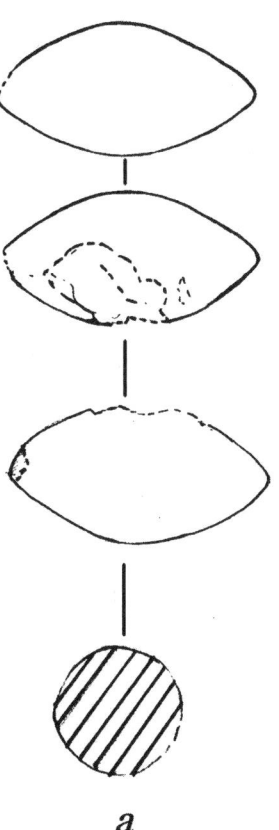

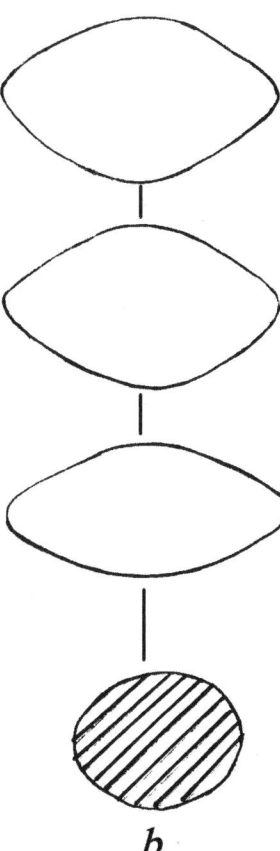

a

b

Figure 51. "Elliptical and globular clay balls" from Lovelock Cave, NV. Estimated wts. 20–40 g. PAHMA Catalog Nos. 1-19231 and -19230. See Loud and Harrington (1931, 109, Plates 53h, g). Used with permission, PAHMA and the Regents of the University of California.

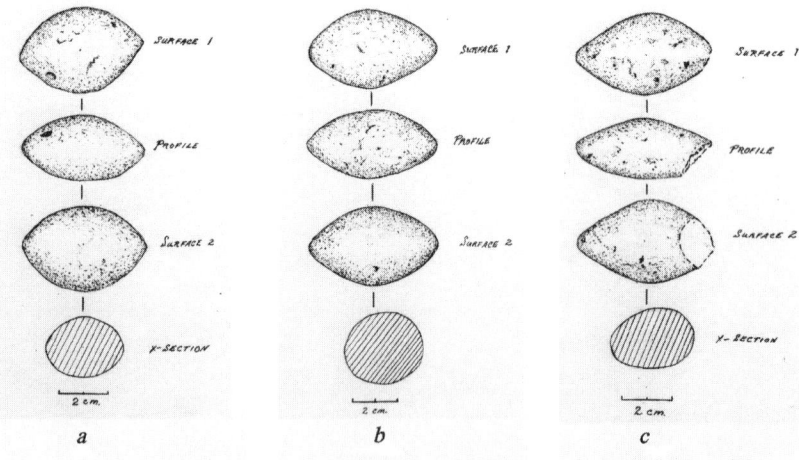

Figure 52. These three basalt bipointed stones from Pyramid Lake, NV, are comparable to T-M Types 4, 1, and 3 (see fig. 7). Royels Collection Catalog Nos. (a) 94-31-2956 (42.1 g); (b) -2957 (70.9 g); and (c) -2958 (50.9 g). Drawings by G. York, 2004. Used with permission, Department of Anthropology, UNR.

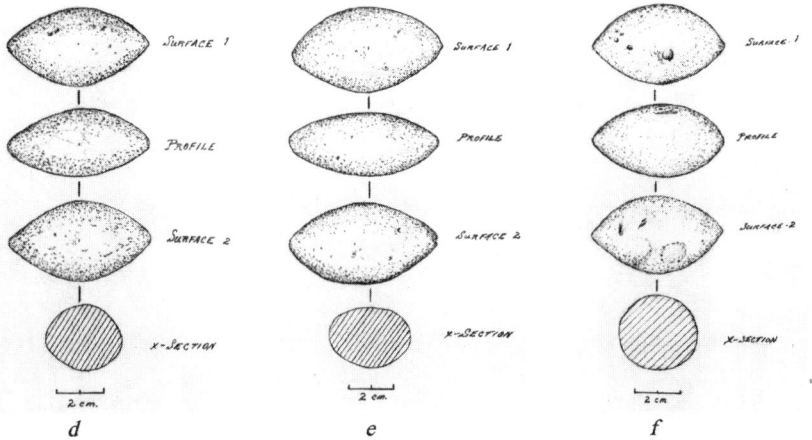

Figure 53. These three basalt bipointed stones from Pyramid Lake, NV, are comparable to T-M Types 1, 2, and 4. Royels Collection Catalog Nos. (d) 94-31-2959 (58.4 g); (e) -2960 (63.9 g); and (f) -2961 (67.8 g). Drawings by G. York, 2004. Used with permission, Department of Anthropology, UNR.

Figure 54. Stone (tuff) balls classified as "sling stones." PAHMA Catalog Nos.: (top, left to right) 1-118195, -118196, -118199, -118200; (bottom) 1-118201, -118203, -118204 (40–70 g). The rare slingstones appellation was probably influenced by their having been recovered from the Indian Island Archaeology Site (LAK-29), a Pomo historic site, Clear Lake, Lake County, CA. Used with permission, PAHMA and the Regents of the University of California.

Figure 55. Replicated baked clay sling balls used by the Eastern Pomo for hunting waterfowl. The accuracy of these replicas is questionable, as they are spherical. Barrett (1952, 145, Plate 14.3) stated that such balls were "not spherical but have two sides decidedly flattened, for the purpose of making them skip over the surface of the water." PAHMA Catalog No. 1-10604. Used with permission, PAHMA and the Regents of the University of California.

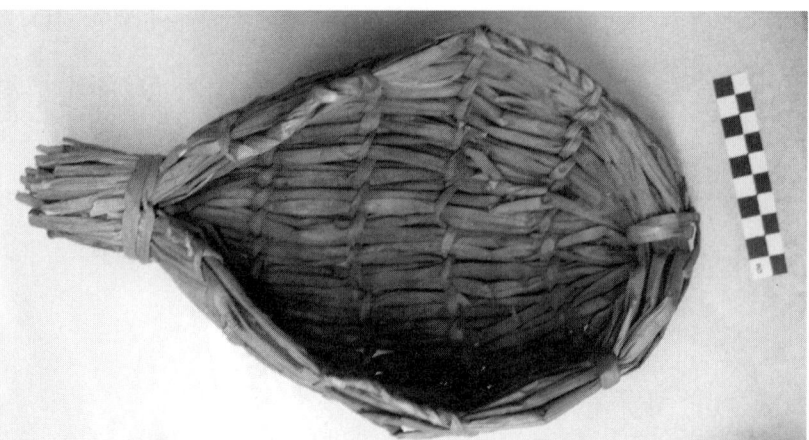

Figure 56. An Eastern Pomo tule basket for carrying clay sling balls. PAHMA Catalog No. 1-10604. Used with permission, PAHMA and the Regents of the University of California.

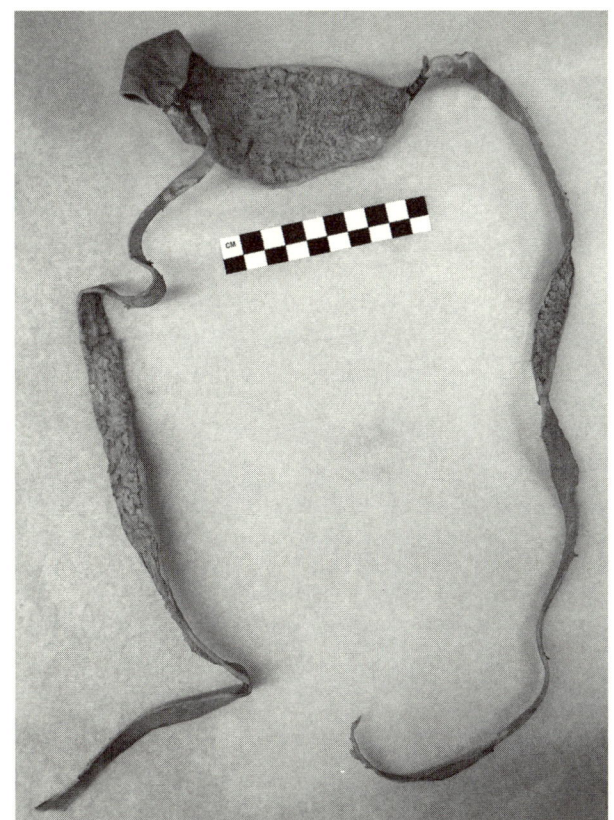

Figure 57. An East-
ern Pomo buckskin
war or hunting
sling. PAHMA
Catalog No. 1-2411.
Used with permis-
sion, PAHMA and
the Regents of the
University of Cali-
fornia.

Figure 58. An Eastern Pomo tule and milkweed-fiber waterfowl sling. PAHMA Catalog No.
1-10605. Used with permission, PAHMA and the Regents of the University of California.

Figure 59. Gigi York measures bipointed stones (probable slingstones) from the Nightfire Island Archaeology Site, Klamath Basin, CA. Used with permission, Klamath County Museum, Klamath Falls, OR.

Figure 60. "Elliptical baked clay balls" (probable sling missiles) dating to ca. 1,100 YA, from the Gunther Island Site (HUM-67), Humboldt Bay, CA. Approximate sizes range 1–5 cm x 1–2 cm midline diameter. Dr. H. H. Stuart Exhibit, Favell Museum. Used with permission, Favell Museum, Klamath Falls, OR.

Figure 61. Two more probable baked clay sling missiles from the Gunther Island Site. Dr. H. H. Stuart Exhibit, Favell Museum. Used with permission, Favell Museum, Klamath Falls, OR.

Figure 62. Gigi York points out the "Slinger Man" petroglyph at Little Petroglyph Canyon, China Lake Naval Air Weapons Station, CA. Used with permission, Command Archaeologist, China Lake Naval Air Weapons Station.

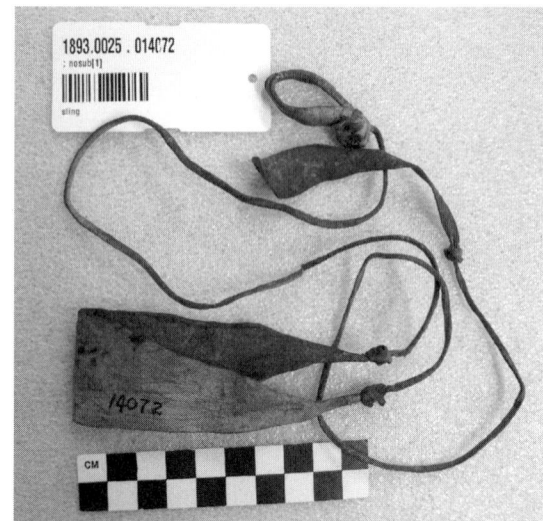

Figure 63. An Inuit sling from Greenland. Note the "banner," or flared end, on the free cord (a decorative element?); this is also seen on slings in the North America Southwest. Chicago Field Museum 1893 acquisition, No. 014072. Used with permission, Field Museum, Chicago.

Figure 64. An Inuit sling from Kotzebue, AK. Note the split pocket and "banner" end element on the free cord. Chicago Field Museum 1896 acquisition, No. 020253. Used with permission, Field Museum, Chicago.

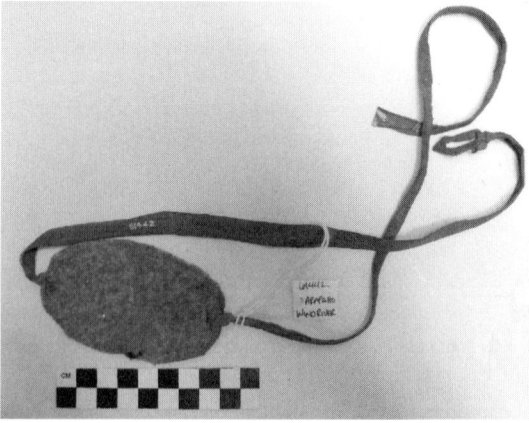

Figure 65. An Arapaho sling from the Wind River Reservation, WY. Field Museum 1900 acquisition, No. 061442. Used with permission, Field Museum, Chicago.

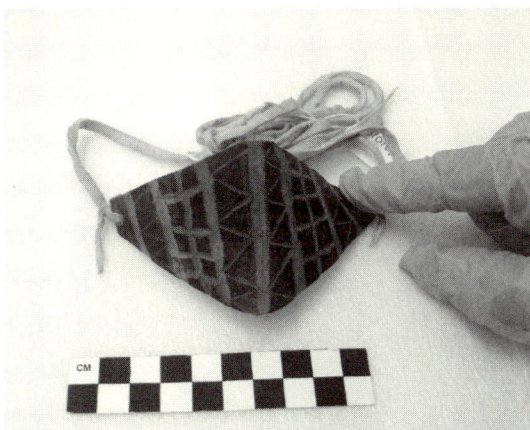

Figure 66. An Uintah Ute decorated sling from Whiterocks, UT. Field Museum 1900 acquisition, No. 061010. Used with permission, Field Museum, Chicago.

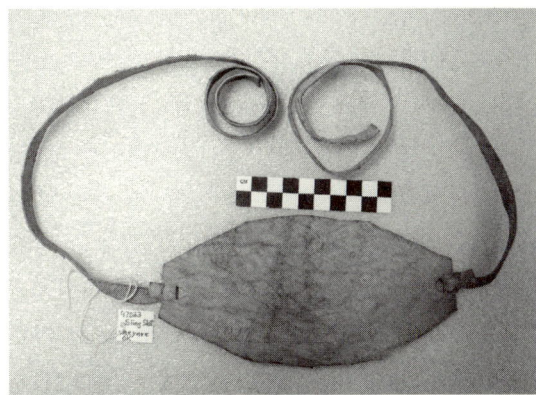

Figure 67 (left and below). Two Cheyenne leather slings from Darlington, OK. Field Museum 1905 acquisitions, Nos. 97032 and 97033. Used with permission, Field Museum, Chicago.

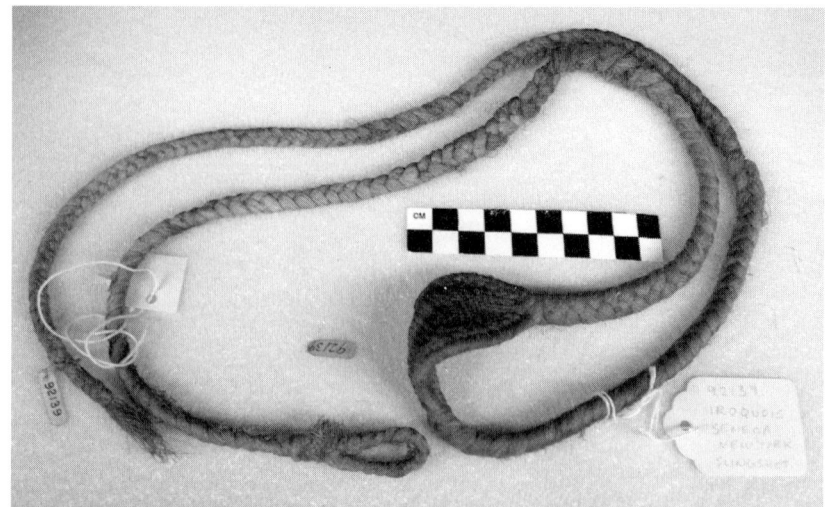

Above: Figure 68. A Seneca Iroquois sling from New York State. Field Museum 1905 acquisition, No. 092139. Used with permission, Field Museum, Chicago.

Right: Figure 69. Common forms of Poverty Point Objects (PPOs) recovered from the Poverty Point Site, LA. From Ford and Webb (1959, fig. 13); used with permission, AMNH.

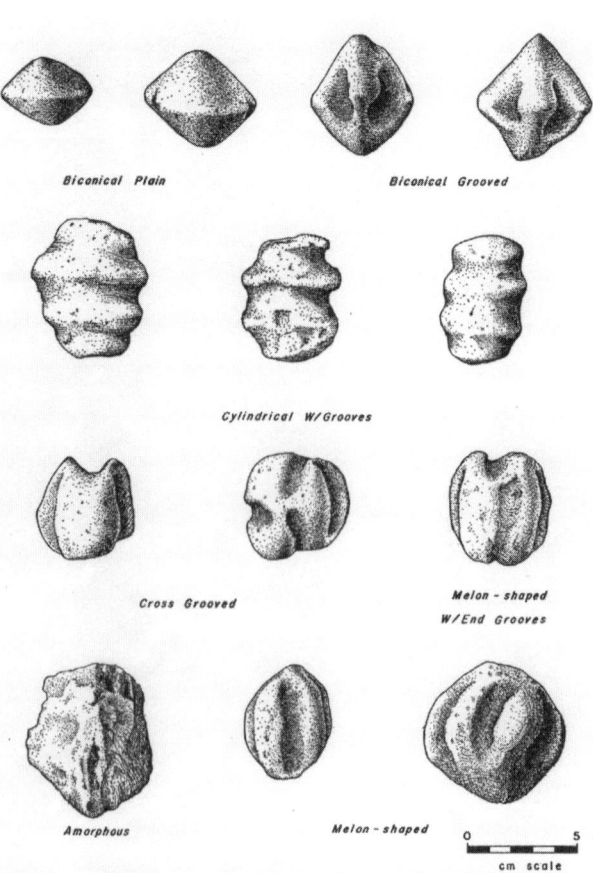

Biconical Plain

Biconical Grooved

Cylindrical W/Grooves

Cross Grooved

Melon - shaped
W/End Grooves

Amorphous

Melon - shaped

cm scale

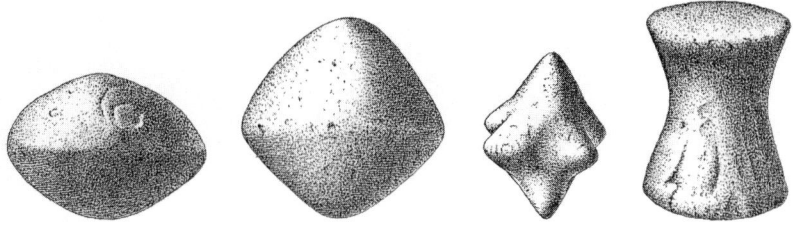

Figure 70. These fired clay objects, 2–4 cm, from Pecos Pueblo, NM, are comparable to, if not actual, common forms of PPOs and BCOs. From Kidder (1932, fig. 123); reprinted with permission, © Yale University Press.

Map 9. North America slingstone survey areas

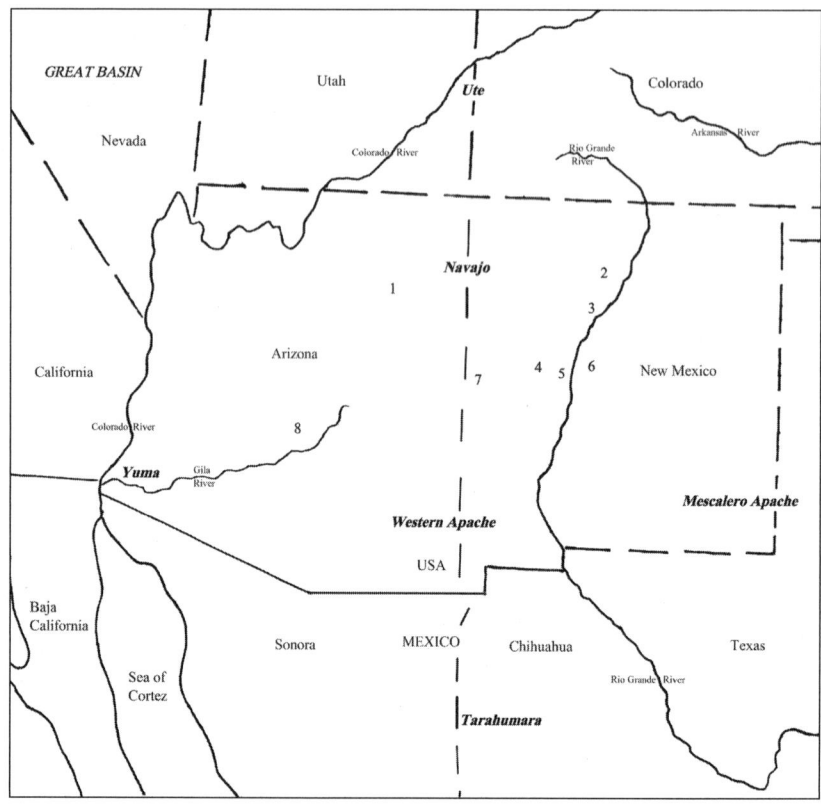

Map 10. North America Southwest locales and peoples discussed. Key: (1) Hopi mesas, including the ruins of Awatovi and Jeddito pueblos, and the Tewa village of Walpi; (2) Pajarito Plateau and the ruins of Otowi pueblo; (3) Astialakwa; (4) Rio Grande pueblos, including San Ildefonso; (5) Acoma pueblo; (6) Tiguex pueblos; (7) Southern Tiwa; (8) Zuni and the ruins of Hawikuh; (9) South Mountain petroglyphs.

Map 11. Locations of Native American groups claiming use or knowledge of the sling in part of western North America. The Klamath Basin, Pomo territory, and Lovelock Cave are indicated. Based on Heizer and Johnson (1952, fig. 68), by permission of the Society for American Archaeology (SAA).

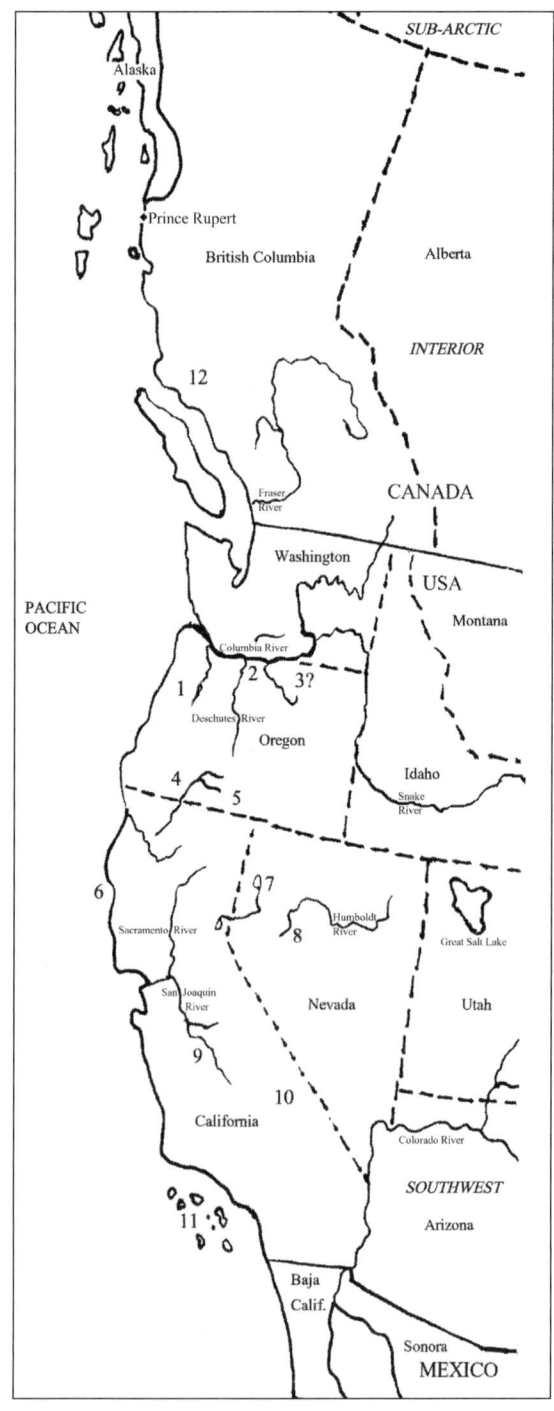

Map 12. North America
West Coast and Great Basin.
Numbers indicate slingstone-
relevant archaeology locales.

Table 2

North America West Coast and Great Basin archaeological find locations of bipointed/biconical stone and clay artifacts (T-M Types 1–4 slingstone correlates [see figures 7 and 8]), slings, and rock art depictions

Map # / Location	Vertical provenience	Material	Local descriptive classifications/Function guesses	T-M Type	Remarks	References
1. Calapooya-Willamette-Columbia Rivers Corridor, OR*	Surface and Buried (?)	Basalts/Obsidians	Chipping stones/Picks/Gaming stones/Bola stones/Ovate bifaces/Stone balls/Throwing stones	1, 2, 4	Seaman notes striking resemblance to New Hebrides slingstones but dismisses the possibility. Suspicious spheroids (balls) are also present.	Pettigrew 1990, figs. 5 (e, g), 6 (h, i), Seaman 1967,174, 175, 200, 201; Strong, Schenck, & Steward 1930, 147
2. Dalles-Deschutes Region, Columbia River, OR	Surface and buried	Crypto-silicates/Basalts	Throwing stones/Bolas/Slingstones/Problematical objects	4. + 1 & 2 probable	Cressman assigns his "girdled bolas" to the Early Period, ca. 9,000–7000 YA, with use of "unmodified bolas" (slingstones) possibly continuing into historic times.	Cressman 1956, 429; 1960, 49, 59, 60, 68, 74, fig. 47(b); 1977, 110, 111; Steward 1928; Strong, Schenck, & Steward, 1930, 4, 5, 10, 12, 73, 74, 89, 90, 125, Plate 19
3. Northern OR	Surface (?)	Stone (Unidentified)	Bipointed objects	1	Only provenience, "Northern Oregon."	F. W. Skiff Collection, 1925, Smithsonian-NMAI Catalog Nos.: 139110.000, 139111.000, 139111.001, and 139111.002
4. Jackson County, SW OR	Surface (?)	Stone	Bipointed object	1	Only provenience, "Jackson County, Oregon."	F. W. Skiff Collection, 1925, Smithsonian-NMAI Catalog No.: 138692.000

Map # / Location	Vertical provenience	Material	Local descriptive classifications/Function guesses	T-M Type	Remarks	References
5. Interior mountains-plateaus-valleys-basins of S Oregon-NE CA.-NW NV *	Surface and buried	Stone, various kinds but mostly basalts	Bolas/Charmstones/Lemon-shaped stones/Biconical stones/Bipointed stones/Slingstones/Gambling and gaming stones/Dog rocks	1–4	The Klamath Basin–Clear Lake area looks to have been slingstone central from ca. 2,500–13,000 ya. T-M slingstones (usually labeled bolas) are found in virtually all Klamath Basin museum exhibits (e.g., Klamath County Museum, Favell Museum, Tulelake-Butte Valley History Museum, Lava Beds NM) and private collections.	Ted Goebel, Personal Communication 2004, re: The Mt. Hebron Paleoarchaic Site; Hector et al. 2006; Howe 1972, 196, 197, fig. 159; 1979, 25–29, 42–46, 59–61; Johnson 1984, 284, 285, 296; Oetting 1989, 70, 71, fig. 17; Riddell 1960a, 89, 108, Fig.19(b); 1960b, 30, 31; Sampson 1985, 235, figs. 10–25(ab); Shapiro et al. 2002, 90, Plate 12; Sundahl and Clewett 1988, 32, 37, 38, fig. 13, 43
6. Humboldt Bay–Gunther Island, N Coast CA	Surface (?) and buried-grave goods and scattered	Baked clay	Elliptical clay balls	1, maybe 2 & 4	Loud notes resemblance to Guam slingstones but essentially dismisses the possibility.	Loud 1918, 377–80, Plate, 20 (1–3, 5); Heizer & Elsasser 1964, 30, 31; Dr. H. H. Stuart 1920s, Gunther Island "Clay Balls," Favell Museum exhibit, Klamath Falls, OR
7. Pyramid and Winnemucca Lakes, NV	Surface and buried-cave deposits	Basalts, maybe limestone	Charmstones/Atlatl weights/Bipointed stones/Sinkers	1–3	T-M Type 3 appears to be the preferred style.	Hattori 1982, 52–54, fig. 22(g); Royels Collection bipointed stones, UNR Anthro. Dept.

Map # / Location	Vertical provenience	Material	Local descriptive classifications/Function guesses	T-M Type	Remarks	References
8. Lovelock and Humboldt Caves, NV	Buried-cave deposits, Lovelock sling found with child's burial.	Basalts and Baked Clay, Apocynum	Elliptical clay ball/ Bipointed stones/ Gaming stones/ Shamen's charms/ Sling pockets	1 & 3	Lovelock Cave is the only known N. American site where both slingstones and a sling were found. The ca. 3,200 ya Lovelock sling is the oldest known, surviving sling in N. America. The two slings recovered from Humboldt Cave likely date to within the last 2,000 years. Suspect clay and stone spheroids (balls) were also recovered from Lovelock Cave.	Bennyhoff & Hughes 1987, 165, 167–69; Heizer & Johnson 1952; Heizer & Krieger 1956, 62, 102–5, Plate 24(i, k); Loud and Harrington 1931, 109, 113, Plate 10, Plate 53 (a, g, h), Plate 57 (b, d); O'Neale 1947; Shackley n.d. (re: R/C dating of sling pertinent Lot 26, Lovelock Cave)
9. Central CA (Clear Lake to Tehachapi Mts.)	Surface and buried	Stone, various kinds, baked clay	Charmstones/ Plummet-like stones/Biconical stones/Bipointed stones or objects/ Cooking balls or stones/sinkers or net weights/Sling-stones	1–4	Heizer describes baked clay objects (BCOs) comparable to T-M slingstones, but his article contains draw-ings only of objects that mostly do not fit. See other references, particularly Kielusiak, for better visuals.	Elsasser 1955; Gifford & Schenck 1926, 93–97, Plate 17 (O–Y), Plate 29 (F&H), Plate 32 (I–Q); Harrington 1948, 95, 97, Plate 25(b); Heizer 1937; Kielusiak 1982 Smithsonian–NMAI Catalog Nos.: (Sonoma County): 043366.000, 118239.000; (Tulare County): 145787.000, 145789.000, 147924.000, 148 213.000, 148214.000, 148216.000, 148218.000, 148220.000–148223.000, 148225.000–148228.000

Map # / Location	Vertical provenience	Material	Local descriptive classifications/Function guesses	T-M Type	Remarks	References
10. Little Petroglyph Canyon, China Lake, CA	———	Rock art	———	———	"Slinger Man" glyphs. To date, only strong candidates (and possibly South Mountain, AZ) native rock art depicting sling use north of Mexico or in Oceania.	Fig. 62 this work; Golio & Golio 2004
11. Channel Islands & S Coast CA (Santa Barbara to Baja California)	Surface and buried, many found with burials	Stone, various steatite, and sandstone most often mentioned	Charmstones/ Plummets/Sinkers/ Bipointed stones/ Drills/Rounded-elongated stones/ Gaming stones/ Cooking stones/ Hammerstones	1 & 4 (at least)		American Antiquity 1907 (re: Rust Collection, San Miguel Is.): Plate 31(1); Gallegos 1991, 29, fig. 3.8 (a); Jones 1956, 233, Plate 122(a); Smithsonian-NMAI Catalog Nos.: (San Nicolas Is.): 063600.000; (Santa Catalina Is.): 076193.000; (San Miguel Is.): 192380.000, 192552.000; (Santa Barbara [LA County]: 130169.000, 118444.000, 201014

Map # / Location	Vertical provenience	Material	Local descriptive classifications/Function guesses	T-M Type	Remarks	References
12. Coastal B.C., Fraser River Canyon, Prince Rupert Harbor, and elsewhere?	Surface and buried	Stone	Biconical stones/ Bipointed ground stone objects/"Pebbles" (included under this term are both unmodified and modified, round, "sling-shot"/"sling-stones")	1 & 4	The biconical/ bipointed stones are large for T-M slingstones (ca. 16 cm L x 8 cm mid line W), but not outside range seen in Oceania. (*Comparable in size to many such stones recovered from Areas 1 and 5.) Though regional archaeologists classify these bipointed stones as weapons, they only consider the "pebbles" to be slingstones. Both the bipointed stones and "slingstone pebbles" are primarily associated with defensive sites dating to ca. 1,000 YA, but some date to ca. 2,000+ YA. Pebble manuports, probable slingstones, dating to ca. 4000 YA, have also been recovered from a drained marsh at the Pit Meadows Locality in SW B.C. Stone and Urcid consider B.C. to be one of only two (Oaxaca Valley, Mexico is the other) pre-Columbian North America cranial surgery (trepanation) centers.	Grant Keddie personal communication 2006; MacDonald 1982, 115, fig. 6.28; Moss & Erlandson 1992, 73; Rose 2003, 350; R. Sagarbarria, personal communication 2008; Schaepe 2006, 686, 687, 691, 694, fig. 14; Stewart 1996, 79; Stone & Urcid 2003, 237–240, 243, 247

Map 13. North America Arctic-Subarctic locales discussed.

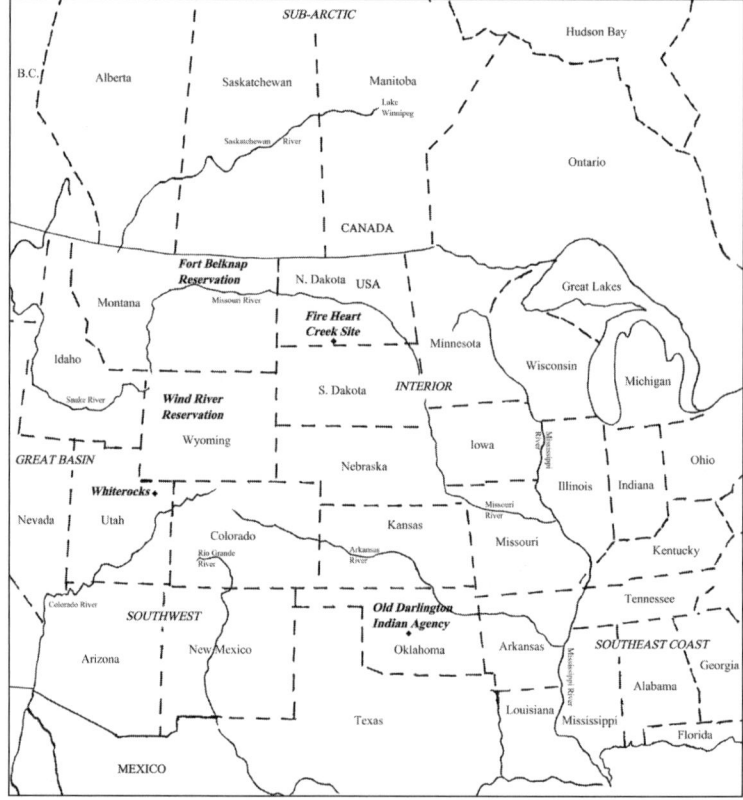

Map 14. North America interior locales discussed.

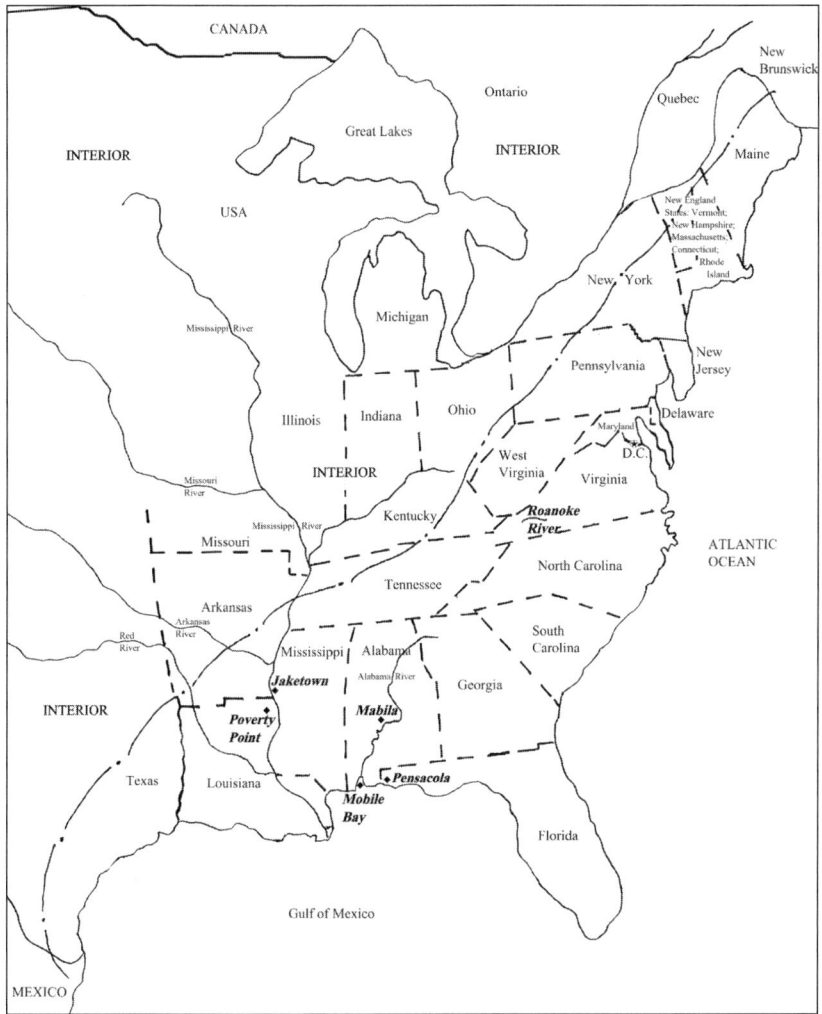

Map 15. North America southeastern and eastern coasts locales discussed.

CHAPTER 8

The Americas Concluding Remarks:
Questions and Issues

As expressed in our introductory remarks, archaeologists engaged in study of the Americas have generally not pursued the study of slingstones. We suggest that this lack of interest has had as much to do with changing trends, politics, in American archaeology as more tangible reasons for deciding what subject matter was worthy of study. In our concluding comments, we will stay on firmer ground and operate on the assumption that this primarily happened because archaeologists assumed that sling missiles were nothing more than unmodified pebbles or, if modified/manufactured, not subject to change culturally, temporally, or in any other significant way that would contribute to our understanding of ancient peoples. These assumptions were premature. Archaeologists should not have operated on these assumptions and should certainly not continue to do so. Sling missiles warrant the same depth of study as projectile points.

The questions that beg for answers, the issues to be pursued, seem almost endless—or are limited only by imagination. Many of those questions and issues we have identified throughout this work, and here we will conclude by highlighting just a few.

CLASSIFICATION AND TYPOLOGY

When we undertook this study from our perch in the Marianas, we looked for artifacts in the Americas that were comparable to Pacific and Old World slingstones, particularly bipointed/biconical ovoids. In the lemon stones and bipointed stones of North America's West Coast and Caribbean Venezuela, we certainly found this comparability. We were surprised to discover other types that, with the exception of universal spheroids, may be unique to the Americas: the bidome or biconical form of Argentina and Uruguay that may have a counterpart among the PPOs and BCOs of North America's southeastern and western coasts. Lenticular and

145

disc types also found in Argentina and Uruguay, with parallel North American types represented by the Virginia patella stones, the Dalles-Deschutes, Oregon, throwing stones, the hockey puck–like slingstones apparently used by the Gros Ventre of Montana and Canada, and odd PPO and BCO forms, such as spool and melon shapes, might have functioned as slingstones.

In tandem with the above primary forms, slingstones can be classified on the basis of variables that are often purpose indicators and perhaps temporal and/or cultural indicators, such as different sizes and weights for different uses, as seen in the slingstones of the Eastern Pomo of California and Stólō of British Columbia. Regarding materials selection, slingstones in the Americas were fashioned out of stone or clay. The Eastern Pomo model, again, is instructive in showing that clay was not simply selected as a substitute when stone was unavailable but was chosen for specific qualities valued in the taking of small waterfowl. However, the Eastern Pomo opted for stone to hunt geese and for use in warfare. Finishing treatments such as intentional pitting or roughening of spheroids, may have been accomplished to increase flight distance—the golf ball effect. The flattening of one or more surfaces, as seen in the "flattened clay sling balls" of the Eastern Pomo, and a common characteristic of northwestern bipointed stones, was most likely, and most often, accomplished for enhanced skipping qualities across water. Pointing versus blunting tips on football-shaped slingstones likely depended on whether the desired end was penetration or knock-down ability. Manuported stones should be subjected to much the same analyses. Ethnohistoric data indicate that similar selection criteria were being applied here as well.

In the course of our Americas research we have come to realize that the slingstones of Oceania also need to be subjected to reanalysis along these lines, as the four T-M types do not accommodate the full range of the phenomenon.

LIMITED DISTRIBUTION OF BIPOINTED SLING MISSILES

The sling was nearly universal, but manufacture and use of bipointed/biconical, ovoid, sling missiles or bullets appears to have been restricted to the Mediterranean, Oceania, Caribbean Venezuela, and the U.S. West Coast. (We concede that this distribution could be even more limited then presumed if the bipointed stone and clay artifacts of Caribbean Venezuela and/or the U.S. West Coast prove not to be slingstones. While we believe the data persuasively indicates that these artifacts were slingstones, to date we lack the ethnohistorical and/or archaeological "smoking gun" to close the case.) This is puzzling, since from a ballistics viewpoint the bipointed design has been accepted as optimum for sling projectiles. Especially confounding is the case of Andean South America, where we know that the sling was a prominent weapon for millennia, certainly as prominent as it was in the Mediterranean and Oceania.

Although we suspect that the answer(s) for this relatively limited use of bipointed sling projectiles lies primarily in the cultural arena, other more tangible reasons must be part of the answer. Again, the situation needs far more study, such as more rigorous comparative ballistics testing of differing types of sling ammunition. While a few such studies do exist (among them Brown Vega & Craig 2009; Richardson 1998), they are insufficient for us to reach conclusions concerning adoption or rejection of the bipointed design relative to other forms.

SHRINES OR SLINGSTONE STASHES?

Cairns of small rocks are found from Tierra del Fuego to the Arctic (*Stone Structures of Northeastern United States* 2007). They have often been interpreted as shrines, monuments, and/or trail markers. Little consideration has been given to the fact that many may have doubled or even solely functioned as stashes of slingstones. (Squier and Davis's [1848, 181] comments concerning possible "small mounds of missiles," notably those adjacent to the Paint Creek fortress in Ohio, are an exception.) Context and composition studies, along the lines of the analyses conducted by the Topics (1989) at the Ostra Site in Peru, could prove fruitful in this regard.

WHAT ABOUT BOLAS?

Use of bolas and slings goes hand in hand, demonstrably so in South America. Was this also true in pre-Columbian North America? The bola has been as understudied as the sling, even in South America. Slings and bolas constitute a parallel universe of weaponry that has been substantially overlooked by archaeologists in favor of studying celebrity projectile points.

We have argued in this work that many of the stone balls and bipointed stones that in North America have been called bola stones, among other things, are likely to be slingstones. We believe the data, in the cases we have explored, point persuasively in this direction. This hardly means it can be stated categorically that the bola was not used in pre-Columbian North America. It is simply high time to look at all those stone balls with fresh eyes and new ideas.

SLINGSTONES, TREPANATION, INJURIES, AND
PHYSICAL ANOMALIES

More in-depth study of human and faunal remains may reveal indirect evidence of sling use.

We have tracked the practice of trepanation because, worldwide, there is a strong, possibly one-to-one, correlation between trepanation as originally practiced (in many locales use as a remedy for other problems, and even total changes in function occurred) and slingstones (Crump 1901, 167; Martin 2003, 334, 340). However, this correlation does not appear to hold true in reverse; there are venues where slingstones occur but trepanation is not known to have been practiced, such as in Micronesia and Hawaii.

Tentatively, we propose that archaeologists can infer from this that where it is known that trepanation was practiced and slingstones to date have not been generally recognized as occurring, they likely do or did occur.

Martin (2003, 334, 340) points out that cranial injuries inflicted by slingstones ("at the end of their range") lend themselves to remedy through trepanation more so than club-inflicted trauma, which would ordinarily leave the victim "beyond help" (see also Crump 1901, 167). Phillip Walker (1989, 1997), an anthropologist at the University of California, Santa Barbara, assumed that nonfatal skull injuries in California's Channel Islands were probably club inflicted. We suggest that given their shapes (often round and ovoid dents) as described by Walker, Martin's above comment, and, as we have proposed, the existence of probable slingstones in the Channel Islands of the requisite shapes, these kinds of injuries are more likely to have been caused by slingstones and/or hand-hurled stones. (Also see Hooton [1930, 312–15] on similar injuries described in his study of human skeletal remains from Pecos Pueblo, New Mexico.) Walker (1989, 321, 322) also briefly describes comparable injuries from other North American locales that, again, are usually attributed to the use of clubs with the possibility of slingstones not considered.

Many torso and limb bone injuries that have been interpreted as club inflicted or "parry fractures" in the Americas (Thorpe 2003) may better conform to sling-stone injuries described in Polynesia. Physical anthropologists studying human skeletal remains in Oceania have recorded anomalies for bones of the arm and shoulder (particularly the ulna and scapula) indicative of sling use (Craib 1998, 85). Comparative studies with American populations could prove informative.

ARMOR, PROTECTIVE GEAR, AND DEFENSIVE ARCHITECTURE

Only incidentally have we addressed the use of body armor and armorlike protective gear. This needs to be looked into further.

Body armor, shields, and particularly protective head gear (leather, wood, feather "helmets") were used in many areas where the sling is known to have been *the* projectile weapon (the Marshall Islands, Hawaii, Tahiti, and Andean South America) or a primary projectile weapon of warfare (Mesoamerica and North America's northwest coast). Study of where these kinds of armor were used yet slingstones have not been identified as weapons of war may be indirect evidence of such use.

North American archaeologists have assumed that armor was devised for protection against pointed or shock weapons, such as spears, arrows, and knives (Ames & Maschner 1999, 200, 212, 213). In some cases, this was so (such as in many areas of New Guinea), but we know from Oceania, Latin America, and the Old World that generally it was more effective in protecting the wearer from hand- and sling-hurled stones (Bancroft 1875, 742; Hassig 1992, 31, 82–84, 173; Korfmann 1973, 40, 41; Métraux 1949, 263; Webster 2000, 66, 79, 102). In noting that Tlingit elk hide and wood armor repelled Russian musket balls but was penetrated by bone-tipped arrows, Ames and Maschner (1999, 200, 212, 213) obliquely (they do not include the sling or stones among the weapons of the northwest) support this view.

As we have discussed in relation to Andean defensive walls, New Zealand pa, and particularly the Poverty Point Site in Louisiana, certain characteristics of site architecture may also be indirect evidence of sling use.

DID ADOPTION OF THE BOW AND ARROW BY WEST COAST AND GREAT BASIN PEOPLES END BIPOINTED SLINGSTONES PRODUCTION?

On the West Coast and in the Great Basin of North America, production of bipointed slingstones appears to have generally ended ca. 2,500–3,000 YA, with the most interesting anomaly being the Gunther Island baked clay sling missiles. This possibly correlates with the introduction—or, probably more correctly, wide acceptance—of the bow and arrow.

We propose that although the sling continued in use on the West Coast and in the Great Basin, it was relegated to a subordinate position and in many cases was replaced as a hunting and combat weapon by the bow and arrow ca. 2,500–3,000 YA. With diminution of the sling, the time and effort to make specialized ammunition lost its importance. Succinctly stated, as skill with the sling was lost, so too was the need for specialized slingstones. Any suitable pebble would now do to occasionally take down a rabbit or a bird. The bipointed slingstones became magical relics from an ancient time functioning now to ensure luck in the hunt or as gaming pieces.

A major problem with this scenario is that it is generally believed that the bow and arrow was introduced no earlier than 2,000 YA into the Great Basin and along the West Coast. This is hardly a settled issue, however, with many archaeologists arguing for earlier and later dates (Ames, Davis, & Fuld 2007, 71; Ames, Fuld, & Davis 2010; Blitz 1988; Justice 2002, 55–59; Nassaney & Pyle 1999; Railey 2010; Webster 1980). The dating range for cessation of bipointed stones production also is arguable. Temporal correlation of these events, then, is critical to advancement or rejection of this proposition.

INDEPENDENT INVENTION VERSUS DIFFUSION

It undeniably appears as if it [the sling] might easily be invented practically anywhere, given stones and a terrain sufficiently open for its use. I am by no means an antagonist of "independent invention," rather the other way about, but where the sling is concerned I am in doubt. The sling has, or has had, a wide distribution all over the the world. There are, however, regions where it never seems to have occurred, and on the other hand others into which it almost certainly has been imported. This speaks for unity of origin. The exact location of this cannot, perhaps, ever be determined.

—K. G. Lindblom, *The Sling, Especially in Africa* (1940)

The sling is very widely used to hunt birds, and serves as a toy for peoples all over . . . and from very distant regions (e.g., Balearic Islands, Arabia, Oceania, Mexico, Peru) one reads that the sling serves also as a fillet or forehead band. Doubtless some enterprising student could add to this brief list of widespread parallels, and could thereby point out even more clearly something which appears to us as quite apparent, namely that the sling is a very ancient implement which has presumably been diffused from some ultimate single source.

—Robert F. Heizer and Irmgard W. Johnson, "A Prehistoric Sling from Lovelock Cave, Nevada" (1952)

We can add little to the above quotes, except to say that we tend to agree. Given our current state of knowledge, or lack thereof, there is little reason to presume an "ultimate single source" for invention of the sling or that the "exact location(s) cannot *ever* be determined." If we have learned anything from the disciplines of history and archaeology, it is that "never" or "ever" should *never* be part of our vocabulary.

When it comes to slingstones, the case for independent invention is more substantial. The two major forms, bipointed ovoids and spheroids, occur naturally as water-tumbled rocks and, even more precisely, as volcanic "tuff balls" and "bombs" (see figures 71 and 72). There appears to be a pattern of first occurrences of these types of modified slingstones in areas of volcanic activity, though this remains to be tested. Suitable volcanic spheroids and elliptical bombs were likely used as slingstones with little to no modification and probably served as models for the fabrication and manufacture of like slingstones. This could have happened in a number of locations quite independently. This hardly rules out diffusion as a mechanism that was responsible for the spread of these forms from different centers. Certainly this appears to have been the case in the Old World and Oceania.

There remain so many avenues to explore, questions to ask, and answers to discover. So let us begin.

Above: Figure 71. A volcanic
bomb, unmodified or slightly
modified, recovered ca. 1927
from Summer Lake, Lake
County, OR. Such volcanic ejecta
may have served as models for
bipointed slingstones. NMAI
Catalog No. 15-6022. Used with
permission, Smithsonian-NMAI.

Right: Figure 72. A "tuff ball."
This spherical volcanic ejecta,
unmodified manuport, recov-
ered from the Chance Gulch
Archaeological Site (5GN817),
CO, is Middle Archaic (ca. 4,000
YA). Courtesy Bonnie Pitblado,
Utah State University, Logan.

References

Agogino, George A.

    1962   Comments on *The Paleo-Indian Tradition in Eastern North America* by Ronald J. Mason. *Current Anthropology* 3(3): 246, 247.

Aikens, C. Melvin

    1993   *Archaeology of Oregon.* Portland, OR: Department of the Interior, Bureau of Land Management.

Aikens, C. Melvin, & Takayasu Higuchi

    1982   *Prehistory of Japan.* New York: Academic Press.

Allen, Jim

    1972   The First Decade in New Guinea Archaeology. *Antiquity* 46: 80–190.

    1996   The Pre-Austronesian Settlement of Island Melanesia: Implications for Lapita Archaeology. In *Prehistoric Settlement of the Pacific.* Ed. Ward H. Goodenough. Philadelphia: American Philosophical Society. 11–27.

Allen, Melinda S.

    2004   Revisiting and Revising Marquesan Culture History: New Archaeological Investigations at Anaho Bay, Nuku Hiva Island. *Journal of the Polynesian Society* 113(2): 143–96.

Allen, Melinda S., & Susan E. Schubel

    1990   Recent Archaeological Research on Aitutaki, Southern Cooks: The Moturakakau Shelter. *Journal of the Polynesian Society* 99(3): 265–95.

American Antiquity

    1907   Archaeological Collections from San Miguel Island, California. *American Antiquity* 9(3): 656, 657.

Ames, Kenneth M., Sara Davis, & Kristen A. Fuld

    2007   Dart and Arrow Points on the Columbia Plateau: Abstracts of the 60th Annual Meeting of the Northwest Anthropological Conference, 14–17 March 2007, Washington State University, Pullman. *Journal of Northwest Anthropology* 41(1): 71–123.

Ames, Kenneth M., Kristin A Fuld, & Sara Davis

    2010   Dart and Arrow Points on the Columbia Plateau of Western North America. *American Antiquity* 75(2): 287–325.

Ames, Kenneth M., & Herbert D. G. Maschner

    1999   *Peoples of the Northwest Coast: Their Archaeology and Prehistory.* London: Thames & Hudson.

Anderson, Atholl

    2006   Polynesian Seafaring and American Horizons: A Response to Jones and Klar. *American Antiquity* 71(4): 759–63.

Anderson, Atholl, Eric Conte, Patrick V. Kirch, & Marshall Weisler
   2003 Cultural Chronology in Mangareva (Gambier Islands), French Polynesia: Evidence from Recent Radiocarbon Dating. *Journal of the Polynesian Society* 112(2): 119–40.
Anderson, Duane C.
   1967 Stone Balls of the Fremont Culture: An Interpretation. *Southwestern Lore* 32(4): 79–81.
Arkush, Elizabeth
   2010 Hillforts and the History Channel: A View from the Late Prehispanic Andes. *SAA Archaeological Record* 10(4): 33–39.
Arkush, Elizabeth, & Charles Stanish
   2005 Interpreting Conflict in the Ancient Andes: Implications for the Archaeology of Warfare. *Current Anthropology* 46(1): 3–28.
Armillas, Pedro
   1951 Mesoamerican Fortifications. *Antiquity: A Quarterly Review of Archaeology* 98: 77–86, Plates I–IV.
Avery, Michael
   1986 Stoning and Fire at Hillfort Entrances of Southern Britain. *World Archaeology* 18(2): 216–30.
Babcock, William H.
   1913 *Early Norse Visits to North America.* Miscellaneous Collections 59(19). Washington, DC: Smithsonian Institution.
Bancroft, Hubert Howe
   1874 *The Native Races of the Pacific States of North America.* Vol. 1, *Wild Tribes.* New York: D. Appleton.
   1875 *The Native Races of the Pacific States of North America.* Vol. 2, *Civilized Nations.* New York: D. Appleton.
Barnett, Franklin
   1993 *Dictionary of Prehistoric Indian Artifacts of the American Southwest.* Flagstaff, AZ: Northland.
Barrett, S. A.
   1910 The Material Culture of the Klamath Lake and Modoc Indians of Northeastern California and Southern Oregon. *University of California Publications in American Archaeology and Ethnology* 5(4): 239–92.
   1952 Material Aspects of Pomo Culture, Part One. *Bulletin of the Public Museum of the City of Milwaukee* 20(1).
Basso, Keith H., ed.
   1971 *Western Apache Raiding and Warfare: From the Notes of Grenville Goodwin.* Tucson: University of Arizona Press.
Bath, J. E.
   1984 *Sapwtaki: Archaeological Survey and Testing.* Micronesian Archaeological Survey Report 14. Saipan: Northern Marianas Historic Preservation Office.
Bean, Lowell John, & Florence C. Shipek
   1978 Luiseño. In *Handbook of North American Indians.* Vol. 8, *California.* Ed. Robert F. Heizer. Washington, DC: Smithsonian Institution. 550–63.
Bean, Lowell John, & Charles R. Smith
   1978 Gabrielino. In *Handbook of North American Indians.* Vol. 8, *California.* Ed. Robert F. Heizer. Washington, DC: Smithsonian Institution. 538–49.

Beckwith, Thomas
    1911 *The Indian or Mound Builder.* Cape Girardeau, MO: Naeter Bros.
Bedford, Stuart, Matthew Spriggs, Meredith Wilson, & Ralph Regenvanu
    1998 The Australian National University–National Museum of Vanuatu Archaeology
          Project: A Preliminary Report on the Establishment of Cultural Sequences and
          Rock Art Research. *Asian Perspectives* 37(2): 165–92.
Bellwood, Peter
    1978 *The Polynesians: Prehistory of an Island People.* London: Thames & Hudson.
    1979 *Man's Conquest of the Pacific: The Prehistory of Southeast Asia and Oceania.*
          New York: Oxford University Press.
    1985 *Prehistory of the Indo-Malaysian Archipelago.* Sydney: Academic Press.
    1987 The Prehistory of Island Southeast Asia: A Multidisciplinary Review of Recent
          Research. *Journal of World Prehistory* 1(2): 171–224.
Bennett, Wendell C.
    1946 The Andean Highlands: An Introduction. In *Handbook of South American
          Indians.* Vol. 2, *The Andean Civilizations.* Ed. Julian H. Steward. Smithsonian
          Institution–Bureau of American Ethnology Bulletin 143. Washington, DC:
          Government Printing Office. 1–60.
Bennyhoff, James A., & Richard E. Hughes
    1987 Shell Bead and Ornament Exchange Networks Between California and the
          Great Basin. *Anthropological Papers of the American Museum of Natural His-
          tory* 64(2): 79–175.
Bird, Junius B.
    1988 *Travels and Archaeology in South Chile.* Iowa City: University of Iowa Press.
Bird, Junius B., & John Hyslop
    1985 The Preceramic Excavations at the Huaca Prieta Chicama Valley, Peru. *Anthro-
          pological Papers of the American Museum of Natural History* 62(1).
Birket-Smith, Kaj
    1929 *The Caribou Eskimos.* Vol. 2. Copenhagen: Gyldendalske Boghandel, Nordisk
          Forlag.
Bishop Museum
    1917 Director's Report for 1916. *Occasional Papers of the Bernice Pauahi Bishop
          Museum of Polynesian Ethnology and Natural History* 4(4).
Blitz, John H.
    1988 Adoption of the Bow and Arrow in Prehistoric North America. *North American
          Archaeologist* 9(2): 123–45.
Blust, Robert
    1996 Austronesian Culture History: The Window of Language. In *Prehistoric Settle-
          ment of the Pacific.* Ed. Ward H. Goodenough. Philadelphia: American Philo-
          sophical Society. 28–35.
Bolton, Herbert E.
    1949 *Coronado Knight of Pueblos and Plains.* New York: Whittlesey House.
Bostwick, Todd W.
    2002 *Landscapes of the Spirits: Hohokam Rock Art at South Mountain Park.* Tucson:
          University of Arizona Press.
Bottoms, Edward, & Floyd Painter
    1989 Bolas and Birds during the Early Woodland Period in Southeastern Virginia.
          The Chesopiean 27(2): 2–5.

Bourke, John G.
 1890   Vesper Hours of the Stone Age. *American Anthropologist* o.s. 3(1): 55–63.
Braidwood, Robert J.
 1967   *Prehistoric Men.* Glenview, IL: Scott, Foresman.
Bram, Joseph
 1941   *An Analysis of Inca Militarism.* Seattle: University of Washington Press.
Brice, Martin H.
 1985   *Stronghold: A History of Military Architecture.* New York: Schocken Books.
Brigham, William T.
 1902   *Stone Implements and Stone Work of the Ancient Hawaiians.* Memoirs of the
       Bernice Pauahi Bishop Museum 1(4). Millwood, NY: Kraus Reprint, 1974.
Broms, R. S. D., & James R. Moriarty
 1967   The Antiquity and Inferred Use of Stone Spheroids in Southwestern Archaeol-
       ogy. *The Masterkey* 41(3): 98–112.
Brosse, Jacques
 1983   *Great Voyages of Discovery: Circumnavigators and Scientists, 1764–1843.* Trans.
       Stanley Hochman. New York: Facts on File.
Brown, Mervyn
 1979   *Madagascar Rediscovered: A History from Early Times to Independence.* Hamden,
       CT: Archon Books.
Brown Vega, Margaret, & Nathan Craig
 2009   New Experimental Data on the Distance of Sling Projectiles. *Journal of Ar-
       chaeological Science* 36: 1264–68.
Buckley, Hallie R.
 2000   A Possible Fatal Wounding in the Prehistoric Pacific Islands. *International
       Journal of Osteoarchaeology* 10: 135–41.
Burch, Ernest S., Jr., & Werner Forman
 1988   *The Eskimos.* Norman: University of Oklahoma Press.
Burger, Richard L.
 1992   *Chavin and the Origins of Andean Civilization.* London: Thames & Hudson.
Burley, David V.
 1998   Tongan Archaeology and the Tongan Past, 2850–150 BP. *Journal of World Prehis-
       tory* 12(3): 337–92.
Butler, Brian M., & Wendy G. Harris
 1995   Shell, Stone, and Coral Artifacts. In *Archaeological Investigations in the Achugao
       and Matansa Areas of Saipan, Mariana Islands.* Micronesian Archaeological
       Survey Report 30. Saipan: Commonwealth of the Northern Mariana Islands
       Division of Historic Preservation.
Cabeza de Vaca, Álvar Núñez
 1999   *The Narrative of Cabeza de Vaca.* Ed., trans., intro. Rolena Adorno & Patrick
       Charles Pautz. Lincoln: University of Nebraska Press. Original Spanish publica-
       tion 1542.
Cannell, Alan
 2002   Throwing Behaviour and the Mass Distribution of Geological Hand Samples, Hand
       Grenades and Olduvian Manuports. *Journal of Archaeological Science* 29: 335–39.
Caraman, Philip
 1975   *The Lost Paradise: An Account of the Jesuits in Paraguay 1607–1768.* London:
       Sidgwick & Jackson.

Casso, Alfonso
    1936   Continuation of Archaeological and Historical Studies in the Region of Oaxaca, Mexico. In *Year Book No. 35.* Washington, DC: Carnegie Institution of Washington. 281–82.

Chang, Kwang-Chih
    1969   *Fengpitou, Tapenkeng, and the Prehistory of Taiwan.* Publications in Anthropology 73. New Haven, CT: Yale University.

Chang, Kwang-Chih, & Ward H. Goodenough
    1996   Archaeology of Southeastern Coastal China and Its Bearing on the Austronesian Homeland. In *Prehistoric Settlement of the Pacific.* Ed. Ward H. Goodenough. Philadelphia: American Philosophical Society. 36–56.

Chartkoff, Joseph L., & Kerry Kona Chartkoff
    1984   *The Archaeology of California.* Stanford, CA: Stanford University Press.

Choe, Chong Pil, & Martin T. Bale
    2002   Current Perspectives on Settlement, Subsistence, and Cultivation in Prehistoric Korea. *Arctic Anthropology* 39(1/2): 95–121.

Christian, F. W.
    1899   *The Caroline Islands: Travel in the Sea of the Little Lands.* London: Frank Cass, 1967.

Clark, Jeffrey T., & David J. Herdrich
    1993   Prehistoric Settlement System in Eastern Tutuila, American Samoa. *Journal of the Polynesian Society* 102(2): 147–85.

Clunie, Fergus
    1977   Fijian Weapons and Warfare. *Bulletin of the Fiji Museum* no. 2. Suva, Fiji.

Codrington, R. H.
    1891   *The Melanesians: Studies in Their Anthropology and Folk-Lore.* New Haven, CT: Behavior Science Reprints, HRAF Press, 1957.

Collins, Michael B.
    1997   The Lithics from MonteVerde: A Descriptive Morphological Analysis. In *Monte Verde, a Late Pleistocene Settlement in Chile.* Vol. 2. Ed. Tom D. Dillehay. Washington, DC: Smithsonian Institution Press. 383–506.

Coon, Carleton S.
    1971   *The Hunting Peoples.* Boston: Atlantic–Little Brown Books.

Cooper, John M.
    1917   *Analytical and Critical Bibliography of the Tribes of Tierra Del Fuego and Adjacent Territory.* Bureau of American Ethnology Bulletin 63. Washington, DC: Smithsonian Institution.
    1944   *Areal and Temporal Aspects of Aboriginal South American Culture.* Annual Report of the Board of Regents of the Smithsonian Institution 1943. Washington, DC: Government Printing Office.
    1946   The Patagonian and Pampean Hunters. In *Handbook of South American Indians.* Vol. 1, *The Marginal Tribes.* Ed. Julian H. Steward. Smithsonian Institution–Bureau of American Ethnology Bulletin 143. Washington, DC: Government Printing Office. 127–68.

Cordy, Ross
    1982   *Archaeological Settlement Pattern Studies on Yap.* Micronesian Archaeological Survey Report 16. Saipan: Commonwealth of the Northern Mariana Islands Division of Historic Preservation.

1993   *The Lelu Stone Ruins (Kosrae, Micronesia): 1978–81 Historical and Archaeological Research.* Asian and Pacific Archaeology Series 10. Manoa: Social Science Research Institute, University of Hawaii.

Cosgrove, C. B.

1929   A Note on a Trephined Indian Skull from Georgia. *American Journal of Physical Anthropology* 13(2): 353–57.

Craib, John L.

1984   Settlement on Ulithi Atoll, Western Caroline Islands. *Asian Perspectives* 24(1): 47–55.

1998   *Archaeological Excavations in the Uyulan Region of Rota.* Micronesian Archaeological Survey Report 33. Saipan: Commonwealth of the Northern Mariana Islands Division of Historic Preservation.

Cressman, L. S.

1956   Klamath Prehistory: The Prehistory of the Culture of the Klamath Lake Area, Oregon. *Transactions of the American Philosophical Society* n.s. 46: 375–514. Philadelphia.

1960   Cultural Sequences at the Dalles, Oregon: A Contribution to Pacific Northwest Prehistory. *Transactions of the American Philosophical Society* n.s. 50(10). Philadelphia.

1977   *Prehistory of the Far West: Homes of Vanished Peoples.* Salt Lake City: University of Utah Press.

Crump, J. A.

1901   Trephining in the South Seas. *Journal of the Anthropological Institute of Great Britain and Ireland* 31: 167–72.

Cruxent, J. M., & Irving Rouse

1958   *An Archaeological Chronology of Venezuela.* Vol. 1. Social Science Monographs 6. Washington, DC: Universidad Central de Venezuela and the Pan American Union.

Cruxent, J. M., & Irving Rouse

1959   *An Archaeological Chronology of Venezuela.* Vol. 2. Social Science Monographs 6. Washington, DC: Universidad Central de Venezuela and the Pan American Union.

Culin, Stewart

1899   Hawaiian Games. *American Anthropologist* n.s. 1(2): 201–47.

1907   *Games of the North American Indians.* New York: Dover, 1975.

Cushing, Frank Hamilton

1988   *The Mythic World of the Zuni.* Ed. & illus. Barton Wright. Albuquerque: University of New Mexico Press. Original publication 1896.

Dam, Hans

1935   *Inselm um Truk: Polowat, Hok und Satowal.* Hamburg: Friederichsen, De Gruyter.

Davidson, Janet

1987   *The Prehistory of New Zealand.* Auckland: Longman Paul.

Deacon, Bernard

1934   *Malekula: A Vanishing People in the New Hebrides.* London: George Routledge & Sons.

Dewar, Robert E., & Henry T. Wright

1993   The Culture History of Madagascar. *Journal of World Prehistory* 7(4): 417–66.

Dillehay, Thomas D.

2000   *The Settlement of the Americas: A New Prehistory.* New York: Basic Books.

Di Peso, Charles C., John B. Rinaldo, & Gloria J. Fenner
 1974   *Casas Grandes: A Fallen Trading Center of the Gran Chichimeca.* Flagstaff, AZ: Amerind Foundation, Dragoon, and Northland Press.
Dorsey, J. Owen
 1891   *Games of the Teton Dakota Children.* American Anthropologist o.s. 4. Millwood, NY: Kraus Reprint, 1964.
Douglas, Bronwen
 1998   *Across the Great Divide: Journeys in History and Anthropology.* Amsterdam: Harwood Academic.
Driver, Harold E.
 1937   Culture Element Distributions: VI, Southern Sierra Nevada. University of California. *Anthropological Records* 1(2): 53–154.
 1940   *Wappo Ethnography.* University of California Publications in American Archaeology and Ethnography 26. Ed. A. L. Kroeber, R. H. Lowie, & R. L. Olson. Millwood, NY: Kraus Reprint, 1965.
 1969   *Indians of North America.* Chicago: University of Chicago Press.
Driver, Harold E., & James L. Coffin
 1975   Classification and Development of North American Indian Cultures: A Statistical Analysis of the Driver-Massey Sample. *Transactions of the American Philosophical Society* n.s. 65(3). Philadelphia.
Driver, Harold E., & William C. Massey
 1957   Comparative Studies of North American Indians. *Transactions of the American Philosophical Society* n.s. 47(2). Philadelphia.
Driver, Marjorie G.
 1989   *The Account of Fray Juan Pobre's Residence in the Marianas, 1602.* Mangilao: Micronesian Area Research Center, University of Guam.
Drucker, Philip
 1941   Culture Element Distributions, XVII, Yuman-Piman. University of California. *Anthropological Records* 6: 3.
 1950   Culture Element Distributions: XXVI, Northwest Coast. University of California. *Anthropological Records* 9: 3.
 1951   *The Northern and Central Nootkan Tribes.* Smithsonian Institution–Bureau of American Ethnology Bulletin 144. Washington, DC: Government Printing Office.
 1955   *Indians of the Northwest Coast.* Bureau of American Ethnology–Smithsonian Institution Anthropological Handbook 10. New York: McGraw-Hill and American Museum of Natural History.
Du Bois, Cora
 1940   *Wintu Ethnography.* University of California Publications in American Archaeology and Ethnology 36. Millwood, NY: Kraus Reprint, 1965.
Duff, Wilson
 1952   *The Upper Stalo Indians of the Fraser Valley, British Columbia.* Anthropology in British Columbia Memoir No. 1. Victoria: British Columbia Provincial Museum.
Dye, Tom, ed.
 1987   *Marshall Islands Archaeology.* Pacific Anthropological Records 38. Honolulu: Bernice P. Bishop Museum.
Edge-Partington, James
 1890   *An Album of the Weapons, Tools, Ornaments, Articles of Dress of the Natives of the Pacific Islands.* Facsimile. London: Holland Press, 1969.

Eells, Myron
    1889   The Twana, Chemakum, and Klallam Indians of Washington Territory. In *Annual Report of the Board of Regents of the Smithsonian Institution, 1887, Part I, Appendix II—Miscellaneous Papers*. Washington, DC: Government Printing Office. 605–82.
Ellis, William
    1827   *A Narrative of a Tour Through Hawaii: or, Owhyhee, with Remarks on the History, Traditions, Manners, Customs and Language of the Inhabitants of the Sandwich Islands*. Honolulu: Hawaiian Gazette, 1917.
Elsasser, Albert B.
    1955   *A Charmstone Site in Sonoma County, California*. Papers in California Archaeology 29. Berkeley: University of California.
    1978   Development of Regional Prehistoric Cultures. In *Handbook of North American Indians: California*. Vol. 8. Ed. Robert F. Heizer. Washington, DC: Smithsonian Institution. 37–57.
Elsasser, Albert B., & Peter T. Rhode
    1996   *Further Notes on California Charmstones*. Salinas, CA: Coyote Press.
Emory, Kenneth P.
    1924   *The Island of Lanai: A Survey of Native Culture*. Bernice P. Bishop Museum Bulletin 12. Honolulu: Bishop Museum Press, 1969.
    1928   Stone Implements of Pitcairn Island. *Journal of the Polynesian Society* 37(2): 125–35.
    1939   Archaeology of Mangareva and Neighboring Atolls. Honolulu. *Bernice P. Bishop Museum Bulletin* 163.
    1965   *Ancient Hawaiian Civilization*. Rutland, VT: Charles E. Tuttle.
    1979   The Societies. In *The Prehistory of Polynesia*. Ed. Jesse D. Jennings. Cambridge, MA: Harvard University Press. 200–221.
Engel, Frederick
    1963   A Preceramic Settlement on the Central Coast of Peru, Asia, Unit 1. *Transactions of the American Philosophical Society* n.s. 53(3). Philadelphia.
Evans, John
    1897   *The Ancient Stone Implements, Weapons and Ornaments of Great Britain*. London: Longmans, Green.
Ewins, Roderick
    1995   Proto-Polynesian Art? The Cliff Paintings of Vatulele, Fiji. *Journal of the Polynesian Society* 104(1): 23–74.
Fagan, Brian M.
    1995   *People of the Earth: An Introduction to World Prehistory*. New York: Harper Collins.
    2003   *Before California: An Archaeologist Looks at Our Earliest Inhabitants*. Lanham, MD: Rowman & Littlefield.
Feest, Christian
    1980   *The Art of War*. London: Thames & Hudson.
Ferdon, Edwin N.
    1961   A Summary of the Excavated Record of Easter Island Prehistory. In *Archaeology of Easter Island: Reports of the Norwegian Archaeological Expedition to Easter Island and the East Pacific*. Vol. 1. Ed. Thor Heyerdahl & Edwin Ferdon Jr. Monographs of the School of American Research and the Museum of New Mexico 24(1). New York: Rand McNally. 527–35.

1981　*Early Tahiti, as the Explorers Saw it, 1767–1797.* Tucson: University of Arizona Press.

1987　*Early Tonga, as the Explorers Saw It, 1616–1810.* Tucson: University of Arizona Press.

1993　*Early Observations of Marquesan Culture, 1595–1813.* Tucson: University of Arizona Press.

Ferrill, Arther

1985　*The Origins of War: From the Stone Age to Alexander the Great.* London: Thames & Hudson.

Fewkes, J. Walter

1907　*Excavations at Casa Grande, Arizona, in 1906–07.* Miscellaneous Collections 50. Washington, DC: Smithsonian Institution. 289–329.

Fitzhugh, William W.

1972　*Environmental Archaeology and Cultural Systems in Hamilton Inlet, Labrador: A Survey of the Central Labrador Coast From 3000 b.c. to the Present.* Washington, DC: Smithsonian Institution Press.

1975　A Maritime Archaic Sequence from Hamilton Inlet, Labrador. *Arctic Anthropology* 12(2): 117–38.

Flint, Richard, & Shirley Cushing Flint, eds. & trans.

2005　*Documents of the Coronado Expedition, 1539–1542: "They Were Not Familiar with His Majesty, nor Did They Wish to Be His Subjects."* Dallas: Southern Methodist University Press.

Ford, James A., Philip Phillips, & William G. Haag

1955　*The Jaketown Site in West-Central Mississippi.* Anthropological Papers 45. New York: American Museum of Natural History.

Ford, James A., & Clarence H. Webb

1959　*Poverty Point, a Late Archaic Site in Louisiana.* Anthropological Papers 46. New York: American Museum of Natural History.

Forde, C. Daryll

1931　*Ethnography of the Yuma Indians.* University of California Publications in American Archaeology and Ethnology 28. Ed. A. L. Kroeber, Robert H. Lowie, & R. L. Olson. Millwood, NY: Kraus Reprint, 1965.

Forster, George

1777　*A Voyage Round the World.* Vols. 1 & 2. Ed. Nicholas Thomas & Oliver Berghof, with Jennifer Newell. Honolulu: University of Hawaii Press, 2000.

Forsyth, I. W.

2004　How to Build and Use a Traditional Apache Sling. Retrieved from http://www.slinging.org/22.html.

Foster, George M.

1944　A Summary of Yuki Culture. University of California. *Anthropological Records* 5(3): 155–244.

Fowler, Catherine S.

1989　*Willard Z. Park's Ethnographic Notes on the Northern Paiute of Western Nevada, 1933–1940.* Vol. 1. Salt Lake City: University of Utah Press.

Fowler, Don D., & Catherine S. Fowler, eds.

1971　*Anthropology of the Numa: John Wesley Powell's Manuscripts on the Numic Peoples of Western North America 1868–1880.* Washington, DC: Smithsonian Institution Press.

Fox, Aileen

    1976 *Prehistoric Maori Fortifications in the North Island of New Zealand.* Monograph No. 6, New Zealand Archaeological Association. Auckland: Longman Paul.

Fredrickson, David A.

    1984 The North Coastal Region. In *California Archaeology.* Ed. Michael J. Moratto. New York: Academic Press. 471–527.

Fritts, Josh

    2002 *The Physics of Golf.* Retrieved from http://ffden-2.phys.uaf.edu/211_fall2002. web.dir/josh_fritts/.

Frost, Everett Lloyd

    1974 *Archaeological Excavations of Fortified Sites on Taveuni, Fiji.* Asian and Pacific Archaeology Series No. 6. Honolulu: Social Science Research Institute, University of Hawaii.

Gallegos, Dennis R.

    1991 Antiquity and Adaptation at Agua Hedionda, Carlsbad, California. In *Hunter-Gatherers of Early Holocene Coastal California.* Ed. Jon M. Erlandson & Roger H. Colten. Perspectives in California Archaeology 1. Los Angeles: Institute of Archaeology, University of California. 19–42.

Garling, Stephanie

    2003 Tanga Takes to the Stage: Another Model "Transitional" Site? New Evidence and a Contribution to the "Incised and Applied Relief Tradition" in New Ireland. In *Pacific Archaeology: Assessments and Prospects, Proceedings of the International Conference for the 50th Anniversary of the First Lapita Excavation—Koné-Nouméa 2002.* Ed. Christophe Sand. Nouméa: Musées et du Patrimoine de Nouvelle-Calédonie.

Geiseler, Wilhelm

    1995 *Geiseler's Easter Island Report: An 1880s Anthropological Account.* Trans. William S. Ayres & Gabriella S. Ayres. Asian and Pacific Archaeology Series 12. Honolulu: University of Hawaii Press.

Gibson, Jon L.

    2000 *The Ancient Mounds of Poverty Point: Place of Rings.* Gainesville: University Press of Florida.

    2007 "Formed from the Earth at That Place": The Material Side of Community at Poverty Point. *American Antiquity* 72(3): 509–23.

Gifford, E. W.

    1932 *The Southeastern Yavapai.* University of California Publications in American Archaeology and Ethnology 29. Ed. A. L. Kroeber, R. H. Lowie, & R. L. Olson. Millwood, NY: Kraus Reprint, 1965. 177–252.

    1936 *Northeastern and Western Yavapai.* University of California Publications in American Archaeology and Ethnology 34. Ed. A. L. Kroeber, R. H. Lowie, & R. L. Olson. Millwood, NY: Kraus Reprint, 1965.

    1940 Culture Element Distributions: XII, Apache-Pueblo. University of California. *Anthropological Records* 4(1).

    1951 Archaeological Excavations in Fiji. University of California. *Anthropological Records* 13(3).

Gifford, E. W., & D. S. Gifford

    1959 Archaeological Excavations in Yap. University of California. *Anthropological Records* 18(2).

Gifford, E. W., & A. L. Kroeber
    1939   *Culture Element Distributions: IV, Pomo.* University of California Publications
           in American Archaeology and Ethnology 37. Ed. A. L. Kroeber, R. H. Lowie, &
           R. L. Olson. Millwood, NY: Kraus Reprint, 1965.
Gifford, E. W., & W. Egbert Schenck
    1926   *Archaeology of the Southern San Joaquin Valley, California.* University of
           California Publications in American Archaeology and Ethnology 23. Ed. A. L.
           Kroeber, R. H. Lowie, & R. L. Olson. Millwood, NY: Kraus Reprint, 1965.
Gifford, E. W., & Dick Shutler Jr.
    1956   Archaeological Excavations in New Caledonia. University of California. *An-
           thropological Records* 18(1).
Goldschmidt, Walter
    1978   Nomlaki. In *Handbook of North American Indians.* Vol. 8, *California.* Ed. Robert
           F. Heizer. Washington, DC: Smithsonian Institution. 341–49.
Golio, J. J., & Mike Golio
    2004   Hohokam Bola Petroglyphs in the South Mountains of Phoenix. *American
           Indian Rock Art* 30: 111–18.
Goodenough, Ward H.
    1996   *Prehistoric Settlement of the Pacific.* Philadelphia: American Philosophical Soci-
           ety.
Gorenstein, Shirley
    1973   *Tepexi El Viejo: A Postclassic Fortified Site in the Mixteca-Puebla Region of
           Mexico.* Philadelphia: American Philosophical Society.
Graburn, Nelson H. H., Molly Lee, & Jean-Loup Rousselot
    1996   *Catalogue Raisonné of the Alaska Commercial Company Collection, Phoebe Ap-
           person Hearst Museum of Anthropology.* University of California Publications
           in Anthropology 21. Berkeley: University of California Press.
Green, Roger C.
    1979   Lapita. In *The Prehistory of Polynesia.* Ed. Jesse D. Jennings. Cambridge, MA:
           Harvard University Press. 27–60.
    1991a Near and Remote Oceania: Disestablishing "Melanesia" in Culture History. In
           *Man and a Half: Essays in Pacific Anthropology and Ethnobiology in Honour of
           Ralph Bulmer.* Ed. A. Pawley. Auckland: Polynesian Society. 491–502.
    1991b A Reappraisal of the Dating for Some Lapita Sites in the Reef/Santa Cruz Group
           of the Southeast Solomons. *Journal of the Polynesian Society* 100(1): 197–208.
Green, Roger C., & Dimitri Anson
    2000   Archaeological Investigations on Watom Island: Early Work, Outcomes of Re-
           cent Investigations and Future Prospects. *New Zealand Journal of Archaeology*
           20(1998): 183–197.
Green, Roger C., & Janet M. Davidson
    1969   Archaeology in Western Samoa, Vol. 1. *Bulletin of the Auckland Institute and
           Museum* 6.
Green, Roger C., & Janet M. Davidson
    1974   Archaeology in Western Samoa, Vol. 2. *Bulletin of the Auckland Institute and
           Museum* 7.
Green, Roger C., & Marshall I. Weisler
    2002   The Mangarevan Sequence and Dating of the Geographic Expansion into
           Southeast Polynesia. *Asian Perspectives* 41(2): 213–41.

Gumerman, George J., & Emil W. Haury
  1979   Prehistory: Hohokam. In *Handbook of North American Indians: Southwest.* Vol.
         9. Ed. William C. Sturtevant & Alfonso Ortiz. Washington, DC: Smithsonian
         Institution. 75–90.
Gunnerson, James H.
  1957   *An Archaeological Survey of the Fremont Area.* University of Utah Anthropo-
         logical Papers 28. Salt Lake City: University of Utah Press.
Haeberlin, Hermann, & Erna Gunther
  1930   *The Indians of Puget Sound.* University of Washington Publications in Anthro-
         pology 4(1). Seattle: University of Washington Press.
Hambruch, Paul, & Anneliese Eilers
  1936   Ponape. In *Ergebnisse der Südsee-Expedition 1908–1910.* Vol. 2, *Ethnographie,
         B. Mikronesien.* Ed. G. Thilenius. Hamburg: Friderichsen, De Gruyter.
Hamilton, A.
  1911   *Rough Notes on Mangaia "Peace" or Ceremonial Axes, and Slings.* Dominion
         Museum Bulletin 3. Wellington, NZ: John Mackay.
Harrington, John P.
  1912   The Tewa Indian Game of "Cañute." *American Anthropologist* n.s. 14(2): 243–86.
Harrington, Mark Raymond
  1948   *An Ancient Site at Borax Lake, California.* Southwest Museum Papers 16. Los
         Angeles: Southwest Museum.
Harrison, Chris
  2006   The Sling in Medieval Europe. *Bulletin of Primitive Technology* 31: 74–79.
Hassig, Ross
  1988   *Aztec Warfare: Imperial Expansion and Political Control.* Norman: University
         of Oklahoma Press.
  1992   *War and Society in Ancient Mesoamerica.* Berkeley: University of California
         Press.
Hattori, Eugene M.
  1982   *The Archaeology of Falcon Hill, Winnemucca Lake, Washoe County, Nevada.*
         Anthropological Papers 18. Carson City: Nevada State Museum.
Haury, Emil W.
  1976   *The Hohokam: Desert Farmers and Craftsman, Excavations at Snaketown,
         1964–1965.* Tuscon: University of Arizona Press.
Hauser-Schäublin, Brigitta, & Gundolf Krüger, eds.
  1998   *James Cook, Gifts and Treasures from the South Seas: The Cook/Forster Collec-
         tion, Göttingen.* Munich: Prestel.
Hayden, Brian
  2008   What were they doing in the Oldowan? An Ethnoarchaeological Perspective
         on the Origins of Human Behavior. *Lithic Technology* 33(2): 105–39.
Hector, Susan M., Daniel G. Foster, Linda C. Pollack, & Gerrit L. Fenenga
  2006   *The Plantation Cache and a New Charmstone Type from Northern California.*
         Report. Sacramento: California Department of Forestry and Fire Protection.
Heizer, Robert F.
  1937   Baked-Clay Objects of the Lower Sacramento Valley, California. *American
         Antiquity* 3(1): 34–50.
Heizer, Robert F., & Albert B. Elsasser
  1964   *The Archaeology of HUM-67: The Gunther Island Site in Humboldt Bay, Cali-*

fornia. University of California Archaeological Survey Reports 62. Berkeley: University of California Press.

Heizer, Robert F., & Irmgard W. Johnson
1952   A Prehistoric Sling from Lovelock Cave, Nevada. *American Antiquity* 18(2): 139–47.

Heizer, Robert F., & Alex D. Krieger
1956   The Archaeology of Humboldt Cave, Churchill County, Nevada. *University of California Publications in American Archaeology and Ethnology* 47(1): 1–190.

Hewett, Edgar L.
1938   *Pajarito Plateau and Its Ancient People*. Albuquerque: University of New Mexico Press.

Heyerdahl, Thor
1953   *American Indians in the Pacific: The Theory Behind the Kon-Tiki Expedition*. New York: Rand McNally.
1961   An Introduction to Easter Island, History. In *Archaeology of Easter Island: Reports of the Norwegian Archaeological Expedition to Easter Island and the East Pacific*. Vol. 1. Ed. Thor Heyerdahl & Edwin N. Ferdon Jr. Monographs of the School of American Research and the Museum of New Mexico 24(1). New York: Rand McNally. 33–90.
1974   *Fatu-Hiva: Back to Nature*. Garden City, NY: Doubleday.

Heyerdahl, Thor, & Arne Skjölsvold
1965   Notes on the Archaeology of Pitcairn. In *Reports of the Norwegian Archaeological Expedition to Easter Island and the East Pacific*. Vol. 2, *Miscellaneous Papers*. Ed. Thor Heyerdahl & Edwin N. Ferdon Jr. Monographs of the School of American Research and the Kon-Tiki Museum 24(2). London: George Allen & Unwin. 3–8.

Higgins, Margaret, trans.
1968   *The Life and Martyrdom of the Venerable Father Diego Luis de Sanvitores*. By Francisco Garcia. Ca. 1683. Ed. Marjorie Driver. Mangilao: Micronesian Area Research Center, University of Guam.

Hill, Matthew E., Jr.
2007   A Moveable Feast: Variation in Faunal Resource Use Among Central and Western North American Paleoindian Sites. *American Antiquity* 72(3): 417–38.

Hiroa, Te Rangi (P. H. Buck)
1927   *The Material Culture of the Cook Islands (Aitutaki)*. Board of Maori Ethnological Research. New Plymouth, NZ: Thomas Avery & Sons.
1938   Ethnology of Mangareva. *Bernice P. Bishop Museum Bulletin* 157.
1957   *Arts and Crafts of Hawaii, Section X: War and Weapons*. Bernice P. Bishop Museum Special Publication 45. Honolulu: Bishop Museum Press.

Holmes, William Henry
1902   Anthropological Studies in California. In *Annual Report of the Board of Regents of the Smithsonian Institution, Report of the U.S. National Museum, 1900*. Washington, DC: Government Printing Office. 155–87.

Honoi, Hare
1918   Did the Maoris of New Zealand Use the Sling? Notes and Queries. *Journal of the Polynesian Society* 27: 226.

Hooton, Earnest Albert
1930   *The Indians of Pecos Pueblo: A Study of their Skeletal Remains*. Department of Archaeology, Phillips Academy. New Haven, CT: Yale University Press.

Horridge, Adrian

1995   The Austronesian Conquest of the Sea—Upwind. In *The Austronesians: Historical and Comparative Perspectives*. Ed. Peter S. Bellwood, James J. Fox, & Darrell T. Tryon. Research School of Pacific and Asian Studies Comparative Austronesian Project. Canberra: Australian National University. 134–51.

Hornbostel, Hans G.

1924   Notes on Stone Implements and Weapons of Guam and the Marianas. Unpublished document. Bernice P. Bishop Museum, Honolulu.

Howe, Carrol B.

1972   *Ancient Tribes of the Klamath Country*. Portland, OR: Binfords & Mort.

1979   *Ancient Modocs of California and Oregon*. Portland, OR: Binfords & Mort.

Howe, K. R.

1977   *The Loyalty Islands: A History of Culture Contacts 1840–1900*. Honolulu: University of Hawaii Press.

Hudson, Charles

1997   *Knights of Spain, Warriors of the Sun: Hernando de Soto and the South's Ancient Chiefdoms*. Athens: University of Georgia Press.

Hughes, Charles C.

1984   Saint Lawrence Island Eskimo. In *Handbook of North American Indians, Arctic*. Vol. 5. Ed. David Damas. Washington, DC: Smithsonian Institution. 262–77.

Hunt, Terry L., & Carl L. Lipo

2006   Late Colonization of Easter Island. *Science* 311 (March 17): 1603–6.

Hunter-Anderson, Rosalind L.

1982   *Settlement Pattern Studies in Nlul Village, Map Island, Yap, Western Caroline Islands*. Micronesian Archaeological Survey Report 20. Saipan: Commonwealth of the Northern Mariana Islands Division of Historic Preservation.

1983   *Yapese Settlement Patterns: An Ethnoarchaeological Approach*. Agana, Guam: Pacific Studies Institute.

1994   *Archaeology in Manenggon Hills, Yona, Guam*. Mangilao, Guam: Micronesian Archaeological Research Services.

2000   Ethnographic and Archaeological Investigations in the Southwest Islands of Palau. *Micronesica* 33(1/2): 11–44.

Hunter-Anderson, Rosalind L., & Brian M. Butler

1995   *An Overview of Northern Marianas Prehistory*. Micronesian Archaeological Survey Report 31. Saipan: Commonwealth of the Northern Mariana Islands Division of Historic Preservation.

Intoh, Michiko

1984   Reconnaissance Archaeological Research on Ngulu Atoll in the Western Caroline Islands. *Asian Perspectives* 24(1): 69–80.

Irwin, Geoffrey

1992   *The Prehistoric Exploration and Colonisation of the Pacific*. Cambridge: Cambridge University Press.

Isaac, Barbara

1987   Throwing and Human Evolution. *African Archaeological Review* 5: 3–17.

Isaac, Glynn L.

1977   *Olorgesailie, Archeological Studies of a Middle Pleistocene Lake Basin in Kenya*. Chicago: University of Chicago Press.

Jacob, Teuku
    1978   New Finds of Lower and Middle Pleistocene Hominines from Indonesia and an Examination of Their Antiquity. In *Early Paleolithic in South and East Asia.* Ed. Fumiko Ikawa-Smith. The Hague: Mouton. 13–22
Jennings, Jesse D.
    1989   *Prehistory of North America.* Mountain View, CA: Mayfield.
Johnson, Jerald Jay
    1984   Ground Stone Assemblages in Northeastern California. Vol. 2. Unpublished Ph.D. dissertation. University of California, Davis.
Jones, Philip Mills
    1956   Archaeological Investigations on Santa Rosa Island in 1901. University of California. *Anthropological Records* 17(2).
Jones, Terry L., & Kathryn A. Klar
    2005   Diffusionism Reconsidered: Linguistics and Archaeological Evidence for Prehistoric Polynesian Contact with Southern California. *American Antiquity* 70(3): 457–84.
Jones, Terry L., & Kathryn A. Klar
    2006   On Open Minds and Missed Marks: A Response to Atholl Anderson. *American Antiquity* 71(4): 765–70.
Joyce, Thomas A.
    1916   *Central American and West Indian Archaeology: Being an Introduction to the Archaeology of the States of Nicaragua, Costa Rica, Panama, and the West Indies.* New York: G. P. Putnam's & Sons.
Judd, Neil M.
    1954   *The Material Culture of Pueblo Bonito.* Smithsonian Miscellaneous Collections 124. Washington, DC: Smithsonian Institution.
Justice, Noel D.
    2002   *Stone Age Spear and Arrow Points of California and the Great Basin.* Bloomington: Indiana University Press.
Kaeppler, Adrienne L., Ed.
    1978   *Cook Voyage Artifacts in Leningrad, Berne, and Florence Museums.* Bernice P. Bishop Museum Special Publication 66. Honolulu: Bishop Museum Press.
Kaeppler, Adrienne L.
    2005   Shielding in Micronesia and Polynesia: A Different Approach to Warfare. In *Shields of Melanesia.* Ed. Harry Beran & Barry Craig. Adelaide, Australia: Crawford House. 259–60.
Kamakau, Samuel M.
    1961   *Ruling Chiefs of Hawaii.* Honolulu: Kamehameha Schools Press.
Kane, Herb Kawainui
    1997   *Ancient Hawaii.* Captain Cook, HI: Kawainui Press.
Keegan, William F.
    1994   West Indian Archaeology Part 1: Overview and Foragers. *Journal of Archaeological Research* 2(3): 255–84.
Keeley, Lawrence H.
    1996   *War Before Civilization.* New York: Oxford University Press.
Keeley, Lawrence H., Marisa Fontana, & Russell Quick
    2007   Baffles and Bastions: The Universal Features of Fortifications. *Journal of Archaeological Research* 15: 55–95.

Kelly, Isabel

1978   Coast Miwok. In *Handbook of North American Indians*. Vol. 8, *California*. Ed. Robert F. Heizer. Washington, DC: Smithsonian Institution. 414–25.

Kennett, Douglas, Atholl Anderson, Matthew Prebble, Eric Conte, & John Southon

2006   Prehistoric Human Impacts on Rapa, French Polynesia. *Antiquity* 80: 340–54.

Kessell, John L., Rick Hendricks, & Meredith Dodge, eds.

1998   *Blood on the Boulders: The Journals of Don Diego de Vargas, New Mexico, 1694–1697.* 2 vols. Albuquerque: University of New Mexico Press.

Kidder, Alfred Vincent

1932   *The Artifacts of Pecos*. Robert S. Peabody Foundation for Archaeology, Phillips Academy. New Haven, CT: Yale University Press.

1964   South American High Cultures. In *Prehistoric Man in the New World*. Ed. Jesse D. Jennings & Edward Norbeck. Chicago: University of Chicago Press. 451–86.

Kielusiak, Carol Mary

1982   Variability and Distribution of Baked Clay Artifacts from the Lower Sacramento-Northern San Joaquin Valleys of California. Unpublished master's thesis. California State University, Sacramento.

Kim, Jeong-Hak

1978   *The Prehistory of Korea*. Trans. & ed. Richard J. Pearson & Kazue Pearson. Honolulu: University of Hawaii Press.

Kirch, Patrick Vinton

1984   *The Evolution of Polynesian Chiefdoms*. Cambridge: Cambridge University Press.

1987   Lapita and Oceanic Cultural Origins: Excavations in the Bismarck Archipelago, 1985. *Journal of Field Archaeology* 14(2): 163–80.

1997   *The Lapita Peoples, Ancestors of the Oceanic World*. Oxford: Blackwell.

2000   *On the Road of the Winds: An Archaeological History of the Pacific Islands Before European Contact*. Berkeley: University of California Press.

Kirch, Patrick Vinton, & Roger C. Green

2001   *Hawaiki, Ancestral Polynesia: An Essay in Historical Anthropology*. Cambridge University Press.

Kiyotari, Tisuboi, ed.

1987   *Recent Archaeological Discoveries in Japan*. Trans. Gina L. Barnes. Tokyo: Centre for East Asian Cultural Studies; Paris: UNESCO.

Klemstein, Curt

2001   Slingstones of the Marianas. Unpublished illustrated pamphlet in possession of the author.

Knight, Edward H.

1880   A Study of the Savage Weapons at the Centennial Exhibition, Philadelphia, 1876. In *Annual Report of the Board of Regents of the Smithsonian Institution, 1879*. Washington, DC: Government Printing Office. 213–97.

Koch, Gerd

1986   *The Material Culture of Kiribati*. Trans. Guy Slatter. Suva, Fiji: Institute of Pacific Studies, University of South Pacific. Original German publication 1965.

Korfmann, Manfred

1973   The Sling as a Weapon. *Scientific American* 229(4): 35–42, 132.

Krämer, Augustin, & Hans Nevermann
  1938   Ralik-Ratak (Marshall-Inseln). In *Ergebnisse der Südsee-Expedition 1908–1910.* Vol. 2, *Ethnographie, B. Mikronesien.* Ed. G. Thilenius. Hamburg: Friderichsen, De Gruyter.
Kroeber, A. L.
  1908   *Ethnology of the Gros Ventre.* Anthropological Papers 4. New York: American Museum of Natural History.
  1925   *Handbook of the Indians of California.* Bureau of American Ethnology–Smithsonian Bulletin 78. Berkeley: California Book, 1953.
Landberg, Leif C. W.
  1965   *The Chumash Indians of Southern California.* Southwest Museum Papers 19. Los Angeles: Southwest Museum.
Lanning, Edward P.
  1967   *Peru Before the Incas.* Englewood Cliffs, NJ: Prentice-Hall.
La Pena, Frank R.
  1978   Wintu. In *Handbook of North American Indians.* Vol. 8, *California.* Ed. Robert F. Heizer. Washington, DC: Smithsonian Institution. 324–40.
Largent, Floyd
  2007   Keeping Ancient Time: John R. Southon's Contributions to AMS Dating. *Mammoth Trumpet* 22(3): 17–19.
Lau, George F.
  2004   Objects of Contention: An Examination of Recuay-Moche Combat Imagery. *Cambridge Archaeological Journal* 14(2): 63–184.
Laut, A. C.
  1905   *Vikings of the Pacific: The Adventures of the Explorers Who Came from the West, Eastward.* New York: Macmillan.
Lavallée, Danièle
  2000   *The First South Americans: The Peopling of a Continent from the Earliest Evidence to High Culture.* Trans. Paul G. Bahn. Salt Lake City: University of Utah Press.
Leakey, M. D.
  1971   *Olduvai Gorge.* Vol. 3, *Excavations in Beds I and II, 1960–1963.* Cambridge: Cambridge University Press.
LeBar, Frank
  1964   *The Material Culture of Truk.* Yale University Publications in Anthropology 68. New Haven, CT: Department of Anthropology, Yale University.
LeBlanc, Steven A.
  2003   *Constant Battles: The Myth of the Peaceful, Noble Savage.* New York: St. Martin's Press.
Lehmer, Donald J.
  1966   *The Fire Heart Creek Site.* Publications in Salvage Archaeology 1. Lincoln, NE: Smithsonian Institution River Basin Surveys.
  1971   *Introduction to Middle Missouri Archaeology.* National Park Service Anthropological Papers 1. Washington, DC: Department of the Interior.
Lessa, William A.
  1975   *Drake's Island of Thieves: Ethnological Sleuthing.* Honolulu: University of Hawaii Press.

Lévesque, Rodrique, ed. & trans.

1992   Saavedra's Voyages-Galvão's Account 1563. Document 1527E. In *History of Micronesia: European Discovery.* Vol. 1. Ottawa: Lévesque. 519–23.

2000   *History of the Mission in the Mariana Islands: 1667–1673.* By Father Peter Coomans. Ca. 1673. Occasional Historical Papers Series 4. Saipan: Commonwealth of the Northern Mariana Islands Division of Historic Preservation.

Liebmann, Matt

2010   The Battle of Astialakwa: Conflict Archaeology of the Spanish Reconquest in Northern New Mexico. *SAA Archaeological Record* 10(4): 40–42.

Lindblom, K. G.

1940   *The Sling, Especially in Africa: Additional Notes to a Previous Paper.* Stockholm: Ethnographical Museum of Sweden.

Linton, Ralph

1923   The Material Culture of the Marquesas Islands. *Bishop Museum Memoirs* 8(5).

1926   *Ethnology of Polynesia and Micronesia.* Department of Anthropology Guide, Part 6. Chicago: Field Museum of Natural History.

1933   *The Tanala: A Hill Tribe of Madagascar.* Anthropological Series 22. Chicago: Field Museum of Natural History.

1943   Culture Sequences in Madagascar. In *Studies in the Anthropology of Oceania and Asia.* Vol. 4. Ed. Carleton S. Coon & James M. Andrews. Papers of the Peabody Museum of American Archaeology and Ethnology, Harvard University. Millwood, NY: Kraus Reprint, 1968. 72–80.

Loeb, Edwin M.

1926a   History and Traditions of Niue. *Bishop Museum Bulletin* 32.

1926b   Pomo Folkways. In *University of California Publications in American Archaeology and Ethnology.* Vol. 19. Ed. A. L. Kroeber & R. H. Lowie. Millwood, NY: Kraus Reprint, 1965.

Loud, Llewellyn L.

1918   Ethnogeography and Archaeology of the Wiyot Territory. *University of California Publications in American Archaeology and Ethnology* 14(3): 221–436.

Loud, Llewllyn L., & M. R. Harrington

1931   Lovelock Cave. *University of California Publications in American Archaeology and Ethnology* 25(1): 1–183.

MacDonald, George

1982   Prehistoric Art of the Northern Northwest Coast. In *Indian Art Traditions of the Northwest Coast.* Ed. Roy L. Carlson. Burnaby, B.C.: Archaeology Press, Simon Fraser University. 99–121.

Martin, Graham

2003   Why Trepan? Contributions from Medical History and the South Pacific. In *Trepanation: History, Discovery, Theory.* Ed. Robert Arnott, Stanley Finger, & C. U. M. Smith. Lisse, Netherlands: Swets & Zeitlinger. 323–45.

Martin, Paul S.

1936   *Lowry Ruin in Southwestern Colorado.* Anthropological Series 23. Chicago: Field Museum of Natural History.

Mason, J. Alden

1968   *The Ancient Civilizations of Peru.* Baltimore: Penguin.

Mason, Otis T.

1889 The Ray Collection from the Hupa Reservation. In *Papers Relating to Anthropology: Annual Report of the Board of Regents of the Smithsonian Institution, for the Year Ending June 30, 1886, Part 1.* Washington, DC: Government Printing Office. 205–39.

1899 Aboriginal American Zoötechny. *American Anthropologist* 1(1): 45–81.

Matthews, Washington

1889 The Inca Bone and Kindred Formations among the Ancient Arizonians. *American Anthropologist* 2(4): 43, 44.

Maudslay, A. P., trans.

1928 *Bernal Diaz Del Castillo: The Discovery and Conquest of Mexico, 1517–1521.* New York: Harper & Brothers.

McCoy, Patrick C.

1979 Easter Island. In *The Prehistory of Polynesia.* Ed. Jesse D. Jennings. Cambridge, MA: Harvard University Press. 135–66.

McIlwraith, T. F.

1948 *The Bella Coola Indians.* Vol. 2. Toronto: University of Toronto Press, 1992.

McIntyre, Loren

1973 The Lost Empire of the Incas. *National Geographic* 144(6): 781.

Means, Philip Ainsworth

1920 Distribution and Use of Slings in Pre-Columbian America, with Descriptive Catalogue of Ancient Peruvian Slings in the United States National Museum. In *Proceedings of the United States National Museum.* Vol. 55. Washington, DC: Smithsonian Institution. 317–49.

Mellaart, James

1967 *Çatal Hüyük: A Neolithic Town in Anatolia.* New York: McGraw-Hill.

Métraux, Alfred

1940 *Ethnology of Easter Island.* Bernice P. Bishop Museum Bulletin 160. Honolulu: Bishop Museum Press Reprints, 1971.

1949 Weapons. In *Handbook of South American Indians: The Comparative Ethnology of South American Indians.* Vol. 5. Ed. Julian H. Steward. Smithsonian Institution–Bureau of American Ethnology Bulletin 143. Washington, DC: Government Printing Office. 229–63.

Milanich, Jerald T.

1994 *Archaeology of Precolumbian Florida.* Gainesville: University of Florida Press.

Miles, Charles

1963 *Indian and Eskimo Artifacts of North America.* New York: Bonanza Books.

Miller, Carl F.

1962 *Archaeology of the John H. Kerr Reservoir Basin, Roanoke River Virginia–North Carolina.* River Basin Surveys Papers 25. Ed. Frank H. H. Roberts Jr. Smithsonian Institution-Bureau of American Ethnology Bulletin 182. Washington, DC: Government Printing Office.

Milner, George R.

1999 Warfare in Prehistoric and Early Historic Eastern North America. *Journal of Archaeological Research* 7(2): 105–51.

Moore. Clarence B.

1913 Some Aboriginal Sites in Louisiana and in Arkansas: Atchafalaya River, Lake

Larto, Tensas River, Bayou Maçon, Bayou D'Arbonne, in Louisiana; Saline River, in Arkansas. *Journal of the Academy of Natural Sciences of Philadelphia* 2nd ser., 16: 5–93.

Moore, D. R., R. L. Hunter-Anderson, J. R. Amesbury, & E. F. Wells
1992   *Archaeology at Chalan Piao, Saipan.* Mangilao, Guam: Micronesian Archaeological Research Services.

Moore, Earl F.
1973   *Silent Arrows.* Trail, OR: Muse Press.

Morgan, William N.
1989   *Prehistoric Architecture in Micronesia.* London: Kegan Paul International.

Morris, Don P.
1986   *Archaeological Investigations at Antelope House.* Washington, DC: Department of the Interior, National Park Service.

Morwood, M. J., F. Aziz, P. O'Sullivan, Nasruddin, D. R. Hobbs, & A. Raza
1999   Archaeological and Paleontological Research in Central Flores, East Indonesia: Results of Fieldwork 1997–98. *Antiquity* 73(280): 273–86.

Moss, Madonna L., & Jon M. Erlandson
1992   Forts, Refuge Rocks, and Defensive Sites: The Antiquity of Warfare Along the North Pacific Coast of North America. *Arctic Anthropology* 29(2): 73–90.

Müller, Wilhelm
1917   Yap. In *Ergbnisse der Südsee-Expedition 1908–1910.* Vol. 2, *Ethnographie, B. Mikronesien.* Ed. G. Thilenius. Hamburg: Friderichsen, De Gruyter.

Mulloy, William
1965   The Fortified Village of Morongo Uta, Report 3. In *Reports of the Norwegian Archaeological Expedition to Easter Island and the East Pacific.* Vol. 2, *Miscellaneous Papers.* Ed. Thor Heyerdahl & Edwin N. Ferdon Jr. Monographs of the School of American Research and the Kon-Tiki Museum 24(2). London: George Allen & Unwin. 23–68.

Mulvaney, John
1978   William Dampier, Ethnography and Elf-Stones. *The Artefact* 3(3): 151–56.

Muñiz, Manuel Antonio, & W. J. McGee
1897   Primitive Trephining in Peru. In *Sixteenth Annual Report of the Bureau of American Ethnology to the Secretary of the Smithsonian Institution, 1894–95.* Washington, DC: Government Printing Office. 11–72.

Murdoch, G. M.
1923   Gilbert Islands Weapons and Armor. *Journal of the Polynesian Society* 32: 173–75.

Nadaillac, Jean-Francois
1884   *Prehistoric America.* Trans. N. D'Advers. London: J. Murray.

Nassaney, Michael S., & Kendra Pyle
1999   The Adoption of the Bow and Arrow in Eastern North America: A View from Central Arkansas. *American Antiquity* 64(2): 243–63.

Nelson, Edward William
1899   The Eskimo About Bering Strait. In *Eighteenth Annual Report of the Bureau of American Ethnology to the Secretary of the Smithsonian Institution, 1896–97, Part 1.* Washington, DC: Government Printing Office. 19–517.

Nelson, Sarah Milledge
1993   *The Archaeology of Korea.* Cambridge: Cambridge University Press.

Newton, Henry
1914   *In Far New Guinea.* London: Seeley, Service.
Nixon, Ursula, trans.
1977   *Astride the Equator: An Account of the Gilbert Islands.* By Ernest Sabatier. 1938. Oxford: Oxford University Press.
Oakley, Kenneth P.
1950   *Man the Tool-Maker.* London: British Museum.
O'Brien, Michael J., & W. Raymond Wood
1998   *The Prehistory of Missouri.* Columbia: University of Missouri Press.
Oda, Shizuo
1981   The Archaeology of the Ogasawara Islands. *Asian Perspectives* 24(1): 111–37.
Oetting, Albert C.
1989   *Villages and Wetlands Adaptations in the Northern Great Basin: Chronology and Land Use in the Lake Abert-Chewaucan Marsh Basin, Lake County, Oregon.* University of Oregon Anthropological Papers 41. Eugene: University of Oregon.
Oliver, Douglas L.
1974   *Ancient Tahitian Society.* Vols. 1–3. Honolulu: University of Hawaii Press.
1989   *Oceania: The Native Cultures of Australia and the Pacific Islands.* Vol. 1. Honolulu: University of Hawaii Press.
Olson, Ronald L.
1936   The Quinault Indians. *University of Washington Publications in Anthropology* 6(1): 1–190.
Onasander
1923   The General. In *Aeneas Tacticus Asclepiodotus Onasander.* ca. A.D. 59. Trans. Illinois Greek Club. Cambridge, MA: Harvard University Press
O'Neale, Lila M.
1947   Note on an Apocynum Fabric. *American Antiquity* 13(2): 179, 180.
O'Neale Lila M., & A. L. Kroeber
1930   *Textile Periods in Ancient Peru.* University of California Publications in American Archaeology and Ethnology 28. Ed. A. L. Kroeber, Robert H. Lowie, & R. L. Olson. Millwood, NY: Kraus Reprint, 1965. 23–56.
Osbourne, Douglas
1966   *The Archaeology of the Palau Islands: An Intensive Survey.* Bernice P. Bishop Museum Bulletin 230. Honolulu: Bishop Museum Press.
Osgood, Cornelius
1937   *The Ethnography of the Tanaina.* Yale University Publications in Anthropology 16. New Haven, CT: Human Relations Area Files Press, 1966.
1940   *Ingalik Material Culture.* Yale University Publications in Anthropology 22. New Haven, CT: Human Relations Area Files Press, 1970.
Osmond, Meredith
1998   Fishing and Hunting Implements. In *The Lexicon of Proto Oceanic: The Culture and Environment of Ancestral Oceanic Society.* Vol. 1, *Material Culture.* Ed. M. Ross, A. Pawley & M. Osmond. Pacific Linguistics Series C-152. Canberra: Australian National University. 211–32.
Oswalt, Wendell H.
1967   *Alaskan Eskimos.* Scranton, PA: Chandler.
1979   *Eskimos and Explorers.* Novato, CA: Chandler & Sharp.

Owen, Bruce
   1995   Warfare and Engineering, Ostentation and Social Status in the Late Interme-
          diate Period Osmore Drainage. Paper presented at the Society for American
          Archaeology 60th Annual Meeting. Retrieved from *http://members.aol.com/
          OwenBruce/saa95_1.htm.*
Parker, Patricia L., & Thomas F. King
   1984   Recent and Current Archaeological Research on Moen Island, Truk. *Asian
          Perspectives* 24(1): 11–26.
Parkinson, R.
   1999   *Thirty Years in the South Seas: Land and People, Customs and Traditions in the
          Bismarck Archipelago and the German Solomon Islands.* Trans. John Dennison.
          Ed. J. Peter White. Bathurst, Australia: Crawford House. Original German
          publication 1907.
Parkinson, William A., & Paul R. Duffy
   2007   Fortifications and Enclosures in European Prehistory: A Cross-Cultural Per-
          spective. *Journal of Archaeological Research* 15: 97–141.
Pennington, Campbell W.
   1963   *The Tarahumar of Mexico: Their Environment and Material Culture.* Salt Lake
          City: University of Utah Press.
   1969   *The Tepehuan of Chihuahua: Their Material Culture.* Salt Lake City: University
          of Utah Press.
Peterson, Warren
   1974   Summary Report of Two Archaeological Sites from North-Eastern Luzon.
          Archaeological and Physical Anthropology in Oceania 9(1): 26–35.
Pettigrew, Richard M.
   1990   Prehistory of the Lower Columbia and Willamette Valley. In *Handbook of North
          American Indians, Northwest Coast.* Vol. 7. Ed. Wayne Suttles. Washington, DC:
          Smithsonian Institution. 518–29.
Pitblado, Bonnie L., & Beth Ann Camp
   2003   2001–02 Excavations at the Chance Gulch Site (5GN817). Report submitted to
          the Colorado Historical Society-State Historic Fund. Retrieved from http://
          www.paleoindian.net/chance-gulch.htm.
Porter, David
   1815   *Journal of a Cruise.* Ed. R. D. Madison & Karen Hamon. Annapolis, MD: Naval
          Institute Press, 1986.
Poulsen, Jens
   1987   Early Tongan Prehistory: The Lapita Period on Tongatatapu and Its Relation-
          ships. *Terra Australis* 12(1/2).
Purdy, Barbara A.
   1981   *Florida's Prehistoric Stone Technology.* Gainesville: University Press of Florida.
Quiros, Pedro Fernandez de
   1595   *The Voyages of Pedro Fernandez de Quiros, 1595–1606.* Vol 1. Trans. & ed. Sir
          Clements Markham. Millwood, NY: Kraus Reprint, 1967. Original publication
          1904.
Railey, Jim A.
   2010   Reduced Mobility or the Bow and Arrow? Another Look at "Expedient" Tech-
          nologies and Sedentism. *American Antiquity* 75(2): 259–86.

Rainbird, Paul
    1996   A Place to Look Up to: A Review of Chuukese Hilltop Enclosures. *Journal of the Polynesian Society* 105(4): 461–78.
Ratzel, Friedrich
    1896   *The History of Mankind.* Vol. 1. Trans. A. J. Butler. New York: Macmillan.
Ray, Erwin R.
    1981   The Material Culture of Prehistoric Taraque Beach, Guam. Unpublished master's thesis, Arizona State University, Tempe.
Ray, Verne F.
    1942   Culture Element Distributions: XXII, Plateau. University of California. *Anthropological Records* 8(2).
Richardson, Thom
    1998   Ballistic Testing of the Sling. *Royal Armouries Yearbook* 3: 44–49.
Riddell, Francis A.
    1960a   *The Archaeology of the Karlo Site (LAS-7), California.* University of California Archaeological Survey Reports 53. Berkeley: University of California.
    1960b   *Honey Lake Paiute Ethnography.* Anthropological Papers 4. Carson City: Nevada State Museum.
Rodden, Robert J.
    1976   An Early Neolithic Village in Greece. In *Avenues to Antiquity: Readings from Scientific American.* San Francisco: W. H. Freeman. 151–59.
Rolett, B. V., & E. Conte
    1995   Renewed Investigation of the Ha'atuatua Dune (Nuku Hiva, Marquesa Islands): A Key Site in Polynesian Prehistory. *Journal of the Polynesian Society* 104: 195–228.
Rose, E. Clifford
    2003   An Overview from Neolithic Times to Broca. In *Trepanation: History, Discovery, Theory.* Ed. Robert Arnott, Stanley Finger, & C. U. M. Smith. Lisse, Netherlands: Swets & Zeitlinger. 347–63.
Rouse, Irving
    1960   *The Entry of Man into the West Indies.* Yale University Publications in Anthropology 61. New Haven, CT: Yale University Press.
    1964   The Caribbean Area. In *Prehistoric Man in the New World.* Ed. Jesse D. Jennings & Edward Norbeck. Chicago: University of Chicago Press. 389–417.
Rouse, Irving, & José M. Cruxent
    1963   *Venezuelan Archaeology.* New Haven, CT: Yale University Press.
Rowe, John Howland
    1946   Inca Culture at the Time of the Spanish Conquest. In *Handbook of South American Indians.* Vol. 2, *The Andean Civilizations.* Ed. Julian H. Steward. Smithsonian Institution–Bureau of American Ethnology Bulletin 143. Washington, DC: Government Printing Office. 183–330.
Rudes, Blair A., Thomas J. Blumer, & J. Alan May
    2004   Catawba and Neighboring Groups. In *Handbook of North American Indians.* Vol. 14, *Southeast.* Ed. Raymond D. Fogelson. Washington, DC: Smithsonian Institution. 301–18.
Russell, Scott
    1998   *Tiempon I Manmofo'na, Ancient Chamorro Culture and History of the Northern*

Mariana Islands. Micronesian Archaeological Survey Report 32. Saipan: Commonwealth of the Northern Mariana Islands Division of Historic Preservation.

Sampson, C. Garth

1985   *Nightfire Island: Later Holocene Lakemarsh Adaptation on the Western Edge of the Great Basin.* Anthropological Papers 33. Eugene: University of Oregon.

Sand, Christophe

2001   Changes in Non-Ceramic Artefacts During the Prehistory of New Caledonia In *The Archaeology of Lapita Dispersal in Oceania: Papers from the Fourth Lapita Conference, June 2000, Canberra, Australia.* Ed. G. R. Clark, A. J. Anderson, & T. Vunidilo. Canberra: Pandanus Books and Australian National University. 75–92.

Sand, Christophe, Jacques Bolé, & André Ouetcho

2002   Site LPO 023 of Kurin: Characteristics of a Lapita Settlement in the Loyalty Islands (New Caledonia). *Asian Perspectives* 41(1): 129–47.

Sanoja, Mario, & Iraida Vargas

1983   New Light on the Prehistory of Eastern Venezuela. In *Advances in World Archaeology.* Vol. 2. Ed. Fred Wendorf & Angela E. Close. New York: Academic Press. 205–44.

Sassaman, Kenneth A., & David G. Anderson

2004   Late Holocene Period, 3750 to 650 B.C. In *Handbook of North American Indians, Southeast.* Vol. 14. Ed. Raymond D. Fogelson. Washington, DC: Smithsonian Institution. 101–14.

Schaepe, David M.

2006   Rock Fortifications: Archaeological Insights into Pre-Contact Warfare and Sociopolitical Organization among the Stó:lō of the Lower Fraser River Canyon, B.C. *American Antiquity* 71(4): 671–705.

Scott, Jeff

2005   *Golf Ball Dimples and Drag.* Retrieved from http://www.aerospaceweb.org/question/aerodynamics/q0215.shtml.

Seaman, N. G.

1967   *Indian Relics of the Pacific Northwest.* Portland, OR: Binfords & Mort.

Seligmann, C. G.

1910   *The Melanesians of British New Guinea.* Cambridge: Cambridge University Press.

Senshui, Zhang

1985   The Early Palaeolithic of China. In *Paleoanthropology and Palaeolithic Archaeology in the Peoples Republic of China.* Ed. Wu Rukang & John W. Olsen. Orlando, FL: Academic Press. 147–86.

Serrano, Antonio

1946   The Charrua. In *Handbook of South American Indians.* Vol. 1, *The Marginal Tribes.* Ed. Julian H. Steward. Smithsonian Institution–Bureau of American Ethnology Bulletin 143. Washington, DC: Government Printing Office. 191–96.

Shackley, M. Steven

n.d.   *Lovelock Cave, Formerly Known as Sunset Guano Cave (NV-CH-18).* Phoebe A. Hearst Museum of Anthropology, University of California, Berkeley. Retrieved from http://hearstmuseum.berkeley.edu/blm/lovelock.html.

Shapiro, Lisa A., William A. Shapiro, William W. Bloomer, & Robert J. Jackson

2002   *Archaeological Investigations at Seven Prehistoric Sites on State Route 89 Between*

Lake Britton and Pondosa Road, Shasta County, California. CALTRANS Project 02-Sha-89. Cameron Park, CA: Pacific Legacy Incorporated.

Sharp, Andrew
  1968   *The Voyages of Abel Janszoon Tasman.* Oxford: Oxford University Press.

Shutler, M. E., & Richard Shutler Jr.
  1966   A Preliminary Report of Archaeological Explorations in the Southern New Hebrides. *Asian Perspectives* 9: 157–66.

Simpson, J. Clarence
  1948   Folsom-Like Points from Florida. *Florida Anthropologist* 1(1/2): 11–15.

Sinoto, Yoshihiko H.
  1979   The Marquesas. In *The Prehistory of Polynesia.* Ed. J. D. Jennings. Cambridge, MA: Harvard University Press. 110–34.
  1988   A Waterlogged Site on Huahine Island, French Polynesia. In *Wet Site Archaeology.* Ed. Barbara A. Purdy. Caldwell, NJ: Telford Press. 113–30.

Skinner, H. D.
  1918   Did the Maoris of New Zealand Use the Sling? Notes and Queries. *Journal of the Polynesian Society* 27: 96.

Smith, Carlyle S.
  1961   The Poike Ditch, Report 16. In *Archaeology of Easter Island: Reports of the Norwegian Archaeological Expedition to Easter Island and the East Pacific.* Vol. 1. Ed. Thor Heyerdahl & Edwin N. Ferdon Jr. Monographs of the School of American Research and the Museum of New Mexico 24(1). New York: Rand McNally.

Speiser, Felix
  1996   *Ethnology of Vanuatu, An Early Twentieth Century Study.* Trans. D. Q. Stephenson. Bathurst, Australia: Crawford House. Original German publication 1923.

Spier, Leslie
  1928   *Havasupai Ethnography.* Anthropological Papers 29(3). New York: American Museum of Natural History.

Spoehr, Alexander
  1957   *Marianas Prehistory: Archaeological Survey and Excavations on Saipan, Tinian and Rota.* Fieldiana Anthropology 48. Chicago: Field Museum of Natural History.

Spriggs, Matthew
  1997   *The Island Melanesians.* Oxford: Blackwell.
  2003   Chronology of the Neolithic Transition in Island Southeast Asia and the Western Pacific: A View from 2003. *Review of Archaeology* 24(2): 57–80.

Squier, Ephraim, & E. H. Davis
  1848   *Ancient Monuments of the Mississippi Valley: Comprising the Results of Extensive Original Surveys and Explorations.* Washington, DC: Smithsonian Institution Publication 1.

Stair, John B.
  1897   *Old Samoa or Flotsam and Jetsam from the Pacific Ocean.* Papakura, N.Z.: R. McMillan, 1983.

Stanford, Dennis J.
  1976   *The Walakpa Site, Alaska: Its Place in the Birnirk and Thule Cultures.* Smithsonian Contributions to Anthropology 20. Washington, DC: Smithsonian Institution.

Steward, Julian H.
  1928   A Peculiar Type of Stone Implement. *American Anthropologist* n.s. 30: 314–16.
  1941   Culture Element Distributions: XIII, Nevada Shoshone. University of California. *Anthropological Records* 4(2).
  1943   Culture Element Distributions: XXIII, Northern and Gosiute Shoshoni. University of California. *Anthropological Records* 8(3).
  1970   News and Notes: Bolas? *Nevada Archeological Survey Reporter* 4(2): 3.
Stewart, Hilary
  1996   *Stone, Bone, Antler and Shell: Artifacts of the Northwest Coast.* Seattle: University of Washington Press.
Stewart, Omer C.
  1941   Culture Element Distributions: XIV, Northern Paiute. University of California. *Anthropological Records* 4(3).
  1942   Culture Element Distributions: XVIII, Ute-Southern Paiute. University of California. *Anthropological Records* 6(4).
Stewart, T. D.
  1958   Stone Age Skull Surgery: A General Review, with Emphasis on the New World. In *Annual Report of the Board of Regents of the Smithsonian Institution, 1957.* Washington, DC: Government Printing Office. 469–91.
Stirling, M. W.
  1938   *Historical and Ethnographical Material of the Jivaro Indians.* Smithsonian Institution–Bureau of American Ethnology Bulletin 117. Washington, DC: Government Printing Office.
Stone, James L., & Javier Urcid
  2003   Pre-Columbian Skull Trepanation in North America. In *Trepanation: History, Discovery, Theory.* Ed. Robert Arnott, Stanley Finger, & C. U. M. Smith. Lisse, Netherlands: Swets & Zeitlinger. 235–49.
Stone Structures of Northeastern United States
  2007   *Reference Materials on Native American Stone Cairns.* Retrieved from http://www.stonestructures.org/html/source-cairns.html.
Strong, Emory
  1969   *Stone Age in the Great Basin.* Portland, OR: Binfords & Mort.
Strong, W. Duncan, W. Egbert Schenck, & Julian H. Steward
  1930   *Archaeology of the Dalles-Deschutes Region.* University of California Publications in American Archaeology and Ethnology 29. Millwood, NY: Kraus Reprint, 1965.
Suggs, Robert C.
  1960   *The Island Civilizations of Polynesia.* New York: New American Library, Mentor Books.
Sundahl, Elaine, & S. Edward Clewett
  1988   An Archaeological Survey of the Ash Creek Wildlife Area, Modoc and Lassen Counties, California. Report for the California Department of Fish and Game. Shasta College Archaeology Laboratory, Redding, CA.
Swanton, John R.
  1946   *The Indians of the Southeastern United States.* Smithsonian Institution–Bureau of American Ethnology Bulletin 137. Washington, DC: Government Printing Office.

Takayama, Jun, & M. Intoh
1978 *Archaeological Excavations at Chukienu Shell Midden on Tol, Truk.* Reports of Pacific Archaeological Survey No. 5. Nara City, Japan: Tezukayama University.

Takayama, Jun, & Richard Shutler Jr.
1978 Preliminary Report of a Pottery Site on Fefan Island, Truk, Central Caroline Islands. *Archaeology and Physical Anthropology in Oceania* 13(1): 1–9.

Taylor, Dee Calderwood
1954 *The Garrison Site.* University of Utah Anthropological Papers 16. Salt Lake City: University of Utah Press.

Thilenius, G., ed.
1936 *Ergebnisse der Südsee-Expedition 1908–1910.* Vol. 2, *Ethnographie, B. Mikronesien.* Hamburg: Friderichsen, De Gruyter.

Thomas, David Hurst
2000 *Places in Time: Exploring Native North America.* Oxford: Oxford University Press.

Thompson, Laura Maud
1932 *Archaeology of the Marianas Islands.* Bernice P. Bishop Museum Bulletin 100. Millwood, NY: Kraus Reprint, 1971.

Thompson, Lucy
1991 *To the American Indian: Reminiscences of a Yurok Woman.* Berkeley, CA: Heyday Books. Original publication 1916.

Thorpe, I. J. N.
2003 Anthropology, Archaeology, and the Origin of Warfare. *World Archaeology* 35(1): 145–65.

Topic, John R.
1989 The Ostra Site: The Earliest Fortified Site in the New World? In *Cultures in Conflict: Current Archaeological Perspectives.* Ed. Diana Claire Tkaczuk & Brian C. Vivian. Calgary, Canada: Chacmool, the Archaeological Association of the University of Calgary.

Topic, John R., & Theresa Topic
1987 The Archaeological Investigation of Andean Militarism: Some Cautionary Observations. In *The Origins and Development of the Andean State.* Ed. Jonathan Haas, Shelia Pozorski, & Thomas Pozorski. Cambridge: Cambridge University Press. 47–55.

Tregear, E.
1892 The Polynesian Bow. *Journal of the Polynesian Society* 1: 56–59.

Tschopik, Harry, Jr.
1951 *The Aymara of Chucuito, Peru.* Vol. 1, *Magic.* Anthropological Papers 44(2). New York: American Museum of Natural History.

Vaillant, George C.
1931 *Excavations at Ticoman.* Anthropological Papers 32(2). New York: American Museum of Natural History.

Van de Velde, Pieter, ed.
1984 *Prehistoric Indonesia: A Reader.* Cinnaminson, NJ: Foris.

Vanstone, James W.
1972 *The First Peary Collection of Polar Eskimo Material Culture.* Fieldiana Anthropology 63(1). Chicago: Field Museum of Natural History.

1980   *The Bruce Collection of Eskimo Material Culture from Kotzebue Sound, Alaska.* Fieldiana Anthropology n.s. 1. Chicago: Field Museum of Natural History.

1985   *Material Culture of the Davis Inlet and Barren Ground Naskapi: The William Duncan Strong Collection.* Fieldiana Anthropology n.s. 7. Chicago: Field Museum of Natural History.

1997   *An Ethnographic Collection from the Northern Ute in the Field Museum of Natural History.* Fieldiana Anthropology n.s. 28. Chicago: Field Museum of Natural History.

Van Tilburg, Jo Anne

1994   *Easter Island: Archaeology, Ecology, and Culture.* Washington, DC: Smithsonian Institution Press.

Varner, Jeannette Johnson, trans.

1987   *The Conquest and Settlement of Venezuela.* By Don José de Oviedo y Baños. Ca. 1723. Berkeley: University of California Press.

Verano, John W.

2003   Trepanation in Prehistoric South America: Geographic and Temporal Trends over 2,000 Years. In *Trepanation: History, Discovery, Theory.* Ed. Robert K. Arnott, Stanley Finger, & C. U. M. Smith. Lisse, Netherlands: Swets & Zeitlinger. 223–36.

Von Hagen, Victor W.

1963   *Realm of the Incas.* New York: Mentor Books.

Voegelin, Erminie W.

1942   Culture Element Distributions: XX, Northeast California. University of California. *Anthropological Records* 7(2).

Wakefield, Elmer G., & Samuel C. Dellinger

1936   The Probable Adaptation of Utilitarian Implements for Surgical Procedures by the "Mound Builders" of Eastern Arkansas. *Journal of Bone and Joint Surgery* 18: 434–38.

Walker, Phillip L.

1989   Cranial Injuries as Evidence of Violence in Prehistoric Southern California. *American Journal of Physical Anthropology* 80(3): 313–23.

1997   Wife Beating, Boxing, and Broken Noses: Skeletal Evidence for the Cultural Patterning of Violence. In *Troubled Times: Violence and Warfare in the Past.* Ed. Debra L. Martin & David W. Frayer. Newark, NJ: Gordon & Breach. 145–80.

Walter, Richard, & Atholl Anderson

2004   *Niue Archaeology Project.* Retrieved from http://www.otago.ac.nz/Anthropology/Pacific/niue/niuetext.html.

Warner, Philip

1988   *Firepower: From Slings to Star Wars.* London: Grafton Books.

Weaver, Guy

1988   Stone and Coral Tools. In *Archaeological Investigations on the North Coast of Rota, Mariana Islands.* Ed. Brian M. Butler. Micronesian Archaeological Survey Report 23 and Southern Illinois University Center for Archaeological Investigations Occasional Paper 8. Carbondale: Southern Illinois University. 255–77.

Webb, Clarence H.

1968   The Extent and Content of Poverty Point Culture. *American Antiquity* 33(3): 297–321.

Webster, David
    1999   Ancient Maya Warfare. In *War and Society in the Ancient and Medieval Worlds: Asia, the Mediterranean, Europe, and Mesoamerica*. Ed. Kurt Raaflaub & Nathan Rosenstein. Cambridge, MA: Center for Hellenic Studies, Harvard University. 333–60.
    2000   The Not So Peaceful Civilization: A Review of Maya War. *Journal of World Prehistory* 14(1): 65–119.

Webster, Gary S.
    1980   Recent Data Bearing on the Question of the Origins of the Bow and Arrow in the Great Basin. *American Antiquity* 45(1): 63–66.

Weisler, Marshall I.
    1994   The Settlement of Marginal Polynesia: New Evidence from Henderson Island. *Journal of Field Archaeology* 21(1): 83–102.
    2000   Burial Artifacts from the Marshall Islands: Description, Dating, and Evidence for Extra-Archipelago Contacts. *Micronesica* 33(1/2): 111–36.

Welch, David J.
    2001   Early Upland Expansion of Palauan Settlement. In *Pacific 2000, Proceedings of the 5th International Conference on Easter Island and the Pacific*. Ed. C. M. Stevenson, G. Lee, & F. J. Morin. Los Osos, CA: Easter Island Foundation. 179–84.

White, J. Peter, & J. E. Downie
    1980   Excavations at Lesu, New Ireland. *Asian Perspectives* 23: 193–220.

White, J. Peter, & James O'Connell
    1982   *A Prehistory of Australia, New Guinea, and Sahul*. New York: Academic Press.

Willey, Gordon R.
    1966   *An Introduction to American Archaeology*. Vol. 1, *North and Middle America*. Englewood Cliffs, NJ: Prentice-Hall.

Wilson, James
    1799   *A Missionary Voyage to the Southern Pacific Ocean, 1796–1798*. New York: Praeger, 1968.

Wissler, Clark, ed.
    1909   Notes Concerning New Collections. *Anthropological Papers of the American Museum of Natural History* 2(3): 307–72.

Wood, J. G.
    1870   *The Natural History of Man*. London: George Routledge & Sons.

Woodbury, Richard B.
    1954   *Prehistoric Stone Implements of Northeastern Arizona: Reports of the Awatovi Expedition, Report 6*. Peabody Museum of American Archaeology and Ethnology 34. Millwood, NY: Kraus Reprint, 1968.
    1979   Prehistory: Introduction. In *Handbook of North American Indians, Southwest*, Vol. 9. Ed. William C. Sturtevant & Alfonso Ortiz. Washington, DC: Smithsonian Institution. 22–30.

Yuping, Wang, & John W. Olsen
    1985   Aspects of the Inner Mongolian Paleolithic. In *Paleoanthropology and Paleolithic Archaeology in the People's Republic of China*. Ed. Wu Rukang & John W. Olsen. Orlando, FL: Academic Press. 243–58.

Zhonglang, Qiu
    1985   The Middle Paleolithic of China. In *Paleoanthropology and Paleolithic Archaeology*

in the People's Republic of China. Ed. Wu Rukang & John W. Olsen. Orlando, FL: Academic Press. 187–210.

Zorich, Zach

  2010   Fall of a Sacred Fortress: The Origins of Ritual Warfare in Ancient Peru. *Archaeology* 65(3): 30–35.

Index

Abnaki Penobscot people, North American
NE, stick sling, 110
Acheulean cleavers, 6
Acho atupat, Chamorro (Marianas) for
slingstones, *Fig. 6*
Achumawi. *See* Pit River people
Acoma Pueblo, New Mexico, 92, *Map 10(5)*
Acorns, Spanish comparison of Chamorro
bipointed slingstones to, 22
Admiralty Islands, 32, 34, *Maps 2, 4, Table 1*
Adzes and gouges, 19, 54, 65, 78
Africa, 6, 7, 58, 150
Agrihan, CNMI, 22, *Map 3*
'Ala stones, Hawaiian slingstones, 57
Alabama River and state, USA, 110, *Map 15*
Alamagan, CNMI, 22, *Map 3*
Alaska, USA, 94, 98, 106, 107, *Fig. 64, Maps
12, 13*
Algonquian peoples, North America, 106
Almonds, comparison of bipointed sling-
stones to, *Fig. 7*
American Museum of Natural History, New
York (AMNH), 31, 32, 34, 76, 90, 100,
108, *Figs. 9, 19, 27–29, 69*
American Indians. *See* Indians; North
America native peoples
Ammonites as charms, 103
Ammunition, sling. *See specific slingstones*
Andes (Andean Mountains), South Amer-
ica, 5, 73, 75, 91, 147; fortified hilltops/
temples, 115, 149; military/warring states,
76, 149; slingers, 76, *Figs. 23, 29;* Tinku
war games, *Fig. 23;* trepanation, greatest
use of, 78, 80. *See also* Bolivia; Inca cul-
ture; Peru; Preceramic Period sites
Angkitkita site, Lif Island, Bismarcks, 32,
Map 4
Apache people, North American SW: Mes-
calero Apache, 89, 90, *Map 10;* Western
Apache, 90, *Map 10*

Arabia, 150
Arapaho people, North American Great
Plains, 108, *Fig. 65*
Archaeology and anthropology, changing
interests and politics, impact on sling stud-
ies, 5, 58, 65, 73, 76, 98, 104, 105, 145, 151
Archaic Period in North American archae-
ology, 107, 111, 112, 115, *Fig. 72. See also*
Chance Gulch site; Patella stones; Pov-
erty Point Complex and site; Roanoke
River
Arctic, 100, 106–8, 147, *Map 13*
Argentina, 75, 77, *Map 7;* domed/biconical
and lenticular/disc slingstones, 78, 108,
113, 145, 146, *Figs. 31, 32. See also* Charrua
people; Uruguay
Arizona, USA, 89, 92, 93, *Maps 10–12, 14*
Arkansas, USA, 116, *Map 15*
Armies, Southern Cook Islands, 52. *See also*
Military; Warriors
Armor. *See* Body armor; Protective gear/
shields
Arrows and arrowheads. *See* Bow and ar-
row; Projectile points
Art, as evidence of a people's activities and
artifacts, 94. *See also* Graphic depictions;
Rock art
As Nieves Quarry, Rota, CNMI, 20
Astialakwa, ruins of, New Mexico, 93, *Map
10(3)*
Asuncion, CNMI, 22, *Map 3*
Athabaskan-Nadene peoples, North
America, 106, *Map 13*
Atlatl, 5, 6, 20, 115; weights, 101, 104, *Table 2*
Attachment modifications for hafting arti-
facts, 9, 10, 78, 109; drilled/bored holes,
10, 99, 100, 109; grooved, 7, 9, 10, 78, 100,
103, 109; perforated, 7, 78, 103
Atupat, Chamorro (Marianas) for sling,
Fig. 8

Auckland Museum, New Zealand, 27, 31, 36, 44, 52

Australia, 4, 6, 17, 32, *Map 2*

Austral (Tubuai) Islands, 53, *Map 5, Table 1*

Austronesian bow, 51. *See also* Tregear's Conundrum

Austronesian language family, 4, 31, 35, 51, 58, 65, *Table 1*

Avifauna, hunting of, other than with slings, 33, 48, 100

Avifauna, terrestrial birds and fowl, sling hunting of, 150; in the Americas, 79, 89, 94, 95, 106, 108; in Oceania, 17, 25, 26, 37, *Table 1. See also* Waterfowl

Awatovi pueblo ruins, Hopi mesas, Arizona, 92, *Map 10(1)*

Ayme, L. H., NMNH Collection, *Fig. 35*

Baboons, 6

Baja California, Mexico, 100, *Maps 8–12, Table 2(11)*

Baked clay balls, 95, 98, 112, *Figs. 55, 60, Table 2(6, 8). See also* Baked Clay Objects (BCO); Poverty Point Objects (PPO)

Baked Clay Objects (BCO), California, 114, 145, 146, *Fig. 70, Table 2(9)*

Baked earthenware. *See* Poverty Point Objects (PPOs)

Balearic Islands, celebrated slingers of the Mediterranean, 8, 22, 150

Ball courts, North America SW, 93

Ballistics of slingstones and thrown stones, 79, 80, 147; accuracy, 10, 22, 45, 49; aerodynamics, 26, 109; effect, 22, 23, 26, 38, 43–45, 47, 49; lethality, 6, 10, 23; range, 6, 47, 63, 109, 110; velocity, 6, 10, 22, 23, 32, 47, 49

Balls of agate, 91

Bandelier, A. F., AMNH Collection, pre-Columbian South American slingstones, *Figs. 27, 28*

Barite, biconical, slingstone, 33. *See also* Angkitkita site; Uranium bullet

Barrett, S. A., 55, 95, 97, 103, *Figs. 55–58*

Basalt slingstones and throwing stones: in the Americas, 97, *Figs. 42–44, 52, 53, Table 2*; in Oceania, 20, 24, 35, 37, 50, 53–56, *Figs. 14, 19, Table 1. See also* Igneous/volcanic rock

Bataan, Philippines, World War II battle, 115

Battlefields and battlegrounds, 7, 24

Battles: Americas, 77, 80; land, 8, 63, 115;

Oceania, 27, 43, 48, 50, 52, 57; sea, 24, 25, 47, 50, 52, *Figs. 17, 18, Table 1. See also* Battlefields and battlegrounds; Military and defensive architecture

Bayou Maçon, Poverty Point, Louisiana, 114

Beads, shell, 19, 96

Beckwith, Thomas, 111

Beechey, Frederick William, 54

Before Present (BP), definition, 4, 96

Belly-of-sling design, Tewa pueblos, New Mexico, 91, *Fig. 39. See also Cañute* game

Bibliotheque Nationale, Paris, *Figs. 11, 21*

Biconical drill, 34

Birket-Smith, Kaj, 106, 107

Bishop Museum, Honolulu, Hawaii, 37, 53, 56

Bismarck(s) Archipelago, 32–35, *Map 4, Table 1*

Blowgun/blowpipe, 33

Boats. *See* Watercraft

Body armor, 149; Gilbert and Marshall Islands coconut fiber and wood, 27, 57; Hawaiian gourd helmet, 57, *Fig. 21;* Spanish steel helmet, 92; Tlingit elk hide and wood, 149

Boiling stones, 104

Bola/Bolas, 7, 45, 80, 147; North American, 93, 94, 99, 100, 101, 147; South American, 75, 78, 93, 99, 100, 147

Bola weights, 6, 7, 9, 10; of bone, ivory, and wood, 100; confusion with slingstones, 93, 99–101, 104, 109, 111; of stone, 77, 78, *Table 2*

Bolivia, 76, *Fig. 27, Map 7. See also* Andes (Andean Mountains); Inca culture; Peru

Bone points, 21, 78, 149

Borax Lake site, California, 10, 98

Bougainville, Solomon Islands, 34, *Map 4*

Bounty mutineers, 54, *Table 1*

Bourke, John G., 90

Bow and arrow, 5, 20, 21, 46, 51, 93; antiquity of, 47, 48, 50, 51, 55, 149, 150; bird hunting, use of, 48; ceremonial, use of, 48, 64; combat, use of in, 35, 36, 38, 44, 50, 51, 64, 65, 73, 92, 110, 149; evidence of , 25, 31; hunting, use of in, 34–36, 64, 103; no evidence of, 24, 31, 37, 44; not preferred or not used, 94; for shooting rats, 57; for sport, 48, 64; technology of, 3, 51, 63, 101; toy, use of as, 25, 50, 53, 55, 57, 58; undetermined use of, 33, 45, 53, 54, 63; as woman's or child's weapon, 27, 64. *See also* Projectile points; Tregear's Conundrum

Bracelets, shell, 19

Brazil historic sling, *Fig. 30*
Breadfruit sap and red soil, used for making slingstones in Chuuk (Truk), 24
Brigham, William T., 37, 56
Brisson, Captain V. A., Pitcairn Island Collection, 54
British Columbia (B.C.), Canada, 94, 95, 98, 105, 106, *Maps 12–14;* bipointed/biconical stones, 98, 105, 106, *Table 2;* fortified sites, 106, 146; pebble slingstones, 106, *Table 2;* Stólō slingstones, 95
British Greenland Expedition of 1586, 107. *See also* Davis, John; Godthaab
British Iron Age: hill forts, 56, 115; sling, combat/warfare projectile weapon of, 111, 115
British Museum, London, 31
Broken Hill Caves, Zimbabwe, 7
Buenos Aires, Argentina, *Figs. 31, 32, Map 7*
Buka, Solomon Islands, 34, *Map 4*
Bullets, in reference to bipointed, ovoid, slingstones/missiles, 11, 109, 146, *Fig. 2*
Bureau of American Ethnology (BAE), *Fig. 36*
Burials, human, 21, 96, 98, 103, 115, *Table 2*
Burley, David, 43

Cabeza de Vaca, Alvar Núñez, 110
Cabot, Sebastian, 107
Cabri, Jean Baptiste, *Fig. 5*
Caches. *See* Stone caches
Calapooia (or Calapooya) country, Oregon, 97, *Map 12, Table 2*
Calendar dates, 4
California, USA, 94, 95, 97, 98, 103, 104, *Maps 10–12;* Central Valley of, 103, 112, 114, *Figs. 45, 46, Table 2(9);* Coast and Channel Islands of, 97, 98, 148, *Figs. 47, 60, Table 2;* northeast area of, 93, 98, 99, 101–3, 105, 114, *Fig. 4, Table 2;* northern area of, 27, 40, 44, 59, 98, *Fig. 3;* northwest area of, 97, 114, 146; southern area of, 62, *Table 2*
Camarin, Marianas canoe house, 22
Canada, 106–9, 146, *Maps 9, 12, 13, 15*
Canal irrigation, 93
Canoes. *See* Watercraft
Canoe and roof breakers/busters, type of outsized slingstones, 21, 57, 96, *Fig. 6*
Cañute game, San Ildefonso Pueblo, New Mexico, 91, *Fig. 39*
Cape Breton, Canada, 107, *Map 13*
Caribbean Sea, 10, 75, 78–80, 145, 146, *Fig. 33, Maps 6–8*

Caroline Islands, 24, 25, 56, *Maps 2, 3*
Catapults, 26, 110
Catawba people, Carolinas, USA, 109
Central America. *See* Mesoamerica
Centrifugal force weapons, 3, 110. *See also specific slingstones*
Ceramics, 19, 65; spheroid, 111. *See also* Clay; Pottery
Ceremonial properties of certain artifacts, 21, 48, 64, 92, 103, *Figs. 6, 14, Table 1. See also* Magic; Sacred properties of artifacts
Chalcatzingo, Mexico, 79
Chalchuapa, El Salvador, 79, *Map 8*
Chamisso, Louise Charles Adelaide de, 26
Chamorros, native people of the Mariana Islands, 21, 22, 26, *Figs. 6, 8*
Chance Gulch site, Colorado, tuff ball manuports, *Fig. 72*
Charleston, Missouri, 111, *Map 15*
Charmstones, 10, 102–5, *Figs. 42, 46, Table 2. See also* Ceremonial properties of artifacts; Magic; Sacred properties of artifacts; Slingstones, special purpose
Charrua people, South America, 77, *Fig. 31. See also* Argentina; Uruguay
Chatham Islands. *See* New Zealand
Cheyenne people, North American Great Plains, leather slings, 108, *Fig. 67*
Chihuahua, Mexico, 89, *Map 10*
China, 6, 7, 11, 20, *Map 2*
China Lake, California, *Fig. 62, Map 12(10), Table 2(10)*
Chipped stone balls, 6
Chipped stone tools, 19, 104
Choiseul, Solomon Islands, 34, *Map 4*
Chokalai, from Pohnpei origin tales, 25, 51
Chugach people, southern Alaska, 107
Chumash plank canoe, California, 105
Chuuk (Truk), 8, 22, 24, 25, *Fig. 9, Map 3, Table 1*
Clay, slingstones of, 3, 8, 10, 11; in Oceania, 20, 23, *Table 1;* in the Americas, 79, 90, 91, 95, 115, 146, *Fig. 55*
Clay balls and pellets, 79, 90, 91, 112, 146, *Figs. 51, 55, 56, 60, 61, Table 2. See also* Baked Clay Objects (BCO); Ceramics; Clay; Lovelock Cave; Pottery; Poverty Point Objects (PPO)
Clear Lake, Lake County, NW California, 95, *Fig. 54, Map 12(9), Table 2(9). See also* Eastern Pomo people; Indian Island site

Clear Lake, Modoc County, NE California, 98, 99, 102, *Fig. 40, Map 12(5), Table 2(5)*. *See also* Klamath Basin

Clubs (weapon), 6, 34, 49, 52, 75, 80, 92, 148, *Fig. 24*; Plains Indian "blackjack" type, 109

Club heads, 7, 9, 10, 92, 104, 109

Colorado, USA, 89, *Fig. 72, Maps 10, 11, 14*

Colorado River, western North America, 90, *Maps 10–12, 14*

Columbia, South America, 77, *Map 7*

Columbia River, North American NW, 98, 100, 105, 111, *Maps 11, 12, Table 2(1, 2)*

Combat weapons, various, use of, 7, 11, 44, 64, 80; in the Americas, 73, 75, 89, 90, 94, 106, 149; in Melanesia, 35–38; in Micronesia, 27; in Oceania, 17, 46, 63, *Table 1*; in Polynesia, 43, 45, 49, 50, 51, 54, 57, 64, 65. *See also* Battlefields; Battles; War and warfare

Commonwealth of the Northern Mariana Islands, (CNMI), 20, *Map 3*. *See also* Mariana(s) Islands; Northern Mariana Islands

Conch shell: gouges/adzes, 78; trumpet, *Fig. 24*

Conflict and hostilities; 38, 43, 110. *See also* Battlefields; Battles; Combat weapons; Military and defensive architecture; War

Cook, Captain James, 36, 44, 45, 57

Cook Islands, 27, 52, *Fig. 20, Map 5*

Cooking stones, 104, 112–14, *Table 2(9–11)*

Copper bells, 93

Coral, slingstones of, 20, 23

Coral limestone, slingstones of, 21, 22, 26, 27, 35, 36, 97, *Fig. 41, Table 1*

Coronado, Francisco Vasquez de, 92

Coyungo site, Peru, *Figs. 25, 26*

Craig, Barry, 31, 34

Cranial trauma, 148; in the Americas, 78, 80, 107, 114, 148; in Oceania, 22, 23, 33, 37, 39, 49, 50, *Table 1*. *See also* Trepan surgery

Creek people, Southeastern USA, 110

Crocker, W. H., NMNH Collection, *Fig. 30*

Crops protection, sling use for, 79, *Fig. 24*

Cubagua Complex. *See* Manicuaroid Series

Cubagua Island, Caribbean Venezuela, 10, 78, *Map 7*

Culin, Stewart, 57, 101–3

Cummings, Rev. William Thomas, 115

Cushing, Frank Hamilton, 90–94

Dalles-Deschutes Region, Columbia River, Oregon, 111, 146, *Map 12(2), Table 2(2)*

Dampier, William, 33

Daniels 1904 Ethnological Expedition to New Guinea, 31

Danish 1605 Greenland Expedition, 107. *See also* Hall, James; Sling Road

Darlington Indian Agency, Old, Oklahoma, *Fig. 67, Map 14*. *See also* Cheyenne people

Darts, atlatl type, 5, 73, 115

Dating (not romantic) techniques, 4

David and Goliath, 3, 6, 25, 90, 107

Davis, John, 107

DeFant, Dave, 23

Deisher Collection, *Fig. 44*

De Soto, Hernando, 110

De Vaca, Cabeza, 110

Diamond-shape, in reference to biconical slingstones and like artifacts, 4, 10, 21, 26, 103, 113, *Figs. 7, 41, 42*

Dickinson, W. R., 32

Diffusionism, 73, 104, 105, 115, 150, 151

Dillehay, Thomas D., 9, 75, 99, 100

Doherty, Moira, 17, 35, 43

Dolphin, HMS, Tahitian slingers battle *Dolphin* at Matavai Bay, *Fig. 18*

Dorsey, Dr. George A., 101, 102

Downes, Lieutenant (U.S. Navy), 49

Drills, a possible function of bipointed stone artifacts, 104, *Table 2(11)*

Driver, Harold E., 73, 79, 89, 90, 94, 95, 100, 106, 108, 109

Du Bois, Cora, 103

Duck hunting, 95

Duff group, Solomon Islands, 34, 35, *Map 4, Table 1*

Duperrey, Commander Louis Isidore, *Fig. 11*

Early *Homo sapiens*, 6, 7

Early man ocean crossings, 32

Earthenware. *See* Poverty Point Objects (PPO)

Easter Island (Rapa Nui), 53–55, *Map 5, Table 1*

Eastern Pomo people, California, 95, 97, 146, *Figs. 55–58*. *See also* Pomo people; Waterfowl hunting

Eastern Woodlands of USA and Canada, 108

Edge-Partington, James, British Museum Pacific Collection, 31, 35, 37

Egg-shape and size, in reference to ovoid

slingstones and like artifacts, 4, 21, 47, 50, 56, *Fig. 7*

Egg stones, enigmatic Paleoindian artifacts, Southeastern USA, 9, 111

El Arbolillo, Mexico, 79, *Map 8*

El Paso Museum of Archaeology, Texas, *Fig. 37*

Elephants, 6, 105

Elliptical clay balls, 98, *Figs. 51, 60, 61, Table 2(6, 8). See also* Gunther Island site; Lovelock Cave

Elliptically chipped stones, Pohnpei slingstones described as, 25

Ellis, Rev. William, 46

Elsasser, Albert B., 98, 103, *Table 2(6, 9)*

Elston, Robert, 20

Emory, Kenneth P., 46, 51, 54, 56, 57, 63, 65, *Fig. 21*

Enemies, 6, 8, 27, 45–47, 50, 64, 96, 114, 115

Eniwetok, Marshall Islands, 26, *Map 3*

Eskimo. *See* Inuit-Aleut peoples

Essex, U.S. Navy frigate, 48

Ethnographic analogs, 103, 104

Evans, John, 77, 111

Fa'ahia site, Huahine Island, Tahiti, 48

Falcon Hill, Nevada, *Fig. 42*

Fana, Tahitian bow and arrow, 55

Favell Museum, Klamath Falls, Oregon, *Figs. 60, 61, Table 2(5, 6)*

Feest, Christian, 3, *Fig. 5*

Fewkes, J. Walter, 91

Field Museum, Chicago, 101, 110, *Figs. 63–68*

Fighting stones. *See* Throwing and fighting stones

Fiji, 37, 38, 39, 43, 44, *Fig. 16, Map 4, Table 1*

Finsch, Otto, 32

Fire Heart Creek site, North Dakota, 109, *Map 14*

Firearms, 64. *See also* Harquebus; Musket

Fired clay objects, 79, 114, *Fig. 70*

Fish spear points, 21

Fishhooks, 19, 65

Fishnet weights, 7, 101, 104, 109, *Table 2(9)*

Fitzhugh, W. M., NMAI Collection, *Fig. 47*

Five-Mile Rapids site, Columbia River, North American NW, 100

Fladmark, Knut, 106

Florida, USA, 9, 109, 110, *Maps 8, 15*

Food processing sites (archaeological), 21

Football-shape, in reference to bipointed and ovoid slingstones and like artifacts, 4, 10, 109, 146; in the Americas, 103; in Oceania, 11, 20, 21, 25–27, *Fig. 7. See also* Mini-footballs

Ford, James A., 112–14, *Fig. 69*

Forsyth, I. W., 90

Fort Belknap Indian Reservation, Montana, 108, *Map 14*

Forts. *See* Military and defensive architecture

Fossils as charms, 103

France, 7

Fraser River Canyon, B.C., Canada, 95, 96, *Map 12(12), Table 2(12)*

Freycinet, Louis Claude, 22

Friendly Islands, the. *See* Tonga

Fry, Sam, and August F. Meyer NMAI Collection, *Fig. 46*

Galvão, António, 26

Gambier Islands. *See* Mangareva (Gambier) Islands

Game balls, 91, 92

Game pieces, 10, 102, 103, 150

Gaming/gambling stones, 57, 91, 101–3, 112, *Fig. 40, Table 1, Table 2 (1, 5, 8, 11). See also Huna Pohaku*

Garling, Stephanie, 32

Gazelle Peninsula, New Britain, 33, *Map 4*

General Secretariat, Organization of American States (GS/OAS), *Fig. 33*

Georgia, USA, 110, 116, *Map 15*

Gerow, Bert A., 103

Gibson, Jon L., 112–15

Gila River, Arizona, 90, *Map 10*

Gilbert Islands. *See* Kiribati

Godthaab (Nuuk), Greenland, 107, *Map 13*

Goebel, Ted, 9, *Table 2(5)*

Golf ball(s): effect (relating to flight distance), 109, 146, *Fig. 28;* slingstones, comparison to, 32, 52, *Fig. 28;* stone balls, comparison to, 34, 111, *Fig. 37*

Golio, J. J. and Mike, 93, 94, *Table 2(10)*

Goodwin, Grenville, 89, 90

Graphic depictions, 5, 7, 93. *See also* Art; Rock art

Great Basin, USA, 57, 79, 93–95, 100, 104, 149, 150, *Maps 11, 12, Table 1. See also* California; Nevada; Oregon

Great Plains, USA and Canada, 107–9

Greeks, 8, 11

Greenland, 106, 107, *Fig. 63, Maps 9, 13. See also* Godthaab (Nuuk); Inuit-Aleut peoples

Gros Ventre people, USA and Canada, 108, 146

Guadalcanal, Solomon Islands, 34, *Map 4*
Gualupita, Mexico, 79, *Map 8*
Guam, Mariana Islands, 20, 21, 23, 25, 32, 97, 98, *Fig. 6, Map 3, Table 2(6)*
Guam Museum, Dept. of Chamorro Affairs, *Fig. 6*
Guarani people, Paraguay, 77
Gulf Coast, North America, 109, 110, 112, *Map 15*
Gulf of Mexico, 109, *Maps 8, 9, 15*
Gunther Island site, Humboldt Bay, California, 98, 149, *Figs. 60, 61, Map 12(6), Table 2(6)*
Gunther Pattern artifacts, California, 98

Hall, James, 107
Hammerstones, 6, 104, 109, *Table 2(11)*
Hand axes, 6
Hand game. *See* Game balls; Game pieces; Gaming/gambling stones; *Huna Pohaku*
Hand-hurled stones, 7–10, 48; combat/warfare use of, 27, 43, 45, 50, 54, 56, 92, 115, 148, *Table 1. See also* Missile stones
Happahs, a people of the Marquesas, 49
Harrington, Mark Raymond, 96, *Figs. 50, 51, Table 2(8, 9)*
Harrison, Chris, 47, 51, 63
Harquebus, 22. *See also* Firearms; Musket
Hassig, Ross, 79
Hawaii, 56, 57, 148, *Map 5, Table 1*; arrow points, 21; gourd helmets, 57, 149, *Fig. 21*; slingstones, 21, 56, 113, *Fig. 22. See also Huna Pohaku*
Hawaiki. *See* Samoa; Tonga
Hawikuh, Zuni, New Mexico, 92, *Map 10(8)*
Hawkins, Benjamin, 110
Head injuries. *See* Cranial trauma
Headband, sling worn as, 50, 150
Hector, Susan M., 104, *Table 2(5)*
Heirlooms, 35, *Fig. 14*
Heizer, Robert F., 96, 114, 150, *Table 2(6, 8, 9)*
Henderson Island, 53, 54, *Map 5, Table 1*
Hervey Islands. *See* Southern Cook Islands
Hewett, Edgar L., 91
Heyerdahl, Thor, 19, 54, 64
Hohokam culture, North American SW, archaeology, 93, 94
Hominids, early, 5, 6
Homo erectus, 32
Homo sapiens, 6, 7
Honey Lake Paiute, California, 102
Honey Lake Valley, California, 102, *Fig. 43*

Honokalani, Hawaii, 57
Ho'olae-maku, Hawaii, 57
Hopi mesas and pueblo people, Arizona, 89, 92, *Map 10(1)*
Hornbostel, Hans G., Marianas Slingstones Collection, 21, *Fig. 6*
Horse, Spanish use of in battle, 77, 110
Hostetter, Bert, 102
Howe, Carrol B., 93, 99, 100, 101, *Table 2(5)*
Hrdlička, Aleš, 94, 107, *Figs. 25, 26*
Human bio-cultural evolution and stone throwing, 5, 6
Humboldt Bay, California. *See* Gunther Island site
Humboldt Cave, Nevada, 73, 96, 97, 100, *Map 12(8), Table 2(8)*
Humboldt Sink, Nevada, 96
Huna Pohaku, Hawaiian slingstones hiding game, 57, 102, *Table 1*
Hunting, ensuring good luck in. *See* Charmstones; Slingstones, special purpose
Hunting, generally and of terrestrial fauna, 5, 6, 76, 109; in the Americas, 73, 75, 79, 90, 94, 105, 106, 149, *Fig. 57*; in Oceania, 24, 35, 36. *See also* Avifauna; Waterfowl
Hunting, other than with slings, 33–36, 48, 64, 73, 75, 103
Hupa people, California, 95

Idaho, USA, 94, *Maps 11, 12*
Igneous/volcanic rock, slingstones and like artifacts of: in the Americas, 151, *Figs. 43, 45–47, 71*; in Oceania, 31, 32, 34, 52, *Fig. 9. See also* Basalt slingstones and throwing stones
Illinois, USA, 109, *Map 14*
Inca culture, Andean South America, 75, 78, 92, *Figs. 24–29. See also* Andes (Andean Mountains); Bolivia; Peru; Thunder
Independent invention, 105, 150, 151
Indian Island site, California, *Fig. 54. See also* Eastern Pomo people
Indian Ocean, 58
Indians, native peoples of the Americas, 77, 109, 110. *See also* North America native peoples
Indonesia, 6, 19, 33, 58, *Map 2*
Injuries, other than cranial, 44, 49, 143. *See also* Cranial trauma
Inuit-Aleut peoples, North America Arctic-Subarctic, 100, 106, 107, *Figs. 63, 64*
Iron Age. *See* British Iron Age

Island Southeast Asia, 19, 21, *Map 2, Table 1*
Ixtlilxochitl Codex, *Fig. 34*

Jaketown site, Mississippi, 112, 114, *Map 15*
Japan and Japanese, 20, *Map 2*; explorers
    and occupations of Pacific islands by, 22;
    samurai, 64
Java, 6, 11
Javelin. *See* Spears and javelins
Jeddito pueblo ruins, Hopi mesas, Arizona,
    92, *Map 10(1)*
Jemez Pueblo people and warriors, New
    Mexico, 93
Jessup, Mrs. Morris K., Expedition, 108
Jesuits, 77
Johnson Archaeological site, California, 114
Johnson, Irmgard W., 96, 150, *Fig. 49, Map
    11, Table 2(8)*
Johnston, Zeb, 102
Juilliard and Gaffron AMNH Donation, *Fig. 29*

Kaʻeleku, Maui, Hawaii, 57
Kamakau, Samuel M., 57
Kamehameha, 57
Kauvai 2 site, Tongatapu, 43, *Map 5*
Kawaipapa, Maui, Hawaii, 57
Kay-kay-my-alth-may, legendary Klamath
    warrior, California and Oregon, 94
Keddie, Grant, *Table 2(12)*
Kenya, Africa, 6
Kicking races, North American SW pueb-
    los, 92
Kidder, Alfred Vincent, 114, *Fig. 70*
Kingsmill Islands. See Kiribati
Kiribati, 27, 45, 106, *Map 3, Table 1*
Kiva ceremonies, North American SW
    pueblos, 92. *See also* Thunder
Kiwalaʻo, 57
Klamath Basin, California and Oregon, 98,
    99, 101, 102, *Figs. 4, 59, Maps 11, 12(5),
    Table 2(5)*
Klamath County Museum, Klamath Falls,
    Oregon, *Figs. 40, 59, Table 2(5)*
Klamath Falls, Oregon, 99, 106, *Figs. 40,
    59–61*
Klamath people, Oregon, 94, 101–3
Kodiak Island, Alaska, 107, *Map 13*
Kona, from Pohnpei origin tales, 25
Korea, 20, *Map 2*
Korfmann, Manfred, 8, 63, 65, 110, *Map 1*
Koro na Yasaca, Fiji, Tonguese attack on, 38
Kosrae, 24, 25, *Map 3, Table 1*

Kotzebue, Alaska, *Fig. 64, Map 13*
Kramer Cave, Falcon Hill, Nevada, *Fig. 42*

La Perouse, Jean Francois, *Fig. 17*
La Quina Cave, France, 7
La Venta, Mexico, 79, *Map 8*
Labrador, Canada, 107, *Map 13*
Lamy, New Mexico, 94
Lapita Cultural Complex, Oceania, 11, 17, 20,
    35–37, 43, 45, *Table 1;* Late Lapita, 24; Late
    Lapita-Transitional, 32; pottery, 19, 38
Lassen County, California, bipointed stones,
    Figs. 43, 44
Las Vegas, Nevada, 102
Latte Cultural Phases, Mariana Islands,
    archaeology, 19–21, *Table 1*
Latte stones, Mariana Islands, archaeology, 20
Le Maire, Jakob, 44
Lead sling bullets/missiles, 8, 11, *Fig. 2. See
    also* Greeks; Macedonians battle with
    Olynthians; Olynthians battle with
    Macedonians; Onasander; Romans
Leakey, Mary D., 6
Lemon-shape, in reference to ovoid
    slingstones and like artifacts, 10, 45, 56,
    102–4, *Fig. 7, Table 1*
Lemon stones, enigmatic California arti-
    facts, 98, 145, *Table 2(5)*
Lif Island, Tanga Group, Bismarcks, 32,
    Map 4
Limestone, slingstones and like artifacts of,
    20, 22, 53, *Fig. 46, Table 2(7)*
Lindblom, K. G., 51, 58, 150
Linguistics, 51, 52, 54, 58
Li-ot, from Pohnpei origin tales, 25
Lithic reduction cores, 6
Lithic Technology, 6
Little Petroglyph Canyon, California. *See*
    China Lake
London Missionary Society, 47
Los Alamos, New Mexico, 91
Losap Atoll, Chuuk, 24, *Map 3*
Loud, Llewellyn L., 95–99, *Figs. 50, 51, Table
    2(6, 8)*
Louisiana, USA, 112, 149, *Map 15*
Lovelock Cave, Nevada, 73, 96, 97, 100, 150,
    Figs. 48–51, Maps 11, 12(8), Table 2(8)
Loyalty Islands, 37
Lumholtz, Carl, 94

Ma, Tahitian sling, 46
Mabila, Alabama, 110, *Map 15*

Macana, obsidian-edged Mexican broad-sword, *Fig. 34*

Macedonians battle with Olynthians, 8

Madagascar, 58, 76

Madeline Plains, California, 102

Magic, 103, 115, 150. *See also* Charmstones; Sacred properties of artifacts; Sling-stones, special purpose

Magnetite balls, 111

Maine, USA, 110, *Map 15*

Malaita, Solomon Islands, 34, *Fig. 13*

Malaysia, 19

Mangaia Island, Southern Cooks, 52

Mangareva (Gambier) Islands, 45, 53, 54, *Map 5, Table 1*

Manicuare Complex. *See* Manicuaroid Series

Manicuaroid Series, Caribbean Venezuela archaeology, 78, 80, *Fig. 33*

Manuports, 76, 101, 146, *Fig. 72, Table 2(12)*

Manus Group. *See* Admiralty Islands

Maoris, native people of New Zealand, 55, 56

Margarita Island, Caribbean Venezuela, 10, 78, *Map 7*

Mariana(s) Islands, 19–23, 101, *Maps 2, 3, Table 1. See also* Commonwealth of the Northern Mariana Islands (CNMI); Northern Mariana Islands; Thompson-Marianas Slingstone Types (T-M)

Marianas Redware, Pre-Latte Phase pottery, Mariana Islands, 19

Marquesa(s) Archipelago, 45, 48–53, 56, 64, *Fig. 19, Map 5, Table 1*

Marshall Islands, 23, 26, 27, 57, 64, 76, 149, *Map 3, Table 1*

Maryland, USA, 116, *Map 15*

Massey, William C., 73, 90, 95, 108, 109

Maui, Hawaii, 57, *Map 5*

McCoy, Patrick C., 55

McIntyre, G. Scott, *Fig. 23*

McIntyre, Loren, Estate of, *Fig. 23*

McPhetres, Sam, 27

Medicine bundles, 103

Mediterranean, 8, 9, 44, 105, 146, 147

Mesoamerica, 73, 75, 79, 80, 89, 91, 93, 115, 149, *Fig. 23, Maps 6, 8. See also* Mexico

Mexico, 73, 79, 80, 91, 94, 97, 106, 150, *Figs. 34–36, Map 8*

Michigan, USA, 109, *Map 14*

Middle East, 9, 10

Military: armies/forces, 52, 77; historians, 47, 51, 64; states, 77

Military and defensive architecture, 26, 76, 106, 149, *Table 2(12);* arsenals, 45, 64, 79, 115; fortified hilltops/temples, 115; forti-fied sites, 38, 44, 76, 106, *Table 1;* forts, 147; hill forts, 38, 53, 56, 115; multivallate earthworks, 115; New Zealand *pa,* 56, 115; redoubts, 93; stone walls, 24, 149

Mini-footballs, in reference to bipointed and ovoid slingstones and like artifacts, 10, 17, 43, 46, *Fig. 7, Table 1. See also* Football-shape

Mishongnovi, Arizona, 92

Missile stones, hand- and/or sling-hurled, 5–9, 38, 45

Missiles, sling. *See specific slingstones*

Mississippi River and state, USA, 112, *Map 15*

Mississippi River Valley, lower, 112

Mississippian Period, North American SE, archaeology, 112

Missouri, USA, 111, *Maps 14, 15*

Mobile Bay, Alabama, 110, *Map 15*

Modoc people, California and Oregon, 99, 100, 103

Moku'ohai, Battle of, Hawaii, 57

Mongolia, 7, 11

Montana, USA, 94, 108, 146, *Maps 11, 12, 14*

Monte Alban, Mexico, 80, *Fig. 35, Map 8*

Monte Verde site, Chile, 5, 8, 9, 77, *Map 7*

Moore, Clarence B., 112

Morongo Uta, Rapa hill fort, 53

Morwood, M. J., 32

Moses, James, 22

Mount Hebron Paleoarchaic site, California, 9, 10, 98, *Fig. 3, Table 2(5)*

Mud, used by boys in the Marianas for making slingstones, 22

Mud ball slingstones, used by Yuma Indian boys, 90

Mulloy, William, 53

Musee de la Marine, Paris, *Fig. 17*

Musket, 38. *See also* Firearms; Harquebus

Musket balls, 44, 49, 149

Nama Atoll, Chuuk, 24, *Map 3*

Nan Kivell Collection, National Library of Australia, *Fig. 18*

Narváez Expedition, 110

National Geographic, Fig. 23

National Library of Australia, Canberra, *Fig. 18*

National Museum of the American Indian, Smithsonian Institution (NMAI), 100, 110, *Figs. 44–47, 50, 71, Table 2(3, 4, 9, 11)*

National Museum of Natural History, Smithsonian Institution (NMNH), 20, 76–78, 90, *Figs. 2, 22, 25, 26, 30–32, 35, 36, 38*

Native Americans. *See* North America native peoples

Navajo people, North American SW, 89, 92, *Map 10*

Naval engagements. *See* Battles

Near East, 9

Near Oceania, 19

Net weights, 7, 101, 104, 109, *Table 2(9)*

Nevada, USA, 9, 89, 94, 96, 100, 102, 103, 105, *Maps 10–12*. *See also* Great Basin; Humboldt Cave; Kramer Cave; Lovelock Cave; Nevada State Museum (NSM); Pyramid Lake bipointed stones

Nevada State Museum (NSM), Carson City, *Fig. 42*

New Britain, Bismarcks, 32, 33, 37, *Map 4, Table 1*

New Brunswick, Canada, 109, *Map 15*

New Caledonia, 36–38, *Fig. 15, Map 4, Table 1*

New Georgia, Solomon Islands, 34, *Map 4*

New Guinea, 31, 32, 35, 65, 149, *Fig. 10, Map 4, Table 1*

New Hebrides. *See* Vanuatu (New Hebrides)

New Ireland, Bismarcks, 32, 33, 37, *Figs. 11, 12, 40, Map 4, Table 1*

New Mexico, USA, 89, 91–94, 114, 148, *Figs. 36, 39, Maps 10, 11, 14*

New World, 4, 6, 8, 77, 79

New York, USA, 109, *Fig. 68, Map 15*. *See also* Seneca Iroquois

New Zealand, 27, 35, 44, 55, 115, 149, *Figs. 14, 20, Map 5, Table 1*

Newfoundland, Canada, 107, *Map 13*

Newton, Rev. Henry, 32

Ngulu atoll, 23, *Map 3*

Nightfire Island site, California, 10, 101, *Figs. 4, 59*

Niue Island, 27, 45, 106, *Map 5, Table 1*

North America native peoples, 57, 73, 89, 94, 99, 100, 102, 105, 106, 110, *Map 11*

North Dakota, USA, 109, *Map 14*

Northern Mariana Islands, 20, *Map 3*; Museum of History & Culture, Saipan, 8, 22, 97, *Figs. 7, 8, 41*

Norwegian 1955–56 Archaeological Expedition to Polynesia, 53, 55

Nova Scotia, Canada, 109, *Map 15*

Nuuk, Greenland. *See* Godthaab (Nuuk)

Oaxaca Valley, Mexico, 80, 106, *Fig. 35, Table 2(12)*

Occam's razor, 76

Ofai ara, Tahitian faced/edged type of slingstone, 47

Ohio, USA, 147, *Maps 14, 15*

Oklahoma, USA, *Map 14*

Old World, 3, 6, 7, 47, 109, 110, 145, 149, 151

Olduvai Gorge fossil man site, Tanzania, 6

Olmecs, first significant use of the sling in Mesoamerica by, 79

Olorgesailie site, Kenya, 6

Olynthians battle with Macedonians, 8

Onasander, 56

Oregon, USA, 36, 94, 99, 100, 101, 105, *Fig. 4, Maps 11, 12*; Northern area-Columbia River corridor, 100, 111, 146, *Table 2(1–3)*; Southern area, 10, 93, 98, 99, 101–3, *Fig. 71, Table 2(4, 5)*

Ostra site, Peru, 5, 76, 147, *Map 7*

Otago Museum, Dunedin, New Zealand, 35, 44, 52, *Figs. 14, 20*

Otowi, ruins of, New Mexico, 91, *Map 10(2)*

Oviedo Y Baños, Don Jose de, 77

Pa, Maori/New Zealand fortified settlements/hill forts, 56, 115, 149

Pagan Island, CNMI, 22, *Map 3*

Paint Creek fortress, Ohio, 147

Paiute peoples, western North America, 102, 112

Pajarito Plateau, New Mexico, 91, *Map 10(2)*

Palau (Belau), 23, 24, *Map 3, Table 1*

Paleoarchaic Period in western North American archaeology, 9, *Fig. 3, Table 2(5)*. *See also* Mount Hebron Paleoarchaic site, California

Paleoindian Period in North American archaeology, 111. *See also* Egg stones; Patella stones; Roanoke River

Palmer, Dr. E., NMNH Collection, *Figs. 36, 38*

Papuan language family speakers, 31, 35

Parkinson, Richard, 33

Patagonia, South America, 77

Patella stones, 111, 146

Payan, Dr. Louis, 103

Payne, Frank and Doris, Klamath County Museum Collection, Oregon, *Fig. 40*

Peace Corps, U.S., 22

Peanuts, © United Features Syndicate, Inc., *Fig. 1*

Pebbles, use of as charms, 103. *See also specific slingstones*

Pecos Pueblo, New Mexico, 114, 148, *Fig. 70*

Pellet bow, 3

Peninsula de Araya, Venezuela, 10, 78, *Map 7*

Pensacola, Florida, 110, *Map 15*

Peru, 3, 5, 76, 97, 147, 150, *Map 7. See also* Andes (Andean Mountains); Bolivia; Inca culture; Ostra site; Preceramic Period sites; Tinku war games

Petroglyphs, 93, *Fig. 62, Map 10(9), Table 2(10). See also* Rock art

Philippines, 19, *Map 2*

Phoebe A. Hearst Museum of Anthropology (PAHMA), University of California, Berkeley, *Figs. 43, 51, 54–58*

Phoenix, Arizona, 93. *See also* South Mountain petroglyphs

Physical, human, anomalies associated with use of sling, 148

Picks, a possible function of bipointed stone artifacts, 104, *Table 2(1)*

Pigs, wild, 6

Pit Meadows Locality, B.C., Canada, 106, *Map 12(12), Table 2(12)*

Pit River (Achumawi) people, California, 102–4

Pitblado, Bonnie L., *Fig. 72*

Pitcairn Island, 53, 54, *Map 5, Table 1*

Pleistocene sites, 6

Plummet stones, *Fig. 47, Table 2(9, 11)*

Po-ha-ku-maa, Hawaiian slingstones, 57

Pohnpei (Ponape), 23–25, 51, *Map 3, Table 1*

Poike Ditch, Easter Island, archaeological excavation of, 55

Polynesian bow, 51. *See also* Tregear's Conundrum

Poma, Felipe Guamán, *Fig. 24*

Pomo people, California, 95, 97, 146, *Figs. 54–58, Map 11. See also* Eastern Pomo people

Porter, Captain David A. (U.S. Navy), 44, 48–50

Port Moresby, New Guinea, 32, *Fig. 10, Map 4*

Portland, Oregon, 36, 97

Portuguese military forces, Paraguay, 77

Pottery, 19, 38, 73; sling balls, 111. *See also* Ceramics; Clay

Poverty Point Complex and site, North American SE archaeology, 112–15, 149, *Fig. 69, Map 15*

Poverty Point Objects (PPO), 112–15, 145, 146, *Figs. 69, 70*

Preceramic Period sites, Peru, 4000+ YA slings recovered from, 76, 97. *See also* Peru

Pre-*Homo sapiens*, 6

Prince Rupert Harbor, B.C., Canada, 106, *Map 12(12), Table 2(12)*

Projectile points, 5, 21, 73, 91, 104, 105, 115, 145, 147; arrowheads, 21, 48, 73, 104, 149; atlatl dart tips, 73, 115; as charms, 103; spear/javelin tips, 21, 54, 73, 115

Projectile weapons, stone tipped, 73

Projectiles, sling. *See specific slingstones*

Protective gear/shields, 57, 94, 149, *Figs. 21, 34. See also* Body armor

Protestant folk, Pohnpei, 25

Pueblo Indian informants, North American SW, 89, 91, 92

Puelche people, Patagonia, 77

Punta Gorda Complex. *See* Manicuaroid Series

Pyramid Lake bipointed stones, Nevada, 9, *Figs. 52, 53, Map 12(7), Table 2(7)*

Pyramids, truncated, 93

Quartz crystals as charms, 103

Quartz slingstones, 43, 123

Raamkokamerkra-Canela people, Sardinha village, Maranhão, Brazil, *Fig. 30*

Radiocarbon dates, 4, 26, 51, 96

Rapa Iti, or Rapa, Island, Australs, 53, *Map 5*

Rapa Nui. *See* Easter Island

Rarotonga Island, Southern Cooks, 52, *Fig. 20, Map 5*

Reef-Santa Cruz Islands, 11, 17, 20, 34, 35, *Map 4, Table 1*

Remote Oceania, 19, 35

Riddell, Francis A., 102, 103, *Fig. 43, Table 2(5)*

Rijks Museum, Holland, 32

Rio Grande pueblos, New Mexico, 92, *Map 10(4)*

Rio Grande River, North American SW, 92, *Map 10*

Roanoke River, Virginia, 111, *Map 15. See also* Magnetite balls; Patella stones

Rock art, 5, 7, 9, 93, 94, *Fig. 62, Maps 10, 12(10), Table 2(10)*

Rocky Mountains/Rockies, western North America, 108

Romans, 11, 37, 51, *Fig. 2*

Rota Island, CNMI, 20, 21, 32, *Map 3*

Roussel, Father Hippolyte, 55

Royels UNR Pyramid Lake Collection, Nevada, *Figs. 52, 53, Table 2(7)*

Rubber, vulcanized, 3

Rust's San Miguel Island Collection, California, *Table 2(11)*

Saavedra, Alvero de, 26

Sabatier, Ernest, 27

Sacred properties of artifacts, 64, 75, 103. *See also* Magic

Sagarbarria, Ryan, 106, *Table 2(12)*

Saipan, CNMI, 21, 22, 25, 27, 97, *Fig. 41, Map 3*

Sahul, 32

Samoa, 43–45, *Fig. 17, Map 5, Table 1*

Samurai, 64

San Cristobal, Solomon Islands, 34, *Map 4*

San Ildefonso Pueblo, New Mexico, 89, 91, *Map 10(4)*

San Lorenzo Tenochtitlan, Olmec site, Mexico, 79, *Map 8*

San Miguel Island, California, *Fig. 47, Table 2(11)*

San Nicolas Island, California, 97, 98, *Table 2(11)*

Sandstone, slingstones of, 24, 91, 97, *Fig. 50, Table 2(11)*

Santa Ana Pueblo, New Mexico, 89

Santa Clara Mound, St. George, Utah, *Fig. 38*

Santa Cruz group, Solomon Islands, 11, 17, 20, 34, 35, *Fig. 14, Map 4, Table 1*

Satawal Atoll, 25, *Map 3*

Schouten, Willem, 44

Scientific American, Map 1

Seaman, N. G., 36, 97, 99, *Table 2(1)*

Seligmann, C. G., 31

Selma, Alabama, 110

Seneca Iroquois, 109, 110, *Fig. 68*

Serrano, Antonio, 77, 78, *Fig. 31*

Shapiro, Will, 97, *Table 2(5)*

Shell ornaments, 19, 96

Shell slingstones and throwing stones. *See Tridacna* shell slingstones and throwing stones

Shock (pointed) weapons, 149. *See also* Bow and arrow; Spears and javelins

Shutler, M. E., 36

Shutler, Richard (Dick), Jr., 36, 37

Simon Fraser University, B.C., Canada, 6

Sinkers, fishing line, 101, 104, *Table 2(7, 9)*

Skiff, F. W., NMAI Collection, *Table 2(3, 4)*

Skill in making of slings: in North America, 95, 110, *Figs. 36, 49, 57, 58, 63–68;* in Oceania, 46, 48, 56, *Figs. 8–10, 16;* in South America, 76, *Figs. 25, 26, 29, 30;* in Tibet, 76

Skill in use of slings, 22, 47, 67, 110, 150; in combat, 23, 26, 46, 47, 49, 57

Skjölsvold, Arne, 54

Skull (head) injuries. *See* Cranial trauma

Sling, preferred projectile weapon in Oceania. *See* Tregear's Conundrum

Sling decoration, 3, 76, *Figs. 25, 26, 29, 63, 64, 66*

Sling defined, 3, 46, 107, 110

Sling Road, Greenland, 107

Sling variations: large or oversized pocket, 44; long, 52, 76; short, 52, *Fig. 30;* split pocket, 53, 107, *Figs. 26, 64;* staff/stick sling, 3, 110; use of braided fiber 46, 56, 110; use of plaited fiber cords 58, *Fig. 29;* use of twisted fiber cords, 58

Slinger Man Petroglyph. *See* China Lake, California

Slingers Bay, New Ireland, 33, *Map 4*

Slings and slingstones, antiquity and longevity of: Arctic-Subarctic, 107; generally and in the Old World, 5–11; in the Interior, 108, 109; in Melanesia, 11, 17, 20, 32, 35–37, *Table 1;* in Mesoamerica, 73, 79, 80; in Micronesia, 20, 24, *Table 1,* in North America, 73; in Oceania, 17; in Polynesia, 43, 44, 46, 48, 52, 56, *Table 1; in* South America, 8, 10, 73, 75, 76, 78, 97, *Fig. 33;* in the Southeast and East coasts, 9, 110, 111; in the Southwest, 90, 91; in the West coast and Great Basin, 9, 10, 96–98, 100, 149, 150, *Figs. 3, 48, 49, 60*

Slingshot, ancient type. *See* David and Goliath; Sling defined

Slingshot, modern type, 3, 110

Slingstone, as Inca thunder god's lightning bolt, 75, 92

Slingstone caches, stashes, and stockpiles, 7, 21, 24, 26, 76, 93, 147. *See also* Stone caches

Slingstones, bipointed and biconical, ovoids: definitive and ballistically optimal design for, 10, 79, 80, 109, 147; earliest occurrences of, 10, 17, 35, 98; limited distribution of, 146, 147; volcanic bombs, nature's model for, 151, *Fig. 71. See also* Acorns; Almonds; Diamond-shape; Elliptical clay balls; Elliptically chipped stones; Football-shape; Mini-footballs; Thompson-Marianas Slingstone Types (T-M)

Slingstones, carrying gear: Eastern Pomo tule basket, *Fig. 56;* Oceania net bags, 23, 36, 37, 63, *Fig. 15*

Slingstones, ceremonial, 21, *Figs. 6, 14, Table 1*

Slingstones, eccentric forms: bidomes, 77, 113, 145, *Fig. 32;* lenticular, disc, and hockey puck–like, 77, 78, 95, 111, 145, 146, *Fig. 31*

Slingstones, modified spheroid types: in North America, 90, 95, 106, *Fig. 55;* in Oceania, 23–25, 32, 38, 44, 50, 52, 55, *Figs. 20, 22;* in South America and Meso-america, 77, 79, 80, 91, *Figs. 27, 28, 35;* use of generally and in the Old World, 4, 8, 10, 145, 146. *See also* Spheroid artifacts of undetermined function(s)

Slingstones, pebbles, water-rounded, and other natural rocks: use of in the Americas, 145; use of generally, in the Old World, and Madagascar, 10, 58, 77, 151; use of in Melanesia, 33, 36, 38; use of in Mesoamerica and South America, 76, 79, *Fig. 27;* use of in Micronesia, 23, 25, 26; use of in North America, 90, 91, 94, 95, 101, 106, 107, *Fig. 54, Table 2(12);* use of in Polynesia, 47, 53, 55–57, *Table 1*

Slingstones, special purpose, 35; Eastern Pomo and Wintun waterfowl hunting, 95, 146, *Fig. 55;* heated in New Zealand for siege use, 56; as hunting charms, 102–4, 150. *See also* Canoe and roof breakers/busters; Ceremonial properties of certain artifacts; Heirlooms; *Huna Pohaku*

Slingstones and like artifacts metric data: generally and for the Old World, 4, 7, 8; for Melanesia, 31–34, 36, 37; for Micro-nesia, 8, 21, 27; for North America, 91, 95–98, 105, 106, 108, 109, 111–13, *Figs. 4, 37, 38, 50, 60, 70;* for Polynesia, 8, 47, 49, 50, 52, 53, 55, 56, 101; for South America and Mesoamerica, 9, 76, 79, 80, *Figs. 28, 33, 35*

Slingstone terminology, 4. *See also* Thompson-Marianas Slingstone Types (T-M)

Smith, Carlyle S., 55

Smithsonian Institution, Washington D.C. *See* National Museum of the American Indian (NMIA); National Museum of Natural History (NMNH)

Society for American Archaeology (SAA), 104, *Fig. 49, Map 11*

Society Islands. *See* Tahiti

Soldato Mexicano, Fig. 34

Solomon Islands, 11, 17, 19, 34, 35, *Figs. 13, 14, Map 4, Table 1*

Sonoma County, California, *Fig. 45, Table 2(9)*

Sonora, Mexico, 89, *Map 10*

South Australian Museum, Adelaide (SAM), 31, 34, *Figs. 10, 12, 13, 15, 16*

South Mountain petroglyphs, *Map 10(9), Table 2(10). See also* Phoenix; Rock art

Southeast Asia, 17, 19, 21, 32, 65, *Map 2, Table 1*

Southern Cook Islands, 45, 51, 52, 55, 56, *Fig. 20, Map 5, Table 1*

Southern Tiwa pueblos, New Mexico, 92, *Map 10(7)*

Southwest, North America, 89–94, *Figs. 36–39, Maps 9, 10*

Spanish/Spaniards, 26, 47, 50, 51, 75, 77, 92, 100, 110, 115

Sparrman, Dr., 45

Spear/javelin sling or thong, 36–38

Spear men, 47

Spears and javelins, 5, 6, 20, 149; in the Americas, 73, 94, 103, 115; in Oceania, 21, 26, 27, 34, 37, 49, 52, 54, 64

Spear thrower, 6, 20, 31. *See also* Atlatl; Spear/javelin sling; Woomera

Speck, F. G., 110

Spherelets, 107

Spheroid artifacts of undetermined function(s), possible slingstones: in Arc-tic-Subartic and Interior of, 107–9; general information and Old World occurrences, 4–8, 10, 11; in North America, 147; in Oceania, 34; in South America, 5, 8–10, 76, 77; in Southeast and East Coasts of, 9, 111–13; in Southwest area of, 89, 91–93, *Figs. 37, 38;* in West Coast and Great Basin area of, 95, 96, 100, *Fig. 51, Table 2*

Spoehr, Alexander, 21

Sport, 38, 48, 64, 75, 109, *Table 1*

Staff sling, 3, 110

Steatite slingstones, 37, *Table 2(12)*

Stewart, T. D., 116

Stick sling, 3, 90, 110

Stiles Ranch site, California, *Fig. 43*

Stockton Mounds, California, 112

Stokes, John F. G., 53

Stólō people, noted for use of outsized stone sling balls, B.C., Canada, 95, 96, 106, 146

Stone axes, 6, 91

Stone caches, 7

Stone hand/hiding game, 101, 102, 112, *Table 1. See also* Gaming/gambling stones; Great Basin; *Huna Pohaku*

Stone stashes. *See* Slingstone caches, stashes, and stockpiles; Stone caches

Stone stockpiles. *See* Slingstone caches, stashes, and stockpiles; Stone caches

Stone throwing, 5, 6, 38, 54, 92

Stonecutters, 77. *See also* Venezuela

Stuart, Dr. H. H., 98, *Figs. 60, 61, Table 2(6)*

Subspheroid artifacts, 4, 6, 8–10, 24

Summer Lake, Lake County, Oregon, *Fig. 71*

Sun god, Inca, 75

Surface Scatter (type of archaeological site), 21

Swords, 6, *Fig. 34*

Taga, House of, ruins, Tinian, CNMI, 20

Tahiti (Society Islands), 45–48, 51, 52, *Fig. 18, Map 5, Table 1;* archery contest/ritual, 48, 64

Taiwan, 19, 20, *Map 2*

Tanala people, Madagascar, 58

Tanga Group, Bismarcks, 32, *Map 4*

Tanna Island, Vanuatu, 36, *Map 4*

Tanna Rockshelter, Tanna Island, Vanuatu, 36

Tanzania, 6

Tarahumara people, Northern Mexico, 79, 90, 94, *Fig. 36(b), Maps 8, 10*

Tasman, Abel Janszoon, 44

Tehuacan, 79, *Map 8*

Tehuelche people, Patagonia, 77

Tension weapons, 3, 110. *See also* Bow and arrow

Tennis balls, slingstones comparison to, 38

Tepehuan people, Northern Mexico, 79, *Map 8*

Tepit (Pohnpei name "David"), 25

Teton Dakota people, North American Great Plains, 108

Tewa pueblo people, North American SW, 89, *Fig. 39, Map 10(1, 4). See also* San Ildefonso; Walpi Pueblo

Texas, USA, 89, 109, *Maps 10, 14, 15*

Thompson, Laura Maud, 21, *Fig. 7*

Thompson, Lucy, 56

Thompson-Marianas Slingstone Types (T-M), 21, 33, 105, 146, *Figs. 7, 8, Table 2;* Type-1, 31, 37, 50, *Figs. 4, 8, 50–53;* Type-2, 31, 50, 78, *Figs. 8, 33, 50, 53;* Type-3, 34, 50, 78, 113, *Figs. 8, 33, 41, 52;* Type-4, 56, 78, *Figs. 8, 33, 52, 53*

Thomson, Robert, 47. *See also* London Missionary Society

Throwing and fighting stones, 27, 45, 54, 106, 111, 146, *Table 2(1, 2)*

Thunder: Acoma and Zuni kiva ceremonies,

imitation of, 92; sling-brandishing Inca god of weather, 75, 92

Tibetan yak herders, 76

Ticoman, Mexico, 79, *Map 8*

Tierra del Fuego, South America, 100, 147, *Map 7*

Tiguex pueblos, New Mexico, 92, *Map 10(6)*

Tinian, CNMI, 20, 21, *Map 3*

Tinku war games, Peru, *Fig. 23*

Tlingit people, North America, 149

Tokyo University, 22

Tonga, 35, 43–45, *Map 5, Table 1*

Topic, John R. and Theresa, 5, 76, 147

Toys, use of slings as, 36, 89, 90, 94, 95, 106, 110, 150, *Table 1. See also* Bow and arrow

Trade/commerce, 43; use of sling by Olmec merchants, 79

Transpacific-Americas contacts, pre-Columbian, 104, 105

Trask Collection, from San Nicolas Island, California, 97

Tregear, Edward, 35, 44, 51, 63–65

Tregear's Conundrum, 35, 51, 63–65

Trepan surgery (trepanning, trepanation), practice of, 148; in Mesoamerica and South America, 78, 80, *Table 2(12);* in North America, 94, 106, 107, 109, 116, *Table 2(12);* in Oceania, 33, 37, 39, 48, 50, 57, *Table 1*

Tridacna shell slingstones and throwing stones, 20, 35, 45, *Fig. 14, Table 1*

Trobriand Islands, 31, *Map 4, Table 1*

Tualatin Plains, Oregon, 97

Tubuai. *See* Austral Islands

Tulare County, California, *Fig. 46, Map 12(9), Table 2(9)*

Tule fiber, 97, *Fig. 56*

Turquoise mosaics, 93

Typees, a people of the Marquesas, 49, 50

Uintah Ute, Utah, *Fig. 66*

Ulithe Atoll, Micronesia, 23, *Map 3*

United States of America (USA), *Maps 9–12, 14, 15*

University of California, Berkeley (UCB), 96, 148, *Figs. 43, 51, 54–58*

University of Nevada, Reno, Anthropology Dept. (UNR), 9, *Figs. 3, 52, 53, Table 2(7)*

University of Oregon, Dept. of Anthropology, *Fig. 4*

University of Queensland Anthropology Museum, 31

Uogoy, Micronesia, 23

Uranium bullet, spent, barite slingstone comparison to, 33

Uriti, Tahitian slingstone, 46

Uruguay, 75, 77, 108, 113, 145, 146, *Fig. 31, Map 7. See also* Argentina, Charrua people

Utah, USA, 89, 94, 112, *Figs. 38, 66, 72, Maps 10–12, 14*

Utah State University, *Fig. 72*

Ute people, western North America 89, *Fig. 66*

Vaito'otia site, Huahine Island, Tahiti, 48, *Map 5*

Vanuatu (New Hebrides), 36, 37, 39, 97, *Map 4, Tables 1, 2(1)*

Vargas, Don Diego de, 93

Venezuela, 10, 75, 77, 78, 80, 145, 146, *Fig. 33, Map 7*

Villagra, Pérez de, 92

Volcanic ejecta, bombs, and tuff balls, 151, *Figs. 54, 71, 72. See also* Igneous/volcanic rock

Wadátkuht (Honey Lake Paiute) people, California, 102

Waika'ahiki, Maui, Hawaii, 57

Waikiu, Maui, Hawaii, 57

Walker, Phillip L., 148

Walpi Pueblo, Arizona, 89, *Map 10(1)*

War canoes, 24, 47, 57, 96. *See also* Battles; Canoe breakers; Watercraft

War and warfare, practices and weapons of: in the Americas, 73, 105, 109, 149; in Melanesia, 34, 36, 37; in Micronesia, 20, 24, 26, 27; in North America, 89, 91, 92, 95, 107, 110, 146, *Fig. 57;* in Oceania, 65, 94, 149, *Table 1;* in Polynesia, 44, 45, 47, 48, 50, 52–54, 56, 63, 64; in South America, 75–77, *Fig. 23. See also* Battles; Combat weapons; Conflict and hostilities; Military and defensive architecture; War canoes; Warriors

Warriors, 6; Marshallese, 27; Mexican and Native American, 93, 94, *Fig. 34;* New Ireland, 33, *Fig. 11;* Polynesian, 44, 46, 47, 49, 50, 52, 57, 64, *Fig. 21*

Washington, USA, 94, 105, *Maps 11, 12*

Watercraft, 32; boats, 26; canoes, 21, 22, 33, 58,

94; Chumash plank canoe, 105. *See also* Canoe and roof breakers; War canoes

Waterfowl hunting, 94, 97, 106, 146, *Figs. 55, 56, 58;* Eastern Pomo use of specialized slings and slingstones for hunting of ducks, geese, and mud hens, 95, 146

Whiterocks, Utah, *Fig. 66, Map 14. See also* Uintah Ute

Williams, John, 52

Williams, Rev. Thomas, 38, 43

Willoughby, Charles, 112, 113

Willow stick slings, 90. *See also* Yuma people

Wind River Indian Reservation, Wyoming, *Fig. 65, Map 14*

Winnebago people, eastern North America, 108

Winnemucca Lake, Nevada, *Fig. 42, Map 12(7), Table 2(7)*

Wintu people, California, 95, 103

Wintun people, California, 95

Woman's weapon. *See* Bow and arrow

Women, roles of, 27, 48, 50, 52, 77

Woodbury, Richard B., 5, 65, 89, 91, 92

Wooden arrow points, 48

Woomera, 6, 20

Xujiayao site, China, 7

Yale Village, Fraser River Canyon, B.C., 96. *See also* Stóló people

Yale University Press, *Fig. 70*

Yap, 23–25, *Map 3, Table 1*

Yavapai people, Arizona, 89

Years Ago (YA), definition of, 4

York, Gigi, *Figs. 50, 52, 53, 59, 62*

Yuki people, California, 27

Yuma people, Arizona, use of willow stick sling and mud balls, 90, *Map 10*

Zacatenco, Mexico, 79, *Map 8*

Zaldivar, Vicente de, 92

Zapotec, Zaachila, Mexico, *Fig. 35*

Zebra, 6

Zimbabwe, 7

Zuni Pueblo, New Mexico, 92, *Fig. 36(a), Map 10(8);* sling-armed twin war gods, 90, 93. *See also* Hawikuh